The publisher and the University of California Press Foundation
gratefully acknowledge the generous support of the
Ahmanson Foundation Endowment Fund in Humanities.

Imperial Encore

BERKELEY SERIES IN BRITISH STUDIES
Edited by James Vernon

Imperial Encore

The Cultural Project of the Late British Empire

———

Caroline Ritter

UNIVERSITY OF CALIFORNIA PRESS

University of California Press
Oakland, California

© 2021 by Caroline Ritter

Library of Congress Cataloging-in-Publication Data

Names: Ritter, Caroline, 1984– author.
Title: Imperial encore : the cultural project of the late British empire /
    Caroline Ritter.
Other titles: Berkeley series in British studies ; 18.
Description: Oakland, California : University of California Press, [2021] |
    Series: Berkeley series in British studies ; [18] | Includes bibliographical
    references and index.
Identifiers: LCCN 2020026934 (print) | LCCN 2020026935 (ebook) |
    ISBN 9780520375932 (cloth) | ISBN 9780520375949 (paperback) |
    ISBN 9780520976283 (epub)
Subjects: LCSH: Cultural industries—Social aspects—Africa—
    20th century. | Great Britain—Colonies—Social aspects—Africa—
    20th century.
Classification: LCC HD9999.C9473 A57 2021 (print) |
    LCC HD9999.C9473 (ebook) | DDC 306.0967/09045—dc23
LC record available at https://lccn.loc.gov/2020026934
LC ebook record available at https://lccn.loc.gov/2020026935

Manufactured in the United States of America

29 28 27 26 25 24 23 22 21
10 9 8 7 6 5 4 3 2 1

For Mom and Dad

CONTENTS

ILLUSTRATIONS

ACKNOWLEDGMENTS

I saved this to be the last section I'd write in a book that has been more than a decade in the making. I am overwhelmed with emotion—to reach this point has felt grueling, exhilarating, and everything in between. More than anything else right now, I am humbled by thinking about all the people who have contributed to my getting here. They've offered all the support, encouragement, and resolve I ever could ask for—the ideas on these pages belong to them as much as they belong to me. Any faults that remain are entirely my own.

I arrived in Berkeley twelve years ago without knowing very much about what graduate school, finishing a PhD, or writing a book would entail. The fact that I got through any of them, let alone all three, is due in tremendous part to the generosity and commitment of James Vernon. Throughout each stage James has believed in where I was headed and has provided the right balance of patience, rigor, and practical guidance to help me get there. His sense of the attributes that make an exceptional teacher-scholar inspire those around him, and I cannot thank him enough for his support and encouragement over these years. I didn't tell James at the time, but as I started to see the titles that came out in his Berkeley Series in British Studies, I knew how excited I would be to have a book there. I also want to thank Robin Manley, Niels Hooper, Jon Dertien, Emilia Thiuri, Kate Warne, and the hardworking team at the University of California Press for their patience and kindness amid all the circumstances that arose over the past two years. Among other things, they secured me the insightful critiques from Charlotte Riley and two anonymous readers whose thoughtful questions and suggestions are imprinted throughout the final product.

It is with pride that I say I come from the British Studies community at Berkeley and I attribute much of my thinking about modern Britain and empire to the reading groups, workshops, and conferences I was and continue to be a part of. I have particularly benefited from an extraordinary group of colleagues, including Jeff Schauer, Katie Harper, Tehila Sasson, Radhika Natarajan, Sam Wetherell, Caroline Shaw, and Penny Ismay, who all lent me their time and wise advice again and again. They, along with the faculty I studied with, including Tabitha Kanogo, Thomas Laqueur, Thomas Metcalf, and Tyler Stovall, pushed me to bring complexity and richness to my scholarship in ways that I am still realizing today. In Berkeley I also met a group of fellow travelers and friends: Nora Barakat, Beatrice Schraa, Hilary Falb, and Chris Church, who shared their optimism, creativity, and humor with me through all the ups and downs of our graduate studies. When I attended the Ninth Annual Decolonization Seminar in Washington, D.C., in 2014, I was very much still figuring out the forms that my ideas about decolonization could take. It was among the conveners and participants of that seminar that I started to think about decolonization as a field all its own. Last, and most emphatically not least, I also must thank Jordanna Bailkin and Philippa Levine, who set examples in both their intellectual acumen and their mentorship that I can only hope to follow.

The most enjoyable part of this project was the research, which took me from Berkeley to London, Nairobi, Accra, and Austin. It was both an adventure and a grind, and it would not have been possible without the support of my graduate institution and my current institution. At Berkeley, the History Department, the Center for British Studies, and the Institute of International Studies provided dissertation and write-up grants that allowed me to spend the time I wanted in the British archives and follow all the unexpected leads I came across. The Center for African Studies provided grants to learn and practice Swahili and conduct research in East and West Africa, without which, I can say with confidence, this project would not be what it is.

Since I joined the Department of History at Texas State University in 2015, I have had the great privilege of working with and establishing friendships with some of the sharpest minds I could have asked for. My colleagues' enthusiastic endorsement of this book helped me greatly through the final stages of research and writing, but what has enriched my thinking even more has been our running conversations about the joys, challenges, and responsibilities of our roles as educators. I want to give special mention to Ana Romo and Margaret Menninger, who each lent thoughtful critiques on drafts as well as astute advice for how to balance the demands of scholarship and teaching. I am also forever grateful to Sara Damiano, who not only contributed the "encore" part of the title, but also her extraordinary mixture of acuity, warmth, and humor, usually during an afternoon coffee walk.

During my research, I received help and insight from dedicated archivists and unsung experts at all the collections and archives I visited. I want to express my particular appreciation to Trish Hayes at the BBC Written Archives Centre, for vetting all the external services files that I requested, and Martin Maw at the Oxford University Press archive, whose answers helped me discover all the reasons to add publishing to my project. In Kenya I received an enormous amount of assistance from Richard Ambani, who has an institutional knowledge of the Kenya National Archives that cannot be matched. I also want to thank the staff of Kenya Broadcasting Corporation, Oxford University Press Eastern Africa, and Ghana Broadcasting Corporation for granting me permission to come to their workplaces and sift through their various records and files. In speaking about doing research away from home, there are two individuals in particular to whom I owe a tremendous debt of gratitude. Jane Judd and Brian Zelly opened their home to me for each of my many, many trips to London and helped spell the loneliness that research abroad could sometimes carry.

It is impossible to think I could have accomplished any of this without my family. My grandparents, Jim, Harriette, Alden, and Helen, instilled in their children and grandchildren the importance of education—plus a stubbornness to see things through. Although they are not all here to celebrate the results, their inspiration will always be a mainstay of our family. Josh, who I met over tacos and beers three years ago, has given me more than words here can capture. He has been my biggest champion and my most challenging debate opponent, and I am eager to see where our next adventure leads. In my sister Bess I have not only a sister but also a best friend and a partner in crime, whom I can always count on even if I am asking at the last possible moment. She has had to live through the doubts and frustrations of this project more than anybody else, and I cannot wait to finally tell her that it is finished.

But without a doubt, what follows here would not have been imaginable without the love and example of my parents. My mom and dad have contributed to this book in more ways than I could ever hope to acknowledge—phone calls and rides to the airport, yes, but even more in how they raised me and my sister to trust our intellect, ask questions, and follow our convictions. Through their lives, they've set an example of dedication, understanding, optimism, and passion that I draw from every day. They are my role models, they are the best people I know, and I dedicate this book to them.

NOTE ON THE TEXT

Throughout this book, I refer to countries by the names current at the time I am referencing. For example, "Gold Coast" denotes Ghana during the colonial period, whereas I use "Ghana" for later time periods.

ABBREVIATIONS

ACE	Aid to Commonwealth English
AOUP	Archives of Oxford University Press, Oxford, UK
AWS	African Writers Series (Heinemann Educational Books)
BBC	British Broadcasting Corporation
BBC WAC	BBC Written Archives Centre, Caversham, UK
CMS	Church Missionary Society
CRO	Commonwealth Relations Office
DDAC	Drama and Dance Advisory Committee, British Council
DTC	Department of Technical Co-operation
EALB	East African Literature Bureau
EAPH	East African Publishing House
ELT	English Language Teaching
ESL	English as a Second Language
FCO	Foreign and Commonwealth Office
GBS	Ghana Broadcasting System
GOS	General Overseas Service
HEB	Heinemann Educational Books
ICS	Institute of Commonwealth Studies
KBC	Kenya Broadcasting Corporation
KIE	Kenya Institute of Education
KNA	Kenya National Archives, Nairobi, Kenya
KPA	Kenya Publishers Association
MIB(T)	Ministry of Information, Broadcasting, and Tourism, Kenya
NAG	National Archives of Ghana, Accra, Ghana

ODA   Overseas Development Administration
ODM   Ministry of Overseas Development
OUP   Oxford University Press
OUP EA   Oxford University Press Eastern Africa, Nairobi, Kenya
UKNA   United Kingdom National Archives, Kew, UK
URSC   University of Reading Special Collections, Reading, UK
USIA   United States Information Agency
VOA   Voice of America
VOK   Voice of Kenya

Introduction

One warm evening in 1963, hundreds of Nigerian citizens crowded outside the largest theater in Lagos. They were there to cram their way into the show advertised on posters overhead, "The British Council brings you *Macbeth*!" At the same time but several streets away, a group of ten men clustered around a market stand. Inside, the owner slowly tuned a transistor set, stopping only when the BBC world news began to fill the stand. Meanwhile, a hundred miles west, the same broadcast played in the Oxford University Press office, where an editor worked late. He was finishing his notes on a manuscript by the Nigerian author Wole Soyinka, the press's latest discovery and proof—the editor believed—that there was still a place for British publishing in Africa.

Together these snapshots capture the prevalence of British culture in one of Britain's former colonies. Three years after independence, one might expect Shakespeare plays and the BBC news would be rare in Nigeria. Yet, instead of disappearing, British plays, broadcasts, and books not only remained but drew large audiences, like the crowds and listeners described above. Was this the encore to empire—a short performance of goodwill before a graceful stage exit? Or was it meant to be another act of a play that showed no sign of ending? Whatever British promoters imagined, the answer really depended on their audience—the playgoers, readers, and listeners across cities, towns, and villages in Britain's former colonies. Were they on their feet, clapping and calling out for more? Or perhaps they had attended out of a mixture of curiosity and habit but now wished the performance would end so they could get on to other things. When taken all together, these questions and their answers exemplify the history this book explains, namely, how a cultural version of the British Empire took root and sustained itself far beyond the formal end of political rule.

1

LOCATING THE CULTURAL PROJECT
OF THE LATE EMPIRE

Imperial Encore traces British cultural relations, British broadcasting, and British publishing in Africa between the 1930s and the 1980s, a half century that contains the last decades of British colonial rule and the first decades of African national rule. However, the cultural project of the late British Empire would always bear the imprint of the moment in which it began. This story begins in the interwar years, which stand in British imperial history as yet another occasion when officials exalted the empire as a solution to their national problems. Whether addressing the political demands of recently empowered groups or the trio of war debt, unemployment, and a tilted balance of trade, British officials sought to resolve— or at least deflect—internal pressures through stronger ties between Britain and its overseas territories. A stronger British world-system, they reasoned, would provide a resounding retort to anyone who dared raise the possibility of relative decline.[1] But exactly how they might accomplish such a mission depended on where in the empire they turned.

To begin with, there was a group which believed Britain's strongest future lay with its white dominions, where they envisioned a cohesive community of nations centered around Britain. This vision, termed the Third British Empire, took visible form in the late 1920s.[2] To preserve imperial unity, Britain was willing to cede constitutional control; in this light, the Montagu Chelmsford reforms in 1919, the Balfour Declaration of 1926, and the Statute of Westminster in 1931 signaled political strength, not weakness, in the imperial system. Meanwhile, the adoption of imperial preference and the emergence of the sterling bloc sustained the economic needs of the empire.[3] But political and economic strategy alone cannot sufficiently capture the dynamic of this stage of British imperialism. Instead, the imperial system rested upon cultural self-confidence, or a series of powerful assumptions constructed around British ideals and practices. British cultural ties between itself and the white dominions were institutionalized through bodies such as the Empire Press Union, the Imperial Relations Trust, and the BBC Empire Service.[4] In London, officials described dominion status as a reconciliation between national autonomy and imperial identity, but they clearly believed the synthetic power of the relationship would always stem from Britain.[5] In sum, the operating principle of the Third British Empire was the shared supremacy of British culture.

The champions of the diasporic cultural empire took the view that their British-ness was a privilege, to be shared among those who shared the same race and language.[6] In turn, they constructed institutions and networks that fostered cohesion by practicing exclusion. To give an example, the BBC Empire Service that started in 1932 broadcast only in the English language. Moreover, if people wished to tune in to the chimes of Big Ben or a soundscape from rural England, they needed to own or have access to a wireless set with a powerful receiver. In another example and another medium, Oxford University Press demonstrated similar priorities in mapping where to open its branch offices. By this period, the press had branches and editorial departments in cities such as Melbourne, Toronto, and Cape Town, but none in the Caribbean, East or West Africa, or Southeast Asia.

In fact, it was these regions—the so-called tropical colonies—that spurred an alternate vision of an enduring empire. This vision granted a central role to colonial development, or to the idea of investing in infrastructure and industry in the colonies. The idea emerged in Britain during the early decades of the century, when officials presented it as a neo-mercantilist solution to problems such as high unemployment in Britain.[7] Such efforts soon suffered setbacks, however, as colonial living conditions exacerbated social unrest and threatened Britain's hold on its territories in areas such as the Caribbean and Africa during the 1930s.[8] Global recession followed by global war forced Britain to take seriously for the first time the labor conditions and standards of living in its colonies, particularly those in Africa, which were seen more and more as an essential part of the empire. Britain responded to these new urgencies by shoehorning questions of welfare into the category of "development," beginning with the commitments of the Colonial Development and Welfare Act of 1940. Here the colonial government committed metropolitan resources to education, health, housing, and infrastructure with the aim of producing a healthier, more efficient, and more dependable workforce. Perhaps predictably, it did not attempt to diversify the export-based colonial economies.[9] Nonetheless, with the advent of such policies, the number of administrators, planners, and experts that comprised the colonial state jumped dramatically from the mid-1940s to the mid-1950s, a period that some scholars later termed the "second colonial occupation."[10]

Although studies of colonial development have focused mainly on political and economic interventions, British officials recognized there was a cultural component to development that could cement their values in the colonies. British development projects exhibited new confidence in the potential of a modern empire that was peculiarly British and rooted in the individualism, democracy, rule of law, and capitalism that Britain produced and relied upon. There was still the matter of devising development that could successfully accomplish the work of liberal modernization. As economic and political conditions around the empire became more contentious than ever, so the British turned to culture. Among the projects that received colonial development and welfare funds in the 1930s and 1940s, the Gold Coast Broadcasting Service, the East African Literature Bureau, and the Colonial Film Unit are but a few examples that demonstrate how British cultural forms were increasingly incorporated into development aims.

Therefore, describing *when* the ideas behind the cultural project took shape is intrinsically tied up with *where* Britain saw the future of its empire. The vision of a diasporic cultural empire and the practice of colonial development coexisted as separate frameworks for thinking through the future of Britain's empire until the mid-1950s. It was not until the prospect of African decolonization and the subsequent pressures of the Cold War that the two separate visions started to come together. In the following chapters, I trace when and how imperial institutions such as the British Council, the BBC, and private publishing firms like Oxford University Press expanded their work into Africa. As they did, their efforts to reach African audiences were aided by the colonial development initiatives that had since become increasingly vital for overarching imperial interests. What I term "the cultural project of the late British empire" is set in Africa because over this period it became clear to Britons that Africa was where Britain's chance to maintain its empire lay. A major narrative arc in this history, then, is British cultural agencies' discovery of African audiences, followed quickly by how those audiences became essential to Britain's future after empire.

EXTENDING THE HISTORY OF EMPIRE

Britain's discovery of African audiences is interwoven with the history of decolonization. The unremitting empire that I depict in this book does not square with the field's prevailing image of the British Empire as a thing that stopped with the transfer of power. Overviews of the British Empire traditionally tell a story of rise and fall, and choose to cut off the fall at a moment in the 1960s.[11] Along the way, as they describe, Britain tried to hold on by linking itself to the dominions, but it could not withstand the rise of the United States or the loss of India, each of which accelerated the pace of the British Empire's decline. Africa is the glaring hole in that narrative. By the middle of the twentieth century the British Empire had reconstituted itself around Africa. In the 1940s and 1950s Britain believed African labor and resources could fill the void left by India—that was precisely why the Colonial Office was willing to invest so many resources and personnel on the continent. The variety that Britain saw in its African possessions allowed for different colonies to occupy different parts of the British imagination. Compare, for example, territories like Southern Rhodesia and Kenya, which offered Britain another chance at a settler empire, with colonies like Nigeria and the Gold Coast, where Britain could most easily measure the success of experiments with development. Even as British administrators received more and more scrutiny from the populations they governed, renewed migration from Britain and a recommitment to the notion of modernizing trusteeship demonstrates that Britain did not see its empire ending any time soon.[12]

Over the 1950s, Britain finally started to see cracks in its empire. The first signs came amid the evolution of the Anglo-American relationship and were quickly followed by reverberations of anticolonial nationalism. The United States had cast a shadow over Britain's practice of empire for a while, but Britain had been able to hold off US disapproval until the middle of the 1950s. Even Suez was not the end-all to America's support of British imperialism, as events in the African colonies would show in the next decade. In other ways, though, the Suez Crisis exhibited how Britain's different attempts to relegitimize imperialism were not working.[13] Now, when Britain looked at its African colonies, it saw the superpowers' rising influence, as well as a series of options open to African leaders. The ideological and cultural contest of the Cold War unfolded across an array of media forms, including the performances, books, and broadcasts examined here, as well as other media, such as artwork, periodicals, and film. In addition, there were individual exchanges—artists, writers, students, professionals—crisscrossing the globe under the banner of diplomacy, but against a Cold War background. In the history that follows here, however, the Cold War largely stayed in the background, while Britain's liberal empire and its discontents remained at center stage.

By the mid-1950s it was evident African populations were not all seduced by the promises of European development. In turn, Britain felt pressure to accelerate the route to self-government in colonies such as the Gold Coast. In other British colonies, such as where there was a settler population to protect, Britain was forced to declare the extent to which it was willing to go to hold on to key colonial possessions. This was on display very clearly in the security regime and protracted violence it imposed on the Kenyan population during the mid-1950s.[14] And by the end of the decade there was no doubt Britain's plans for imperial unity and modernizing trusteeship had not worked out in the ways it had intended. Indeed, confrontations such as Mau Mau and Suez were determinant in both how and when Britain gave up political rule in Africa.

But I want to emphasize that there was a whole other story going on too, in that cultural initiatives did not relent—and were in fact strengthened—during the events that marked the waning and then formal end of empire. Throughout the state of emergency in Kenya, for example, British cultural work proceeded apace. British organizations published schoolbooks on East African oral histories, staged plays in the British Council's center in Nairobi, and transmitted educational and cultural programs over the BBC. For their proponents, these moments were not the signs of a failing empire, but of a reinvigorated one—one that would be marked by a renewed commitment to building a thriving public sphere.

Suez and Mau Mau might appear in most imperial histories as crises, or moments when the jig of empire was up, but these moments also led to new overtures to nonwhite populations in Africa and other parts of the world. After Suez, in 1957, the British government granted funds for the BBC to broadcast in African languages and for the British Council to expand its drama export to the developing world. After Mau Mau, in 1960, the BBC posted a permanent correspondent

to Nairobi for the first time and signaled that African audiences now took programming priority over European settlers. These activities are what I mean when I
say that the cultural project of late empire accelerated during decolonization. The
initiatives were informed by and intersected with the political and economic circumstances of late colonialism, but they were not confined to the period of British
rule. Instead, with renewed strength, they continued past it.

What all of this is to say is that the political history of the end of the British
Empire must be realigned with a cultural history of reinvigorated imperial ambi-
tion. Political histories of British decolonization have explained that by 1960
both sides of the political spectrum in Britain agreed that Britain should grant
independence to its West and East African colonies. The left had adopted the
language of self-determination in addition to international cooperation, while
the Conservative-led government portrayed African independence as the logical
fulfillment of Britain's imperial mission.[15] Even in this telling, African independence was not predetermined. Rather, it fell out of the complicated interplay
between Britain's adherence to the principles of self-government, the construction of popular legitimacy in an African nation, and divergent ideas about what
Britain's role in postcolonial Africa would be.[16] Nor would independence end this
interplay. In what has been called the "imperialism of decolonization," the same
process continued into the postcolonial period when Britain and other international powers wielded great influence over African decision-making.[17] In a
way reminiscent of the cultural self-confidence behind the Third British Empire,
British officials recognized that decolonization could make room for a new type
of empire to take shape. Britain did not expect to drop out of the picture after
transfer of power in Africa, but instead saw itself as having a head start over its
international competition. Britain's confidence that it would retain a role means
that the history of the British Empire should not end just because the Union Jack
came down.

TRACING THE CULTURAL PROJECT ACROSS
INSTITUTIONAL AND NATIONAL BOUNDARIES

In short, Britain used the domain of culture to maintain its imperial influence
after the end of formal political rule. It worked through the institutions at the
center of this study: the British Council, the BBC World Service, and Oxford
University Press. To be sure, as these are long-lasting and wide-reaching institutions, plenty of histories trace the evolution of each of them. Many of the aforementioned volumes are either presented as official histories or are authored from
within, with all relying heavily on how the institution and its employees defended
their work and understood their impact in the world.[18] Meanwhile, in a separate
literature, social scientists and policy makers have examined agencies such as the

British Council and the BBC under the label of cultural diplomacy and Britain's use of "soft power."[19] As different as they may seem, official histories and the social science studies share a similar fixation on identifying the uniqueness of each institution and proving the contribution it has made and continues to make to British public diplomacy.

This book aims to break British cultural relations out of the institutional and diplomatic boundaries to which it has been confined so far. My approach emphasizes that what are sometimes seen as separate topics, like the histories of broadcasting and publishing, actually unfolded in quite similar manners and became interwoven with one another over the period. By bringing them together in a single study and positioning their history within the complicated interests of decolonization, this book underlines that these British institutions operated as part of a broader, systematic effort to spread British values and the English language around the world. At the same time, the cultural project of empire was indeed a *project*—an ongoing and loosely defined aim pursued by an array of individuals and agencies through a collection of different forms. The initiatives that I describe relied on both new and old media. New media such as radio offered Britain the ability to spread language and traditions of expression across a vast space cheaply. Within colonial development, the media was a crucial part of the message and reflected Britain's specific vision of modernity. Yet, when deciding how to use their resources and personnel, the British used old standbys—the traveling theater troupe and small print-runs of books—just as often as they used new media. It is important to put those histories in the same study, because only then can I show how the same group of cultural artists and even the same relatively small canon dominated British cultural outreach to Africa. For example, during the 1960s William Shakespeare's plays were produced and distributed around Africa in performance, book, and broadcast forms, most particularly *Julius Caesar*, which was translated into at least seven African languages. The same can be said of the works of African literary figures such as Wole Soyinka and Ngũgĩ wa Thiong'o, who enter the story partway through the period. The cultural project spread across agencies and media forms, but it can be understood as a single project: a combined effort to forge cultural connections between Britain and Africa.

THE LASTING POWER OF BRITISH CULTURE

Anyone who writes a book on "culture" and "imperialism" is following in well-known footsteps. When Edward Said published *Culture and Imperialism* during the mid-1990s, he presented a critique of cultural imperialism that he and others had already been making for decades.[20] Even when formal colonial rule ended, Said reminds us, imperialism lingered—in economic, ideological, and social practices, and especially in cultural forms.[21] Among other critics of cultural imperialism, the most important for the particular history I tell here are those whom Said terms "the post-imperial writers of the Third World," referring to esteemed authors such as Ngũgĩ wa Thiong'o, Chinua Achebe, Wole Soyinka, and Tayeb Salih, who were born and educated in British colonial Africa and started publishing literary works during the years of African independence. As Said describes, these postcolonial writers "bear their past within them . . . as urgently reinterpretable and redeployable experiences, in which the formerly silent native speaks and acts on territory reclaimed as part of a general movement of resistance, from the colonist."[22] Like Said, these authors' powerful insights highlight the gap in British imperial history. Their writing reminds us of the importance of understanding how British cultural imperialism unfolded both during and after the formal end of the British Empire.

The experiences of African authors such as Ngũgĩ and Achebe did not just frame this history, they were at its core, while the authors themselves offered a significant means through which British cultural agencies sought to gain more legitimacy. During decolonization, British publishers and broadcasters recognized that African independence could put an end to their designs in Africa. As part of their effort to prove their usefulness to African states and publics—and thus ensure Britain's continued presence—British agencies set out to show how they encouraged and supported African culture. Therefore, the first time an author such as Ngũgĩ wa Thiong'o is mentioned in this history is when British publishers identified him as a useful figure for Britain's cultural aims. British publishers had their reasons for publishing Ngũgĩ—and for continuing to do so, despite the fierce indictments of imperialism and colonialism that Ngũgĩ penned. In one of his strongest condemnations, *Decolonising the Mind*, the Kenyan wrote about the brute totality of imperialism and condemned the alienating persistence of the English language in Britain's former colonies—precisely the structures and language that British publishers relied on for their global profits.[23] Ngũgĩ denounced his publishers for being exploitative through their structures and language—and yet, they still saw reason to publicize his words widely. British cultural agencies believed that figures such as Ngũgĩ brought a new level of authority to their long-standing imperial mission.

CENTRAL ARGUMENTS AND THEIR SIGNIFICANCE

The above discussion showcases the two interconnected arguments in this book. First, this book challenges when the history of the British Empire should end. My work is significant for the larger study of empire because it examines the period after formal British rule—that is, a period largely absent from traditional histories of empire. As studies of development and overseas aid increasingly show, the handover of political power was by no means a bookend to many of the ways Britain engaged with Africa.[24] But Britain's engagement in Africa extended beyond development and overseas aid. After the colonial government left, British cultural agencies used conditions and advantages from the colonial period to delineate new and lasting roles for themselves in the postcolonial setting. The reconfiguration was more gradual than political independence (when most imperial histories choose to end), and it did not resort to relocating decolonization to the metropole (as histories of migrants and race in Britain often do.) Still, the success of these efforts helped ensure Britain continued to influence the politics and attitudes of people in newly independent states and afforded Britain greater prestige in global politics than would otherwise be the case. Put simply, this book joins the call for extending the timeline of British imperialism beyond the formal dissolution of the empire.

As much as this is a history of continuity, it is also one of reinvention. As it lost its empire, Britain reinvented the culture that it projected to the world. At the beginning of the period of study, the British officials I examine held a narrow view of British culture that celebrated its prestige and fixedness. However, decolonization forced those officials to replace that understanding with one oriented around a plural group of values and practices, such as disinterested news and high editorial standards. What remained constant throughout the period, however, was how British actors continued to cast themselves in the position of handing down a specific culture to Africans. Moreover, as this history demonstrates, British officials believed their success at demonstrating the universality of British cultural work hinged on the degree to which they could demonstrate African buy-in. Therefore, proponents of British cultural imperialism set out to incorporate a select amount of postcolonial culture and recast it as the evolved global British culture they now promoted. In their willingness to provincialize how they had once seen British culture, British actors also revealed the colonizing impulse that remained a core part of British cultural imperialism. The reworking of British cultural imperialism, therefore, was also about the cultural extension of imperialism.

That brings the discussion to the second main argument in this book, which is that the postcolonial critique did not disarm British cultural imperialism—in fact, it ran alongside and sometimes even strengthened it. As the act of publishing Ngũgĩ demonstrates, British cultural agencies sometimes found reason to encourage criticism—even when they were the target. During the years after African independence, agencies such as the BBC and British publishing firms boasted about fostering African input and encouraging dissenting voices as a means of proving that they served an important role in postcolonial societies. The fact that British agencies now competed against a chorus of thought and were able to persist nonetheless thus gave a new, powerful legitimacy to the British cultural mission more broadly.

THE AFTERLIVES OF EMPIRES AND ARCHIVES

As Christopher Lee declared in a volume on the aftereffects of the 1955 Bandung Conference, there is a fundamental challenge to writing a history of decolonization because it is an experience that is "at once uniquely individual in scope . . . and in retrospect seemingly universal."[25] Even when confining a study to one imperial power and one continent, as I do here with the British in Africa, the course of decolonization is still protracted and uneven. When confronting the challenge of writing a history of decolonization in British Africa, I had to make decisions about which archives to visit, which threads to pursue, and which case studies to select. As a guiding principle, I aimed to highlight distinct experiences that would demonstrate the overall shape of British cultural activity in Africa while simultaneously recognizing the range of encounters and varied realties of individual communities and nation-states. Therefore, in what follows I draw from examples from East and West Africa that are broadly illustrative of British agencies' concerns, the challenges they faced, and the responses their work provoked.

The six chapters that follow are divided into two parts, with the first examining the late colonial period and the second examining the decades after African independence. The three chapters in part 1 demonstrate how British agencies sought to spread British culture by sending British drama performances, books, and broadcasts into colonial Africa. The opening chapter, "Shakespeare in Africa," examines Britain's official cultural diplomacy body, the British Council, and shows how the council's officials and advisers confidently decided which performers and performances to send overseas under the banner of British national culture. Chapter 2, "Bringing Books to Africans," looks at publishing and shows how missionaries, development agents, and commercial publishers all used the rhetoric of a civilizing mission to build a book publishing industry in East Africa that complemented the metropolitan industry in Britain. Then, chapter 3, "This Is London . . ." shifts to the field of broadcasting and examines the debates between colonial officials and BBC broadcasters over the types of British content they should transmit to Africa.

If the first part of the book focuses on the efforts by British officials to construct a framework that would convey their culture, the second part examines how they ensured it would last. The chapters in part 2 all begin in the early 1960s, or the moment captured by the snapshots that began this introduction. These chapters mirror the first half of the book and carry forward the history that began in the late colonial period. First, chapter 4, ". . . Calling Africa," continues the history of the BBC in postcolonial Africa, when British broadcasters faced a competitive field for the first time and looked for ways to make their broadcasts appeal to African audiences. Chapter 5, "Patrons of Postcolonial Culture," shows how British publishers set out to demonstrate their usefulness to African states and African writers. The ways in which British cultural agencies shifted how they understood the mission of liberal empire becomes quite apparent by chapter 6, "From Culture to Aid to Paid," which shows British Council officials searching for remnants of a liberal empire that might no longer exist.

This work thus draws inspiration from and is proud to join the field's growing interest in examining the different and intersecting "afterlives of empire." By that, I refer to all of the ways that empire and—even more vitally—decolonization embedded itself in and lived through institutions, identities, and political units, be they the welfare state, blackness and whiteness in Britain, or the European Union.[26] This study takes cues from those examples but repositions the inquiry away from the metropole, to illustrate that decolonization also fundamentally changed and then lived on through British institutions and identities overseas.

One of the most poignant questions to come out of the afterlives of empire scholarship has been about locating decolonization's archives. Although from different geographical fields, here I found that Jordanna Bailkin's answer to the question "Where, then, did the empire go?" aligns quite significantly with the methodologies that Africanist historians such as Jean Allman and Jeffrey Ahlman promote in their studies of Ghana right at and after independence.[27] Like Allman and Ahlman, my research for this project brought me across national and continental borders. As I traced a broad range of British and African actors, I tried to lessen my reliance on state and institutional archives, but as the following chapters make obvious, I was not always successful in this endeavor. However, both what was present in the archives and what was absent made its imprint on how I came to view decolonization. I describe the late colonial period as one when many British cultural agencies did not seem to be concerned with how African audiences perceived their activities. Indeed, very few African voices—and certainly no non-elite voices—appear through the archives unmuted during this era. The archives reveal that British officials' preoccupations clearly represented a historical instance of what Gayatri Spivak pointed at when she famously asked "Can the Subaltern Speak?"[28] Most of the British officials in the first half of this history did not consider whether the subaltern could speak because they believed the subaltern should be listening—to Britain.

When I reached the second part of the period under study—that is, the decades after African independence—I assumed that while some aspects of research would become more difficult, other aspects would open up. In particular, I anticipated it would be easier to find crosscurrents and exchanges between different archives, different media forms, and different types of actors. But this turned out to be only half true. In this portion of the volume, and in contrast to the late colonial period, I show that British agencies depended on African audiences, states, and writers; correspondingly, African archives and voices appear in greater frequency in the endnotes. At the same time, British agencies still exerted a great deal of control over when and how they received counter-evidence or critique. This means that

British officials did not set out to listen to Africans speaking as much as they tried to appropriate those voices for their own uses. The British actors' answer to Spivak's question therefore remained to a great degree the same—and the fact that it did explains a great deal about the global British culture at which this history arrives.

In the course of decolonization, British cultural agencies realized it was imperative to redefine the national culture that they were tasked to promote. They thus set out to rebrand both themselves and their work as dynamically global while remaining British at their core. In many ways, this construction of global British culture both stems from and shares a great deal with what Antoinette Burton and Isabel Hofmeyr delineate as the imperial commons, a space and a resource that "presumed shared values but also sponsored debate, doubt, critique."[29] Moreover, as they go on, "as with all commons, access [is] uneven and dependent on wealth, location, levels of literacy."[30] Although ostensibly no single power had rights or control over the commons, there were still clear signs of its British origins—for starters, through the prevalence of the English language—and that remained true after empire's formal end.

When tracing when and how the English language appears in the history of global British culture, it becomes apparent that in many ways it *is* that narrative. Throughout the first part of the history told in *Imperial Encore*, British cultural agencies promoted and reinforced an exclusive idea of English that mapped closely with the categories of race and class as another tool for differentiation within the British world. During decolonization, those same agencies reframed how they spoke about and taught their language, replacing a rigid set of rules with a fluid language that had endless accents and variants. What was more, after losing their territorial empire, British authorities were buoyed by any and all signs that their language was in demand. It signaled the enduring mission of liberal empire, a deep faith in progress and uplift, and their continued commitment to what Britain could contribute to the world.

RACE AND THE DIFFERENT MEANINGS
OF *POSTCOLONIAL*

One of the themes of this volume is the repeated questioning by both British and African actors of "Who and what is African culture?" This was a question that, for example, BBC producers struggled over when they created a program called *African Theatre* and then found themselves debating policies about whether an author's race or national origin qualified them and their writing as African. As their question implies, the understanding of race is important for one of the main shifts that I show in this volume, which is that British officials stopped tailoring their cultural outreach to East and West Africa toward white settler and elite audiences only, and instead started to direct their work much more toward black non-elite African populations. To make that point, therefore, I highlight the different ways British individuals spoke about and imagined their theatergoers, readers, and listeners after African independence. Otherwise, in my discussion when I speak generally about African audiences (or—as was much more often the case—the failure to attract African audiences), I refer to black Africans.

Finally, when I was considering how different British and African individuals imagined and articulated the relationship between the metropole and its former colonial subjects, I found it useful to distinguish between the temporal and critical uses of the term *postcolonial*. Many of the British individuals who appear in this history expressed a desire to construct a positive (or at least symbiotic) relationship between Britain and Africa that would survive past the end of colonial rule. For them, the dates of independence marked the start of the postcolonial in a temporal sense, that is, the time that came next, after the colonial. In their conversations with one another and in their writings, they thus portrayed a postcolonial period that was different from what had come before but that also reflected a joint history that continued forward without struggle. This stood in stark contrast to how several of the African writers and politicians who appear in the following pages framed their understandings of colonialism and what could follow it. These individuals could not imagine how there could simply be a "next" framework that was not still grappling with and trying to disentangle itself from the tentacles of colonialism. Therefore, when they deployed the term *postcolonial*, they described something far more complicated than simply the period that followed the colonial. For them, it was truly an imperial encore, but one that showed no signs of ending.

PART ONE

Cultural Imperialism during the Late Empire

Shakespeare in Africa

The British Council and Drama Export

When the British Council first hung posters for a performance of *Macbeth* in Lagos in 1963, the council's representative wondered aloud whether anyone would attend. By the time the performance came around a few weeks later, his worries had evaporated. From his office window that afternoon, he watched crowds flock throughout the center of the capital. With James Cairncross and Judi Dench in the title roles, some of the playgoers had traveled more than a hundred miles for the chance to attend opening night. There was a black market for tickets, which were now selling at £2 10s. over face value. During the ninety minutes after the curtain rose that evening, there was never a moment the audience was silent. During the first act, the playgoers laughed uproariously, seeing a white man who believed in witches. A few minutes later, they booed and hissed loudly as Lady Macbeth entered the stage. Later that evening, when James Cairncross began to recite "Tomorrow and tomorrow and tomorrow," a chorus of audience voices finished the rest of the soliloquy with him. By the final death, the front rows appeared to be ready to rush the stage, and the stage manager was heard yelling, "Curtain—down!... Curtain—down!" At last the curtain fell, closing on the first night of the Nottingham Playhouse Company's tour to West Africa.[1]

How a small repertory company from the East Midlands came to perform to a packed house in Nigeria is the story of this chapter. The Nottingham Playhouse Company followed its Lagos performance with fifty more shows in cities and towns around Nigeria, Ghana, and Sierra Leone—newly independent nations all of them. The British officials behind the tour had planned it very carefully, believing every detail—from the venues to the scenery to the plays themselves—was vital for what they considered a new phase of Britain's overtures to its former empire. The Nottingham players traveled to West Africa under the auspices of the British Council, an organization founded in the 1930s with the purpose of projecting national culture overseas. Through this quasi-state organization, the British government expected to influence audiences in Europe, which the council did for the next two decades. However, by the 1950s there were several in Whitehall who believed the council's geographical priorities were dated and no longer served the national interest. Over the next decade, British overseas representation became consumed with the global Cold War and with audiences largely outside the Western world. The Nottingham players' trip to West Africa was part of that large pivot. The discussions leading up to the tour, as well as the changes prompted by its success, reveal how the Cold War and decolonization not only affected where the British Council worked but challenged the entire premise of its pursuits.

The West Africans who attended the Nottingham performances in 1963 comprised a new audience for the British Council. Up until that point, the council designed its cultural export around a very select audience. In most parts of the world, that audience was elite, educated, and urban, which meant that black colonial subjects were all but excluded.[2] It was an approach that reflected the times and attitudes the British Council was born in, but it was also more than that, as many in the council believed their target audience guided the standards of their work. As this history describes, even when the council expanded the areas where it worked, council officers were reluctant to change their way of thinking. This pitted them against officials in the overseas departments of the British government who maintained that if Britain were to remain a global power, it must generate broader appeal in every sense of the term. With its experience in cultural export and its position next to but not within Whitehall, the British Council appeared best suited for the task of selling Britain to postcolonial audiences around the world—provided, that was, the council was willing to shift emphasis away from its traditional high-minded approach. Such were the political circumstances that brought drama export to the forefront of British cultural relations to Africa in the early 1960s.

Within the British arts, drama proved most malleable to the shifting demands being made of cultural relations. During the first decades of its work, the council had viewed drama alongside art, music, and dance as the fields to showcase the very best of British talent. After the 1950s, when the British government instructed the council to orient itself toward mass audiences, the council's officials started to lean more heavily on drama because they believed it was more obviously entertaining than the other arts, even to foreigners who did not completely understand what they saw. Even more importantly, as the council's officials came under pressure to defend continued arts funding, they recognized drama could tick off several boxes at once, including educational aims that were in line with Britain's new attention to development in Africa. Therefore, the changes that occurred in the council's cultural export were not limited to where it went and what audiences it performed to. Starting in the 1960s the council began orienting the form and content of its drama export in Africa around educational objectives and the needs of postcolonial audiences.

By focusing on the council's work in drama, then, this chapter examines large changes that occurred to Britain's cultural export in the early 1960s. To understand how those changes played out, it is necessary to pause and examine the British Council's internal organization and who got to decide what comprised British culture. Over the first three decades after its establishment in the 1930s, the council grew from a handful of departments and representations around the world to an organization with thousands of officials who worked in over seventy territories, including twenty in Africa.[3] British Council officials were divided between home and overseas posts, the former at the British Council headquarters in London and the latter at the council's representations, or what it termed its overseas offices. The council rotated its officials between London and overseas every three years, so a typical council career might begin with a three-year assistant representative post in colonial Nigeria, then three years in London in the council's Service Conditions department, then three years as a representative in Brazil, and so on. This showed how the council really differed from the British government's overseas departments; the council did not want to hone regional expertise among its officials, but rather preferred to think of their broad experience as a strength. During the 1940s and 1950s, the council slowly added colonial Africa to the areas of the world where it worked. After receiving instruction from the Colonial Office to open a new representation, the council dispatched one man to the urban capital, where he would find an office space, hire a few local staff, open a small library of British books and periodicals, and then look around for what the British Council would do there. This meant the council's influence and activities varied greatly across its representations in Africa, but a constant was that almost all decision-making took place in London. (Looking back on this era, representatives bemoaned the labor involved in writing back and forth to London to get something as small as a replacement mosquito net for the office.)[4] That certainly included all decisions about Britain's cultural export, or what and whom the British Council sponsored to go abroad. The history that follows here is about drama performances that were dreamed up in Britain, arranged from Britain, rehearsed in Britain, and then sent to different parts of Africa.

Yet, although much of the deliberation over British drama export to Africa actually took place in London, even there, it was not council employees who made the primary decisions about what was and was not British culture. The officials in the council's arts department relied upon a group of esteemed advisers in fields such as art, music, and in this instance theater. The content of British cultural exports rested in these advisers' hands, and in the process of determining which performers and performances to send under the label "British national culture," they also set the standards and relative values that propelled the British Council's entire arts program. In addition to relying on the advisers for their esteemed knowledge, taste, and contacts, the council's officials cherished the professional authority they lent to the organization's work. In the history that follows here, we will see how the drama advisers' opinions translated into British Council policies and actions. It becomes clear that the council's institutional layers and especially its reverence for its advisers' authority reinforced a certain view of cultural knowledge as something that emanated from the top and was handed down. Furthermore, such a top-down understanding of cultural knowledge mapped very neatly onto the council's entire mission to prescribe content and values from the British metropole outward to the rest of the world. As decolonization prompted large changes to the British Council's cultural export, however, we will see whether the council's top-down and centralized view of British culture also came under challenge.

CULTURAL OUTREACH TO SPECIFIC AUDIENCES

"No country to-day can expect to be understood by others if it remains aloof and passive."[5] The London *Times* hailed the appearance of the British Council in the mid-1930s as evidence Britain had at last caught on to the tangible merits of cultural promotion. The group of businessmen and Foreign Office officials behind the creation of the new body wanted to see the British government take a more active, planned role in promoting the ideas and feats that distinguished Britain from other cultures and civilizations. Among the distinctions they named were the English language, British literature and arts, and British political thought. In interwar Europe there was nothing new in the idea that promotion abroad of language, literature, and other aspects of national life could be a means of encouraging understanding and goodwill, particularly when "understanding and goodwill" translated to political alliances and economic trade partners. Indeed, by the 1930s all the other leading Western European nations had been engaging in this type of work for decades, and France and Germany considered it a crucial component of their respective foreign policies. The model for an institutionalized body of cultural promotion was the Alliance Française, which began in 1883 and expanded to centers all over the world, overseeing the teaching of the French language and arranging lectures and exhibitions on French arts.[6] The British Foreign Office estimated that by the 1930s, the French spent 6 million francs a year on this form of cultural promotion. From Italy the Dante Alighieri Society served a similar role, and though the Germans did not yet have a centralized institution, they were working hard to fortify national pride and *Deutschtum* in Germans around the world.

What *was* new about the British Council was that Britain was finally joining in this form of national promotion.[7] Until then, the British government had held a very utilitarian stance vis-à-vis national culture, both within and beyond its borders. (In 1930s Britain there were no state subsidies to the arts, no national theater, and no Arts Council.) This did not simply reflect the Treasury's ethos of cheap government; it was founded in a belief that British culture did not need any promotion because it spoke for itself. Leading British figures described how self-promotion was not only undignified, it was unnecessary. However, by the late 1920s and 1930s, as all other European nations stepped up their cultural presence overseas amid the global depression, the British government was forced to consider new methods of preserving its material interests. While some of the initiatives that date to this period, such as the BBC Empire Service, aimed to preserve imperial ties, the impetus that propelled the British Council was focused on regions outside the British world. Individuals in the Foreign Office had pushed hardest for the council's creation in the early 1930s, and in turn they expected their diplomatic and strategic agenda to dictate where the council would work. Giving these officials greater sway was their control over the British Council's revenue, which came from an annual grant-in-aid in the Foreign Office vote. During the 1930s, the council primarily worked in areas the government deemed strategically critical (western and southern Europe and the Middle East) and areas in which it sought to stimulate commercial trade (Central and South America). Although the British government directed where the council went, it did not provide consistent instructions about the specific content of the council's work.[8] In 1940 the council received a royal charter that described its aims in similarly amorphous language as that from the council's establishment: "the promotion of a wider knowledge of the United Kingdom and the English language abroad and the development of closer cultural relations with other countries."[9] What precisely this broad language could mean would be debated continuously over the next four decades.

In all the nations where it started to work in this period, the British Council focused its activities on elite urban audiences. Britain had begun the state-sponsored export of culture to keep up with its European neighbors; therefore, the council's initial efforts in the field mimicked the Alliance Française and similar organizations. In major cities like Madrid, Buenos Aires, and Cairo, the council worked through a centrally located British Institute from which it offered English classes, provided British books and newspapers, held British art exhibitions, and hosted lectures by well-known British academics.[10] The sites and the activities both sent strong signals about the presumptive audiences as urban, literate, and possessing a certain degree of leisure time—and that was true across all places the council worked. Yet, as the British Council's institutional structure and sense of mission took shape, there were large differences between its approach to cultural relations with the Western world and that in an area like the Middle East. When working in nations such as France and Italy, British Council representatives regularly described how Britain and the host made parallel contributions to modern civilization and the arts. The council heralded the notion of cultural interchange and organized exchanges between British and visiting symphony orchestras and dance companies. In these places, the council's desire for international exchange led to a relatively narrow sense of cultural work, but British officials were confident audiences would understand and fully appreciate what they saw.

It was a large contrast to the council's work in the Middle East, where British officials dropped any talk of exchange but also came to work across a much broader group of fields. The council's Middle East representative oversaw activities in nine areas—some independent nations, others British mandated territories, and still others British colonies. Across the entire region, however, British Council officials held the base view that there was none of the "cultural equality" they saw in European nations.[11] Therefore, in place of any cultural exchange, the council viewed its role as a disseminator of culture—where culture stood in for Western thought more broadly. At its British Institutes in the Middle East, the council provided lectures, books, and services on topics such as engineering, agriculture, science, and medicine. The council also opened or sponsored numerous elite schools around the region, where expatriate and elite children received British-style educations. Although the council's activities abutted fields such as agriculture or education, the British government insisted the council was a cultural body, not a development agency. In Whitehall's view, the crucial distinction was that the council's work was limited to elite, well-educated urban populations. That would continue to be the case as the British government deployed the council to other areas of the world.

After being ignored by the British Council in the 1930s, the empire became an area for expansion in the 1940s. The push to extend the council's work into the British colonies came from key individuals inside the council, such as the chairman Lord Lloyd, who interpreted the council's broad mission as part of a grander imperial vision. Lloyd believed in what had become an old-fashioned way of thinking about the British Empire, wherein the British people had a duty to carry out the noble task of civilizing other populations.[12] In 1940 Lloyd was appointed secretary of state for the colonies, which he held concurrently with his position as chairman of the British Council for the next year. He was thus able to initiate the council's entry into other parts of the colonial empire such as West Africa and the Caribbean. The council recruited former colonial administrators to join its new empire division and investigate the type of work the council should pursue in the colonies. Council officials did not feel they needed to explain that in these areas of the world a two-way exchange was impossible and that, instead, it was Britain's role to impart cultural knowledge to local audiences. However, as the council began to open representations in West Africa and the Caribbean, it ran into conflicts with some of the colonial administrations who were reluctant to cede any ground to an alternative body. For instance, in the mid-1940s the Gold Coast governor Sir Alan Burns insisted to London that his government could better carry out all the British Council's functions. Burns and other colonial governors did not want to share newly available development funds with the council, nor did they want any interference in their efforts to enlarge their own information apparatus. When the council defended the strategy behind maintaining its appearance as an independent body, Burns acquiesced slightly to allow the council to work on libraries and an interracial institute in Accra.[13] Even so, the British Council representative assigned to the Gold Coast spent most of the 1940s resisting the colonial government's attempts to absorb his work into the government Public Relations Department.[14]

The Gold Coast governor's complaint was a call to examine whether Britain should silo the domains of culture, development, and propaganda in the colonies. Like other government officials in the Colonial Office and the British Treasury, Burns wanted to see firm steps to rein in the council's amorphous mission. His hopes were met during postwar austerity and a push to seek out and erase possible overlaps between different parts of government spending. In August 1948, the Colonial Office issued a definition document between itself and the council that aimed to demarcate the separate categories of culture and development. The British Council received charge of the former, which the policy limited to drama, music, exhibitions, lectures, and specialty films and broadcasts—activities the definition document described as nonpolitical. Meanwhile, the Colonial Office retained full responsibility for work in the burgeoning domain of colonial development.[15] Through the definition document, the Colonial Office sought to curtail the broader understanding of culture that the council had adopted in certain parts of the world. But, in spelling out what constituted a cultural activity and what a development objective, British officials realized how slippery those spheres really were. The most concrete distinction in the definition document was that of whom Britain sought to influence with its different activities. The definition document instructed the council to cull audiences from the top echelons of society, while the Colonial Office had charge over the population as a whole. For the most part, education and library activities fell in the category of development because they were oriented toward general audiences. A division along this line meant the British Council could offer a course on British life to UK-bound students but could not teach English to secondary students. In a similar vein, the council could lend out recordings and films of Shakespeare and Dickens but not hold film screenings on malaria prevention or soil erosion.

Therefore, even if the council had wanted to expand its reach to wider parts of the colonial population, it no longer could. Of course, it was not clear that the council's officials were all that interested in engaging with colonial subjects anyway. As part of an organization that only engaged with elite populations in other parts of the world, the council's first representatives in colonial Africa focused their attention on only the uppermost echelons of colonial society. For example, upon arriving in Kenya in 1947, the representative Richard Frost decided the council's primary objective in the settler colony was to promote interracial harmony "by a mixture of example and persuasion."[16] Over the following years, Frost measured his success by whether European groups such as the Nairobi Musical Society, the Arts and Crafts Society, and the East African Natural History Association were willing to strike any "European only" language from their constitutions—although he did not consider whether any of the organizations actually admitted nonwhite members. Meanwhile, he discounted Asian and African groups and movements because he believed they worked against the color-blind society he was trying to build.[17] Frost's starry-eyed attitude toward race relations was typical of British Council representatives in colonial Africa who believed they could promote British culture and values in a manner that was outside politics.

By limiting itself to only a narrow segment of associational life, the council had difficulty generating interest among African populations. As in Kenya, British Council officials in the Gold Coast spent most of their energy during the colonial period establishing and running a cultural center in the capital where—they hoped—Europeans and Africans would come together for dramatic performances, art exhibitions, and music recitals. But year after year, the council representatives reported back to London that African attendance at its events was painfully small. They noted this could not be due to anti-British sentiment, because the Alliance Française branch in the Gold Coast had the same experience. The council's officials in West Africa offered telling explanations for the council's lack of appeal. Writing in 1958 after Ghana's independence, for example, one representative observed a "noticeable dearth of cultural institutions, groups, and societies" in Ghana as well as "an almost total lack of intellectual curiosity amongst Ghanaians."[18] Across colonial Africa, the British Council oriented its work toward elite, mostly European audiences and then expressed surprise its events did not attract much African interest. But in a damaging manner, as the next section will reveal, the low attendance among Africans reinforced ideas within the council that African populations could not understand or appreciate British culture.

As the British Council spread to more and more parts of the world, everywhere it oriented itself toward highly educated urban audiences. In western Europe, where the council began its work, the British believed a larger portion of the population could understand British culture than in non-western parts of the world, where the council only appeared interested in reaching a small, mostly expatriate portion of the population. As much as it set parameters around the council, the British government left it to the council to determine how it would tackle its vague assignment to project British culture to these audiences. Which performers?

Which performances? Where should they go? The next section looks more closely at how the council decided which performers and performances were worthy of the label "British national culture." In so doing, it reveals how the council used its target audiences to defend the high-minded thinking behind its decisions.

ALL THE WORLD'S A STAGE

The British Council's work in drama export reveals not only the performers and performances the council was willing to label "British national culture," but also the audiences it determined were most important for Britain's cultural relations in the mid-twentieth century. The council began incorporating drama and dance performances into its work during the late 1930s. Representatives from organizations such as the Society of West End Theatre Managers and the Critics' Circle comprised a drama and dance advisory committee that took up the task of recruiting and sponsoring British companies to go on overseas tours. The council could not afford to fund an entire overseas tour, but the advisory committee arranged for small advances—up to £1,000 or so—to be repaid against any earnings. Just like in the council's other fields of work, the advisory committee's main criterion was that it promoted metropolitan culture of the highest standard, or the best Britain had to offer. The committee members established a policy that the British Council would only sponsor tours by professional companies like the Royal Ballet or the Old Vic Theatre Company, and that they were not interested in considering groups or works that they were not intimately familiar with.[19]

The certainty with which the council's advisers proclaimed what should represent British culture implicitly reflected ongoing anxiety about the decline of culture inside Britain.[20] Just as with its committees on music, film, and books, the council's drama advisers came from the political and cultural elite. They represented a London-centered, elite version of the stage, which they had clear financial, political, and cultural interests in preserving. When the drama advisers spoke about theatrical traditions in Britain during their meetings, they did not mention the rowdy Victorian music hall, variety shows, or even the "repertory" of provincial theaters. Instead, they idealized a stage that was conservative and refined and that satisfied the tastes of metropolitan bourgeois audiences.

In the middle of the twentieth century the council's advisers feared this form of traditional theater was coming under challenge from multiple directions. First, they were still uncomfortable with some of the new aesthetics and politics theatrical modernism had introduced onto the British stage and some of the new dramatists, such as George Bernard Shaw, who had gained inclusion in a more modern canon. Though the West End only slowly accepted the Irish Fabian, Shaw was a mainstay for regional repertory theaters that started to appear around Britain in the first part of the century. The relative success of some of these provincial companies represented a second challenge to London theater—a movement to democratize the stage beyond the capital. After the introduction of Arts Council funding in 1946, which made it easier for new groups to enter the field, regional theater grew even more. By far, however, the largest threat to British theater in the first half of the twentieth century came from the cinema. By the late 1930s, twenty-three million Britons attended the cinemas each week, where they saw—among other things—a preponderance of Hollywood films. In terms of theater attendance, the arrival of cinema was most devastating for popular theater forms such as the variety show, but audiences diminished in all types of theater over the first half of the century. By the outbreak of the Second World War British theater had become the domain of small relatively specialized segments of society.[21] In a certain manner, this pattern reinforced the British theater tradition that members of the cultural elite sought to preserve. They saw in the stage a cultural form that could resist massification and Americanization, a place where aesthetic and critical standards could be upheld.[22]

British theater performance, then, fit neatly into the British Council's design for cultural export. The drama experts who advised the council on which performances were worthy of export were able to deny their own anxieties about the future of British theater and national culture. In projecting a national theater tradition to outsiders, the British Council was also safeguarding a particular and unchanging version of its culture. For that to continue being true, however, the council had to uphold its standards concerning which performers and performances went overseas under its name. For the first several decades of its drama export, the council used its anticipated audiences to justify its choice performances and vice versa. If Britain sought to attract and impress influential individuals, the council reasoned, it must deploy only the most highly esteemed performances. At the same time, the same officials explained, the British Council preferred to work with elite audiences because those were the most likely to understand and be impressed by the types of culture the council wanted to promote. As the council worked to come up with a consistent understanding of "British culture," its advisers' criteria excluded the clear majority of overseas populations.

Initially, the British Council hoped to see British theater companies realize their national responsibility and commit to performing only British *works* when touring overseas. Instead the council settled for getting the right British *companies* to go overseas. In 1947, the British Council was very excited to add its name to a commercial tour in Australia and New Zealand by the Old Vic Company. The council's drama advisers agreed that the Old Vic and its headliners, Laurence Olivier and Vivian Leigh, certainly represented the best of British theater. When the council asked to see the company's program, it received in response a list of three diverse pieces: the Shakespeare drama *Richard III*, the Sheridan comedy *The School for Scandal*, and a modern Thornton Wilder play *The Skin of Our Teeth*.

During the next drama committee meeting, the council's advisers unanimously commended the first two selections. However, they were very unhappy with the third because its author was American. The council demanded the Old Vic select an alternative play by a British author instead, but the protests were to no avail.[23] Although the British Council's name was on the tour, it was the theater company that was paying for the actors' passages and letting its headliners perform away from Britain for such a long period, so the final decision did not rest with the council. Nevertheless, despite the problematic origins of one of the three pieces, the British Council celebrated the Old Vic's tour to Australia and New Zealand as one of its crowning achievements from the period.[24]

Over the next decade this pattern of acquiescence became common for the British Council—on certain matters at least. In 1957 the British Council gave approval for the Glyndebourne Opera to represent Britain at the Théâtre des Nations festival in Paris. Glyndebourne's program comprised two Italian operas—Verdi's *Falstaff* and Rossini's *Le Comte Ory*—with the latter in French. The drama advisers arranged for council sponsorship and maintained that the company's program and international cast still fell under their mandate to promote British culture overseas. After all, they reasoned, such high-quality selections projected an important message about British musical taste. (Plus, the costumes were British and the baritone singing Falstaff was Welsh!)[25] But it would be misleading to imply the British Council was becoming more flexible in its overall approach to national culture during the 1950s. Yes, the council made allowances, even going so far as to sponsor non-British works, to uphold what it deemed the standards of high culture. At the same time, the council made clear it was only interested in working with a select group of well-established companies and did not want to associate with any of the newer, more political types of groups or works that were emerging in Britain during the period. In 1959, the year after Glyndebourne went to Paris, Joan Littlewood's Theatre Workshop was invited to the same festival. The company expected to perform *The Hostage*, a play that examined Irish nationalism and contained lines the council's drama advisers thought were insulting and derogatory to England. The British Council refused to give any endorsement or funding.[26]

As they were making these decisions, the British Council's advisers and officials saw themselves as defenders of cultural standards, particularly as the council increasingly came under attack for its activities and audiences. The British press had been attacking the British Council since its start, with the most consistent and vicious attacks coming from the Beaverbrook newspapers. During the 1940s, hundreds of articles in the *Daily Express* and the *Evening Standard* divulged details about the council's extravagant expenses, pedantic events, and inconsequential audiences. Although Lord Beaverbrook's feud with the British Council was well known, the stories still struck a nerve during economic austerity. One member of the British public stated, "As a worker and tax payer I resent being ordered to work harder, to smoke, eat and bath [*sic*] less and to save more, to help maintain a useless and extravagant herd of officials and to give dubious foreigners luxurious entertainment quite beyond the means or dreams of the British working classes."[27] Taxpayers were not the only ones asking whether the British Council's activities were beneficial and vital to Britain, as government officials too were questioning if this was the best way to fight the Cold War. During the late 1940s and early 1950s, the British Council saw repeated reductions to the funds it received from the three overseas departments.[28] (Once the council began working in the colonies and Commonwealth, its funding came from those departments as well as the Foreign Office.) Being part of Britain's broader efforts in overseas information, which also included the BBC external services and the United Kingdom Information Services, was a double-edged sword: the council was not alone in lobbying for additional funds but the council also needed to distinguish its particular value, or what it offered that the BBC and information services did not.

The British Council believed its work in the performing arts critically distinguished it from other information services. Throughout the 1950s, council officials continued to argue that they alone influenced elite, high-minded populations (or crucial "neutrals and waverers" when phrasing their defense in Cold War terms) in contrast to the groups of students and clerks the other information services targeted.[29] Yet, within the government grant-in-aid, the portion for the arts was shrinking even faster than the rest of the council's funding. The 1952 estimates reduced the arts allocation to only 1 percent of the British Council's entire budget, a snub that the chair of the drama advisory committee saw as so egregious he felt obligated to resign.[30] He was one among many inside the council who believed high culture was the organization's raison d'être. Even though they had a smaller budget to work with, the drama advisers' decisions over the rest of the 1950s reflected how important they regarded their standards. The council's arts proponents accused the British government of falsely thinking that *Hamlet* was *Hamlet* and it didn't matter if Laurence Olivier was in the role, while they—and, they presumed, their audiences—knew it was Olivier that made all the difference.[31]

As the British Council incorporated the colonial empire into its overseas activities, it did so with a firm understanding of a cultural hierarchy that relegated colonial subjects to the bottom. British Council officials believed audiences in Western countries had sophisticated tastes and high standards and must be served only the very top performances from Britain. They assumed audiences in other places were less discerning. Therefore, when the Oxford Repertory Company proposed traveling to the United States in 1945, the drama committee opposed it. The committee members believed Britain could not send just an "ordinary English rep company" to the United States, where artistic standards were high, but acceded to the idea that Oxford could go to the West Indies, where they assumed performance standards were much lower.[32]

As Britain's work in overseas representation grew, the British Council's willingness to sponsor only a select type of theater company became a hindrance to its larger mission. The council had a policy that it would only give financial support to professional companies. Throughout the 1940s, it refused to sponsor any amateur companies "on the grounds that the standards of their performance fell below professional competence."[33] But as tours such as that of the Old Vic to Australia received acclaim and press, it prompted other British Council representatives to contact the London headquarters and request they receive equal attention. The council acknowledged that amateur companies and university groups were more likely to be available for lengthy tours and could meet the new demand. Yet, when the question of reversing the amateur policy first came up in the early 1950s, council executives decided against it, saying there was a limited amount of public funding to go around, and the council should assist the highest-quality performances first.[34] But a decade later, after the council had secured greater funds to use on drama tours, it found itself hamstrung by its own policy. For example, when the Royal Shakespeare Company informed the British Council it was going to stop doing foreign trips, the council's drama advisers lamented that they were left with only one established company (the Old Vic) to call on.[35]

It was at this point, in the early 1960s, that the British Council finally widened the field from which it selected its drama tours. At the end of 1961, the council removed its ban on sponsoring amateur and provincial companies. Council officials made it clear they did not want to change in any way the cultural programs they already offered and that they expected Western audiences would continue receiving the same respected performers as before. Instead, the looser policy toward amateur and provincial theater was meant to serve the new area for drama export—namely, the former empire.[36] Although the council had acquiesced on so many other components of its cultural program before, the decision to broaden the field for drama export was significant in what it would mean for the British Council's work in a decolonizing and developing world.

"A FUNDAMENTAL RE-ORIENTATION"

The significance of the council's policy change is only apparent when examined alongside larger changes that had begun to take place within Britain's broader cultural relations program. Since first put forward in the early 1950s by a committee under Lord Drogheda, there was a growing idea in Britain that cultural relations should be more oriented around education than around culture, especially in regions where Britain saw a need for development. The British government formed the Drogheda committee to investigate Britain's combined overseas representation and particularly how Britain stacked up against other nations. The committee's report confirmed something the BBC and British Council had argued for years, which was that British austerity cuts were a self-inflicted wound on Britain's power and prosperity and that the damage continued to grow the more other nations built up their services. Although the Drogheda investigation led to an immediate injection of funds, Britain still lagged far behind other nations. (To give just one example, Britain's £12.5 million annual allotment for overseas representation was still paltry in comparison to the £65 million the United States spent on comparable services each year.)[37] At least the new funds were a turn in the right direction, council officials thought, and they could breathe a sigh of relief that their organization would not be starved into nonexistence. However, as a little more time went by and these officials absorbed more of the Drogheda report's implications, they started to see how cultural work as they previously practiced it was in danger of disappearing.

The Drogheda report's real significance rested in its demand that the council redefine the role of the arts. The Drogheda committee sharply criticized the council's tendency to see any single form of cultural export—whether an art exhibition, an opera tour, etcetera—as having a purpose all its own. Instead, the report stressed, the British Council must adhere to the same thinking as the BBC did when designing its schedule: use entertainment to lure a foreign listener, then get him to stay for the news and commentary.[38] In other words, the report reiterated the government's stance that British cultural export was only meant as a means and never an end. To the council's arts champions, the message became even clearer when the Drogheda committee advocated for a "fundamental reorientation . . . a change of emphasis from cultural to educational work and from the more developed to the less developed parts of the world."[39] The report instructed that moving forward, the council should direct its attention and funding to the Middle East, South and Southeast Asia, and the British colonies. This was where the government wanted to see the council make a large push in fields such as English-language teaching and specialist education, at the expense of what it had been doing in western Europe or the white dominions.[40] Thinking again about the drama advisers' preferences and patterns, it might appear the council's traditional drama activities had reached the beginning of the end.

If one expected to see this moment as the last time the British Council sponsored an Old Vic tour to Australia, they would be very wrong. By the late 1950s the council's drama advisers and officials found a way to continue much of their old pattern and still act in line with the Drogheda recommendations. The key, they realized, lay in emphasizing that drama did multiple things simultaneously: not only was it cultural, it was also *educational*. The drama advisers believed this small rhetorical change would make a big difference. That was particularly because following the Drogheda report the British government had started providing the British Council additional funds to expand its English-language teaching in the developing world. The program included an allotment for drama work that contributed toward the teaching of English, and in the 1959–60 fiscal year that allotment was £12,000, or about a quarter of the council's entire music and drama budget.[41] In 1959, after learning the Old Vic planned another commercial tour to Australia, the drama advisory committee brainstormed how they could attach the British Council name. They proposed adding a six-week stopover in India to the tour, where the esteemed company would perform in Madras, Calcutta, Bombay, and Delhi (the only cities that had what they deemed suitable theaters). The advisers' interest was plain; by stopping in India, the Old Vic's tour furthered English instruction in a developing nation. In other words, they hoped to see the British Council capitalize on the new funds without having to adjust what they saw as its standards.[42]

This instance from the turn of the decade was important for what it revealed about what many in the British Council characterized as their relative values and core audience. As a government-funded organization, the council could not ignore directives to shift its attention toward the decolonizing and developing world. Yet several inside the council—the arts departments and advisers first and foremost—undertook that shift only reluctantly. The same was true for the decision two years later to begin sponsoring provincial and university companies: while it was a practical solution in response to growing demand and increased funding, there was still an underlying regret among council officials that they were giving up some of the standards that marked their brand. At this stage, although only two years had passed, efforts within the council to resist or find a work-around were much less likely to succeed. By the early 1960s, British cultural relations organizations could not deny any longer the post-imperial world in which they now operated.

"WHAT WE IN BRITAIN ARE BEST EQUIPPED TO DO"

However loud the complaints about what British cultural relations were losing, there were others within the council who viewed decolonization as an immense opportunity. The Drogheda report did not immediately impact the council's work in Britain's colonies because the definition document still parceled educational work to colonial governments. But with independence, the restrictions no longer applied, and the British Council was free to work in many more fields than it ever had before. Council officials in both London and overseas posts quickly interpreted that a larger role would equal a larger British Council, which would equal more funding.[43] At the same time, it also required more diplomacy: the council's continued presence was at the bequest of the national government, so the British Council would constantly have to prove either its benign conduct or its overwhelming usefulness. It was a "delicate position," as one council representative remarked after Ghana's independence in 1957, but a position that nevertheless appeared more advantageous than the prior period.[44]

As more African nations attained independence the urgency to find new ways to appeal to their citizens only intensified. With independence in Nigeria (October 1960) and Sierra Leone (April 1961) the Commonwealth Relations Office (CRO) gained two more West African nations in the early 1960s. The British high commissioners in these former colonies soon joined the chorus of concern that Britain lacked a way to appeal to wide numbers of West Africans. Like in Ghana, the council was known for putting on stodgy events such as orchestra concerts and art exhibits, at which African attendance had always been low. Meanwhile, the Americans and the Soviets had each recently sponsored very popular events, including tours by a jazz ensemble, a circus, and an ice show.[45] Seeing the excitement that arose around their rivals' events, CRO officials declared that Britain could not afford to wait for the long-term effects of Commonwealth scholarships or other forms of assistance to set in. They demanded the council supply something with an immediate and broad appeal, even if, as the high commissioner in Nigeria exposited, it meant the council had to get creative.[46]

However, the British Council was reluctant to attach its name to the types of activities the CRO had in mind because it wanted to protect the reputation it had cultivated. The council representative in Sierra Leone explained that any lapse, like a popular music or sporting event such as what the high commissioners suggested, would signal the British Council had become a purveyor of popular entertainment, thus ruining its hard-earned reputation for high quality. As a cautionary tale, he described what had happened to the United States Information Services in Freetown, which added more popular entertainment to its radio broadcasts and quickly saw its reputation dwindle.[47] The British Council might have been changing its pattern of work in West Africa, but it did not want to swing too far in the other direction or pander blatantly. So, when the idea of sending a major British tour to West Africa first came up in 1961, the Commonwealth Relations Office wanted to see a variety show or something with obvious popular appeal, while the British Council countered with a combined lecture/recital tour by a British theater director and an actor. The British government did not get behind the council's idea, and it fell through.[48]

The following year the British government and the British Council found an option entertaining enough for the British government and cultured enough for the council. Their plan was to send sixteen members of the Nottingham Playhouse Company on an extended tour around West Africa in 1963. Nottingham was the council's second choice (the Windsor Rep was not free that year), but, having decided by that point to widen the field from which it chose its drama tours, the council was very satisfied with the option. In particular, having become used to having to coax companies to work with the council, the drama advisers commented how impressed they were by the director and actors' enthusiasm at the opportunity. It is worth noting that even though it was a regional theater, the

Nottingham Playhouse was still a professional company with a national reputation as an exemplar of the revitalized repertory movement in Britain.[49] Like the members of many regional theaters in the postwar period, the Nottingham actors were committed to reaching new theater audiences and experimenting with different theater styles—and that was likely a large reason for their enthusiastic response to the opportunity to go to West Africa. Although the council's advisers had long resisted sponsoring provincial theater companies, they discovered new benefits when they finally did so, as they were working with actors who were also willing and enthusiastic ambassadors.

Just as it had in earlier decades, the British Council believed the content of the tour mattered almost as much as the performers. In the months leading up to the actors' departure the British Council worked with the company to set the program. The council had decided immediately that one of the three plays should be *Macbeth*, since it was a set book for West African school certificate exams that year. It took longer to determine the other two selections, mostly because the council's drama advisers were very concerned African audiences would not be able to understand the material. (Although the council's drama advisers admitted not knowing very much about West Africa, they felt certain that African audiences were less sophisticated than those in South Asia.) They finally agreed on a repertoire of Shakespeare and Shaw: *Macbeth*, *Twelfth Night*, and *Arms and the Man*, a small-cast play so some of the actors could have an occasional rest. The council's advisers were pleased with the program, feeling the comedies would keep the material accessible, while the repertoire and headliners, James Cairncross and Judi Dench, kept it a distinguishably British event.[50]

When the Nottingham Playhouse Company kicked off its tour in Lagos, Nigeria, on 11 January 1963, the actors were not sure what at all to expect. In a radio interview back in Britain, one cast member recalled his shock on opening night during *Macbeth*, a play he had previously believed he knew quite well. "At moments when we didn't really expect it at all they laughed with great enthusiasm. This was very bracing and we said we'd better be careful not to let this happen next time. It didn't ever really completely fall away because *Macbeth*, if you're not careful, can be quite a funny play."[51] Although they were taken aback at first, over the next ten weeks the British actors became more accustomed to the demonstrative audiences, which they described as a refreshing change. The same cast member continued, "When we were doing *Twelfth Night*, which was very popular, I remember one night in particular, a lot of school children as well as grown-ups. At the moment when Sebastian was clearly going to meet and recognize Viola the audience went up in a burst of enormous spontaneous applause. Now you'd never get that in England, you'd never get such a warmth and response."[52] During later tours of Shakespeare in Africa, other British actors would express very similar sentiment and that they felt their performances were more authentic in front of African audiences.

FIGURE 1. The Nottingham Playhouse Company after arriving at the Accra Airport from Nigeria. The National Archives, Kew, United Kingdom, INF 10/127/1 (1963).

Demand alone made the tour a hit from the start. There was a black market for tickets in Lagos, where the Nottingham players opened in the national theater. Then, at a later stop, an opportunistic businessman printed up and sold a duplicate batch of tickets. The fraud was not discovered until audiences arrived at the theater, and then the actors had to delay their performance until two hundred extra seats could be found and squeezed into the hall. After so many of their events had scanty turnouts, the British Council officials in West Africa were surprised to learn playgoers from an entire surrounding area were willing to travel and pay so they could see Shakespeare in this form. After the first few performances, however, British officials in West Africa realized how large a success they had on their hands and scrambled to capitalize. They started to look for ways to increase audience numbers however possible, even if it meant moving performances from indoor theaters and cinemas to open air spaces. For instance, one of the company's upcoming stops was in Nsukka in southeastern Nigeria, where the council had reserved the main theater, which could seat a few hundred people. But after seeing the turnout for the first several stops, the council decided to move the performance to the open-air sports stadium instead. The Nottingham players ended up performing on a makeshift stage to an estimated audience of thirteen hundred Nigerians. As with most of their stops, the British actors did not have much time to rehearse or get used to the stage before the first performance; however, that only added to the sense of unworldliness they later used to describe these performances. In one anecdote, for instance, Judi Dench recalled the vultures that would perch atop the cinema screen behind the stage and remembered thinking, "For goodness' sake twitch when you're killed, they're waiting to pick your bones."[53]

In their reports back to London, British Council representatives emphasized repeatedly what terrific ambassadors Britain had gained with the Nottingham tour. The local British officials were struck by the Nottingham players' flexibility to adapt to rudimentary set design, perform in sports stadiums, and accommodate difficult travel conditions. They explained to London that these well-known actors were exemplars of the personal qualities and traits the London headquarters must look for from then on when deciding who to send to an area of the world like West Africa. As further evidence that visiting company members' personal demeanors could make or break a tour's success, the council's West Africa representatives went into detail about the Nottingham actors' genuine interest and interactions with Africans off the stage. As they described it, the "free, unfussy, unself-conscious way in which the Company mixed with local people of all kinds—Governors to schoolgirls" made an enormous contribution to Britain's cultural message.[54] Britain's official information services set out to capture this in their promotional photographs, such as one photograph of John Neville meeting playgoers after a performance in Ghana (figure 2). From afar, the image would appear strikingly familiar to someone back in Britain—a celebrity surrounded by gushing schoolgirls—and was intended to convey there was no barrier between British and West African individuals. Visitors like the Nottingham actors provided the British Council's local offices an opportunity to demonstrate that Britons were genuinely interested in African history and culture. One noticeable instance of this occurred during the company's final night in West Africa. For the send-off celebration, a headmaster in Sierra Leone arranged for his students to perform a scene from *Julius Caesar* in Krio, a language the British colonial government discouraged during its rule but that was resurgent after independence. After the performance, the British visitors lauded praise on the student performance and really emphasized the Krio added liveliness and excitement to the scene that the English language did not capture.[55]

Both the British Council and the British government deemed the Nottingham tour a grand success, albeit for different reasons. The council's drama advisers evaluated the tour primarily through the content and the performance. They knew prior to the tour that the Nottingham company sought to adapt the works to audiences who might not be able to follow all the dialogue but could still follow the

FIGURE 2. John Neville of the Nottingham Playhouse Company after a school matinee performance of *Macbeth* in the Ghana Institute of Art and Culture in Accra. The UK Central Office of Information captioned, "John Neville is surrounded by a group of youthful admirers, some of those who packed the hall to capacity." The National Archives, Kew, United Kingdom, INF 10/127/2 (1963).

action without difficulty. With the comedies, the performers succeeded to a wild degree, especially with *Twelfth Night*, which local British officials declared Africans found colorful, vivid, and highly entertaining.[56] But the council's drama advisers in London were disappointed to hear that some reviews of *Macbeth* were tepid. They assumed at first it was because less educated playgoers had simply not understood the material or performance. A few months later, however, they heard something that gave them pause: the loudest dissatisfaction came from the council's traditional audience of Europeans and university-educated Africans, while the council's new audience of secondary and college students had responded enthusiastically.

In other words, the council was having some success attracting postcolonial audiences, but to continue in that direction might involve losing some of the esteem it had once enjoyed. This was something the council's drama advisers were going to have to continue thinking about, and that would take some time.

While the council's drama advisers evaluated the tour's success through its content, British officials celebrated the political impact. With this tour, many felt that the British Council had finally achieved in West Africa what it was meant to: culture that had measurable political value. In their reports back to London they highlighted audience figures and how Britain stacked up against foreign competitors. In Ghana, where nearly fifteen thousand people saw the Nottingham performances, the UK high commissioner reported that the three-week trip did more to cement Anglo-Ghanaian friendship than a year or more of diplomatic activity.[57] The council representative in Eastern Nigeria echoed those sentiments, "This is without doubt the greatest single impact [the British Council has] made on the Region since Independence and possibly before. . . . Some 7,000 people (from the Governor-General downwards) saw the Company in action, over 1,500 column inches of space were devoted to it in the Eastern Nigerian press, [and] there was extensive coverage on the radio and television."[58] In Northern Nigeria the British Council representative compared the British tour to what other nations were doing in the field and concluded theirs was not only bigger, better, and more organized, but of more value to local audiences. The deputy high commissioner in Eastern Nigeria also positioned Britain's success against its competitors. "Neither the American Holiday on Ice show nor the Russian Circus troupe made anything like the impact which the Nottingham Players have made. In bringing this Company to perform Shakespeare, we have provided not only exactly what the Eastern Nigerians like best, but exactly what we in Britain are best equipped to do."[59]

Since African independence, the British Council had been looking for how it could serve African and British interests simultaneously; with the Nottingham tour in 1963, the council believed it was finally on to something. The Nottingham tour fulfilled three demands being made of British cultural outreach in postcolonial Africa. First, theater provided entertainment, and the tour therefore satisfied Britain's aim to stay competitive with the United States, the USSR, and other international powers. Second, drama export was a cultural activity that was consistent with what the British Council had been doing overseas since the organization's start; therefore, it quieted anxiety about a slipping mission. Last, the presentation of known plays in English—plays that appeared on exams at that—fell under the category of education and was thus part of the growing developmentalist mission that defined Britain's continued presence in the region. The increasing importance of drama to Britain's cultural relations was reflected in the government's grant-in-aid. For the 1956/57 fiscal year, the government grant-in-aid allotted the council £15,000 to support drama and music tours overseas. Seven years later, that amount was £160,000. But the government allotted that funding with specific instructions to the council's advisers that they could not concentrate all their activities in the developed world; instead, they must pay attention to demand from areas such as Africa and South Asia. The council found itself assessing a much different set of local, political, and artistic factors as it tried to spread British culture to more and more parts of the world.[60]

BRINGING SHAKESPEARE TO THE PEOPLE

Following the Nottingham Playhouse's accomplishments in West Africa, the British Council had mixed success as it tried to be more flexible in its approach to drama export to Africa. First, the council experimented with new formats for its British tours that were increasingly scaled down in size and even more oriented toward education. This pattern started to reveal itself later in 1963 when the council arranged for producer Peter Potter to lead a group of seven actors on a nine-week tour to Mauritius, Uganda, Sudan, and Ethiopia. Though the program also featured Shakespeare and Shaw, this tour was organized a little differently than the Nottingham Playhouse tour. In each colony or country, Potter's group linked up with a local company or drama group and cast local residents in small roles and as extras in the productions. For example, in Mauritius the cast for *Julius Caesar* contained over one hundred extras from the island's European and African communities. In addition to giving seventeen performances in Mauritius, Potter and the professional actors also delivered lectures and acting demonstrations at schools, thus increasing the number of ways they interacted with the public.[61] The next year Peter Potter returned to East Africa and repeated the experiment with another of Shakespeare's plays. This time he and three British actors led amateurs in productions of *A Midsummer Night's Dream* in Mauritius and Ethiopia and then traveled around Ethiopia, Uganda, and Libya performing Shakespeare recitals in primary and secondary schools.[62] Potter's entire tour covered four nations for only £2,450, a fraction of the £15,000 cost to send the Nottingham Playhouse to West Africa or £40,000 to send the Old Vic back to India.[63] Indeed, cost and flexibility were big factors in why the British Council's drama export to Africa evolved into scaled-down tours that focused on students.

With both the Nottingham Playhouse and Peter Potter tours, both the lower cost and the higher likelihood of availability solved the difficulty the council had in meeting demand, especially now that the British government expected it to practice cultural relations with the entire world, not just developed nations. It also helped resolve something the council's drama officials had been rather anxious about—what to do for the major Shakespeare anniversary that was fast approaching. The year of 1964 was the Shakespeare Quatercentenary, an anniversary that

British Council officials imbued with almost as much importance as a monarch's jubilee. British Council officials and drama advisers did not want to see the anniversary go unnoticed anywhere and had already planned to spend half of the music and drama budget for 1964 on Shakespeare Quatercentenary tours.[64] Even so, they recognized they were not capable of sending a well-known company to every region of the world, especially because the major British companies would also have demanding schedules at home.[65] But the past couple of years had demonstrated that what the council had once deemed lesser companies or just a few relatively unknown individuals could still accomplish quite a lot.

After the mid-1960s, the typical format for British drama export to sub-Saharan Africa was the one- or two-person Shakespeare school tour. A big contrast to the large company tour, the council had made some use of this type of drama tour before, such as Rosalinde Fuller's trips to the Middle East, South Africa, and East Africa performing a recital of monologues, including scenes as Ophelia, Juliet, and Lady Macbeth. The council continued to use Fuller throughout the 1960s.[66] By the late 1960s and throughout the 1970s, the council arranged for many similar recital tours, often working with a handful of British actors over and over. Even when the Nottingham Playhouse's follow-up tour was canceled, the conciliatory arrangement was one of these two-person tours; in 1969, Judi Dench and James Cairncross returned to West Africa with a Shakespeare recital. When it was only a couple of actors, the trip did not need nearly as much advance planning—in fact, sometimes it was only one or two months before departure when the details came together. What typically happened was the drama advisers and London officials contacted the actors and passed along any requirements, leaving the in-country British Council representatives to schedule performances around the country. For many of the tours, the pair of actors would give a couple of performances in theaters in large cities, but would then spend a good deal of their time in university and school halls or in rural areas giving performances to schoolchildren. Most tours had simple costumes, but no scenery.[67] By this point, then, it was obvious that the British Council's drama export had moved away from its singular focus on the caliber and prestige of its performers. Instead, drama export to Africa and other parts of the developing world now centered on content and how it met educational objectives.

By the 1970s, the British Council's drama export to Africa was almost entirely an educational endeavor. This is obvious when looking at how the council determined the material for these tours; it was no longer a decision made in the metropole but instead usually hinged on a nation's curricular needs and requests. In a memoir titled *The Bard in the Bush,* John Fraser, an actor who traveled several times under the council's auspices, recalled how a typical conversation with the council's drama department would go, such as this call-up to go to West Africa in three weeks.

"What they want is Shakespeare."

"What play?"

"The tour has been arranged for school-children, and they've asked specifically for the plays they're studying. It'll help them with their exams."

"Plays? You mean more than one? In three weeks?"

"If you can manage it, they'd like *Macbeth, The Merchant of Venice, The Taming of the Shrew, Henry V, Twelfth Night*, and perhaps *Julius Caesar* and *The Tempest* for Cameroon."

"I see. Just *The Complete Works* in fact. Easy. Three weeks . . ."[68]

Fraser and the actor Suzan Farmer ended up giving forty-nine performances of extracts from *Macbeth* and *The Merchant of Venice* in eight weeks. (The tour went one week longer than planned because an aborted coup in Nigeria closed the airports.) The British Council officials in Nigeria praised the couple for their willingness to accommodate any audience and circumstance—including doing scenes on table tops pushed together or on the verandah of a school principal's house.[69] The representative in Cameroon counted the tour as an undoubted success and ended his comments with a request for more of the same. He received it: the following year Eleanor Thomas and Gareth Armstrong did another tour of West Africa, this time giving sixty performances of extracts from *Romeo and Juliet* and *Twelfth Night*, that year's set texts for secondary exams. Council officials such as the English Language Teaching adviser in Cameroon and the representative in Sierra Leone were particularly pleased to see an additional educational element to the tour: after each performance, Thomas and Armstrong would stay and answer students' questions about the text and how it could be interpreted.[70] Thomas did a follow-up tour with another actor to West and North Africa the next year, this time modeling their program even more to the plays and poetry in that year's "O"- and "A"-level studies. Even more than before, the council's officials lauded how it was an ideal use of their organization's resources. The representative in Ghana declared, "This seems one of the most worthwhile ways of spending British Council arts money since it met an obvious need."[71]

During the same time that it shifted toward more frequent but more barebones tours, the British Council also pursued another new way to spread British drama in Africa—this time through African university students. The approach illustrated how much the council's attitude toward drama export had changed over just a few years. However, as British officials would discover, it also opened a new avenue for critique of British culture in the former colonies. The first time the council sponsored an African university student tour was in 1964 to get out of the dilemma mentioned earlier around the Shakespeare Quatercentenary. Just one year after the Nottingham visit, the council did not have the time or funding to organize another large-scale British tour to West Africa for the Shakespeare anniversary. At the same time, the Commonwealth Relations Office told the council that West Africa was becoming a high diplomatic priority and it was essential they not lose any of the momentum or enthusiasm they had just generated.[72] The council's representatives in Nigeria began searching for an alternative solution, beginning by looking at local drama groups that had performed Shakespeare plays in prior years. This brought them to the University of Ibadan's Travelling Theatre. This touring company was the brainchild of Geoffrey Axworthy, a British academic who moved to Nigeria in 1956 to build a drama program at University College Ibadan. After independence, the school became the first university in West or Central Africa to offer degrees in drama and theater arts, and local British Council representatives recognized Axworthy as being behind "the nucleus of the beginnings of professionalism in Nigeria."[73] Axworthy's ambitions in Nigeria extended beyond Ibadan, and so in 1961 he created the Travelling Theatre in which university students would take their performances on tour to remote parts of the country. British Council representatives did not pay much attention to the theater group until its second year when Axworthy selected a British play—Shakespeare's *The Taming of the Shrew*—and thus caught their attention. (Every year the council's representatives sent London a list of all the occasions local groups performed British works—they saw it as a way of measuring the success of their promotional efforts.) The council was pleased to see the group follow that up in 1963 with *The Comedy of Errors*. It made sense that soon thereafter, when they were searching for a means to celebrate William Shakespeare, the council remembered this group. In 1964 the British Council's local office in the Western Region gave the Travelling Theatre £1,000 to take a Shakespeare festival around Nigeria.

The Travelling Theatre recaptured the enthusiasm and response the council had with the Nottingham tour, but also added a degree of novelty and reached more rural areas. The Ibadan group's itinerary took them to all the cities and towns the Nottingham company had visited, and then added more stops that had been out of reach. About a month before each performance, the tour's advance man would travel to the town and ask to be taken to the largest space available, which was most often a football (soccer) field. He would also meet with the head of the electricity company (to arrange lighting) and with local leaders, and he would assign a few individuals to put up posters. When the entire group arrived a few weeks later, they would drive through the center of town yelling "Come to the Shakespeare tomorrow!" through loudspeakers and passing out hundreds of handbills.[74] The students used the next afternoon to erect their set—a replica of an Elizabethan stage built onto a lorry's large trailer (figure 3)—and then began the three-hour performance as soon as it got dark. The show, which was titled "A Shakespeare Festival," comprised excerpts from seven plays linked together by a tape-recorded narration. British onlookers who caught the performance were struck by the setting more

FIGURE 3. Members of the University of Ibadan Travelling Theatre rehearsing a scene from *The Taming of the Shrew* (1964). Photo courtesy of Tom Hebert.

than anything else. After praising the freshness and vigor the cast brought to the performance, one British official exclaimed, "But it was all this combined with the novelty of presentation which gave the performances their real appeal, the stage appearing by magic out of a 'lorry' and standing floodlit in the centre of a dark, open space."[75] This caught the attention of none other than the Nottingham artistic director, John Neville, who declared he would use the same setup should he do a return tour.[76] After the Travelling Theatre finished its tour, Axworthy estimated a total of sixty thousand Nigerians had seen it perform. About twenty thousand of them were from the Eastern Region, where the local council representative detailed the spontaneous participation and sometimes-riotous enthusiasm of audiences at all seven shows. He proudly summarized that through the Travelling Theatre the British Council had found "a little 'Nottingham Playhouse.'"[77]

The Ibadan group was the first of several African traveling theaters the British Council funded that stated an aim to bring theater to the people. In the mid-1970s, a drama lecturer in Malawi described what had become a widespread pattern of university students "setting out in land-rovers, lorries, buses and kombies from Ibadan, Legon, Makerere, Nairobi, Ife, Lusaka, Chichiri, and Zomba to entertain, educate and keep the universities in touch with the communities who supported them."[78] Though scattered across the continent, many of these ensembles looked to their local British Council office as a source for funding. The British Council's support was small (in the realm of £1,000, for example, or in-kind assistance, such as loaning them Land Rovers and drivers) and the council was only one of several sponsors. In the council's eyes, university students were a good way to sponsor local performance because their education made them more likely to perform British works. Indeed, following the Ibadan tour, other university groups included Shakespeare in their programs. With these performances, the British funders acknowledged that they were merely observers and had no influence over the students' diverse interpretations. These included Shakespeare in translation, as with the Makerere group's performance of *Julius Caesar* in Swahili in 1964, or adapted to African settings, as the Malawi group did in 1974 when it set *Julius Caesar* to present-day southern Africa. (The actor playing Brutus dressed in a member of parliament's suit, while the actor playing Antony wore a tracksuit.)[79] Nevertheless, the British Council excitedly pointed to these examples as evidence British culture was still relevant in postcolonial Africa.

Therefore, British officials were not prepared for the criticism the university theaters attracted during the 1960s and 1970s. Both British onlookers and the students themselves celebrated the premise of the university traveling theaters—the image of the educated elite volunteering to go into rural areas and bring "theater to the people." Like the British actors who visited Africa, the university groups boasted about how they made do with whatever performance space was available, while their proponents described in detail "the ordinary housewife, the market vendor, the factory worker, and the barefoot urchin" who formed their audiences.[80] One of the cofounders of Makerere Free Travelling Theatre in Uganda explained, "The whole point of the tour was to get people to discover they liked drama and to demonstrate that there is a vast popular audience for drama in East Africa now."[81] Implicitly—or sometimes explicitly—the university traveling theaters reproduced the assumption that the masses did not have a performance culture already and it was the duty of the educated elite to bring it to them. Over time, however, the students' lack of experience with rural audiences, their foreign repertoire, and the relatively uncritical manner they reproduced Western ideas of performance attracted criticism from African literary and intellectual circles and even the press and public. Critics portrayed the model as a colonial holdover that was out of touch with other more authentic and effective trends in African theater.[82] In 1965, the year after its Shakespeare Festival, the University of Ibadan Travelling Theatre went on the road again, but this time the students left Shakespeare behind. After seeing their performance of Nkem Nwankwo's *Danda* at the Lagos City Stadium, one newspaper finished its review with the statement, "This will be an important hint to Professor Geoffrey Axworthy that the Nigerian audience needs more

Nigerian plays than Shakespeare's plays."[83] Over the rest of the 1960s and early 1970s, university groups became more radical in design, first moving away from foreign works, and then challenging the presence of non-African elements in theater altogether.[84] Rather than acting as evidence that there was a place for British culture in postcolonial Africa, they now led the charge against it.

THE LEGACY OF SHAKESPEARE IN AFRICA

Colonial independence had a significant impact on the shape and content of British cultural export, affecting both who Britain strove to reach and how it thought it could best do so. Britain denied importance to black audiences until the middle of the 1950s, when it realized it was fighting the Cold War in the wrong ways and the wrong places. Even after Whitehall officials determined they needed a better way of appealing to audiences in the developing world, it took several more years—and the incentive of funding—before the British Council came around. The council's reluctance was rooted in how its advisers believed that the mission to promote British culture overseas bequeathed a much more important responsibility of preserving British standards and values. Therefore, up until the early 1960s, the council's arts export reflected the powerful assumption that elite audiences reinforced high cultural standards and vice versa.

Facing the end of British colonial rule, the British Council widened its view of its audiences, first incorporating more areas of the world, and then later extending its reach to more segments of the population. The evidence is seen in how the council changed the performers and styles it was willing to sponsor. First, when the council wanted to cover more regions of the world, it changed its drama export policy to include British provincial companies. Then later, when the council sought to reach wider audiences in former colonies, it changed from sending full companies and large-scale productions to sending one or two British visitors performing recitals of excerpts, believing that this accomplished the central purpose of British cultural relations but in a much cheaper and simpler manner. Within a decade, British drama export to Africa shifted from lofty cultural aims to more tangible educational objectives. Thus, decolonization had forced the council to demonstrate a flexibility it was unwilling to consider in an earlier period. The result was that by the late 1960s, British drama export embodied a much broader understanding of the performers and performances that could be labeled British culture.

And yet, reviewing the actual texts of British drama export across these decades, one can see how little the canon changed. British drama export centered around William Shakespeare's plays throughout this period of study; in fact, almost every drama tour the British Council sponsored during these decades had at least one Shakespeare play in its program. After decolonization, the pattern changed only in that other British works dropped out somewhat while Shakespeare became even more prominent. Yet, while British officials consistently reached for Shakespeare as the embodiment of their national culture, they did so for different reasons at different times. In the beginning of the period, when Britain had just begun to promote itself overseas, the council's drama advisers vaunted performances of Shakespeare that exemplified the rarefied English culture they aimed to propagate. A quarter of a century later, British agencies still staged Shakespeare for postcolonial audiences but had re-branded them; no longer English and highbrow, now the performances were universal and accessible. This allowed British arts advisers the leeway to celebrate Shakespeare in all its different forms, including translations and interpretations, and to commend African groups' productions as their (Britain's) own achievement.

The council's officials imagined that British works such as Shakespeare's plays served as a sort of universal language with the capacity to unite artists and audiences from different parts of the world regardless of any past or ongoing conflicts. When British individuals introduced a visiting company, art exhibition, or another council-sponsored event, they invariably invoked the long-standing history between their nation and their hosts. In these introductions, they portrayed Britain's history in Africa as something that deserved celebration for its longevity, which the British Council's continued outreach now stood for. Reading it again, there was almost a naivete to the British Council officers who professed that decolonization was an opportunity to share their culture with a larger section of the African population. In their eyes, Shakespeare's plays in the hands of an African company was the symbol of what the British-African relationship could and would look like moving forward. But even as British authorities posited the possibility of and encouraged what they called an intercultural Shakespeare, they still expected African publics to be enthralled by the English playwright.

British authorities were so eager to mark their success in postcolonial Africa that they obscured the true politics of the climate in which they worked and the critique that they encountered. Like other British cultural agencies at this same time, the council demonstrated a willingness to expand its understanding of British culture by relying upon and reinforcing other colonial institutions. Britain continued to fund drama export to Africa under the aegis of development and educational aid whereby metropolitan officials diagnosed the new nations' needs and remedies. British authorities relied upon the prominent position of Shakespeare's texts in the curricula and on school certificate exams without a glimpse of recognition that they were using one expression of hegemonic power to justify another. Therefore, they could not see the true extent of the postcolonial critique that took shape around them, or that it was about more than just a call to see more African participants and languages on the stage. When African intellectuals reflected on the legacy of British drama export, they portrayed it as a mission to propagate a determinedly limited understanding of performance with the explicit aim of eliminating all others. The renowned Nigerian playwright Wole Soyinka made this point in an essay titled "Towards a True Theatre," where he explained how crucial it was that East and West Africans think imaginatively beyond "the dictates of the British Council pre-historic strictures," and that there was more to performance than theater buildings and formal scripts.[85] He was followed by the Kenyan writer Ngũgĩ wa Thiong'o, who lobbed a much sharper attack at the British cultural mission that had imposed such a totalizing notion of theater—"a structure of values, assumptions, political outlook, language, audience. . ."—it left little space through which African groups could challenge it. Writing during the 1970s, Ngũgĩ decried, "The Kenyan people may want to look back to history and realize that no civilization on earth has ever thrived on blind imitation and copying; that foreigners, no matter how well intentioned, no matter how clever and gifted, no matter how original, can never develop our culture and our languages for us."[86] Like the British authorities who propagated Shakespeare's works, they too felt that a Shakespeare performance was never just that—it was part of a larger political and cultural project that extended throughout every facet of the colonial encounter.

2

"Bringing Books to Africans"

Publishing in Colonial East Africa

"Books in all their variety are the means whereby civilization may be carried triumphantly forward." When Winston Churchill uttered this particular sentiment during the opening of the National Book Fair in 1937, he was speaking about the strength of the book trade in Britain. Churchill did not mention British books in overseas markets; yet, it was overseas where British publishers most took his words to heart.[1] At that precise time, British publishers had started showing interest in expanding their industry's reach, particularly in the Asian and African colonies, where they imagined endless untapped markets. They seized upon and started repeating Churchill's words as testimony that there was more purpose to their work than just markets and profits. As they saw it, and as they would explain again and again over the following decades, the British publishing industry had a central place inside the grander civilizing mission behind British imperialism.

This chapter traces the overlapping efforts of British institutions to publish books in colonial East Africa. As will quickly become apparent, the twinned activities of producing books and encouraging colonial subjects to read them were interwoven through several constituent elements of British colonial rule, including the rhetoric of a civilizing mission, the development of imperial trade, and the inequalities of colonial education. To connect them together, the chapter traces the career of a man who was fond of repeating Churchill's call to carry civilization forward with books. Charles Granston Richards arrived in East Africa in 1935 to start as manager of the Church Missionary Society (CMS) Bookshop. Over the following decade, he developed the CMS Bookshop into what he declared to be one of East Africa's first publishers. Like other British officials in this story, Richards defined book publishing narrowly as an activity that required mechanical reproduction on a somewhat large scale. Instead of acknowledging the various origins or material forms books could take, he and those he worked with described books in a self-evident manner: a permanent item with a formal cover and purposeful spine that was the result of a writing, editing, and publishing process designed to deliver the author's intended meaning.[2] This also meant that when Richards and others told the history of the book in Africa, they skimmed over indigenous publishing initiatives and the Islamic manuscript trade, and they certainly did not acknowledge the writing or reading of texts before the advent of moveable type. Instead, Richards saw himself as following earlier generations of European missionaries who, as he understood it, first encouraged the shift from orality to literacy and introduced the book to Africans.[3]

Richards believed his calling was to continue the mission of bringing the book to Africa, even when it took him away from Christian publishing specifically. In 1948, the colonial governments in East Africa started a state literature bureau and asked Richards to direct it. This he did for fifteen years before moving to another British agency: Oxford University Press, which needed a man to head its new branch in Nairobi. As Richards's career progressed between these agencies—a mission press, a development project, and a commercial firm—so will this chapter's discussion, which will examine how each phase of British publishing in East Africa helped create the conditions for the next. By the mid-1960s, when the chapter finishes, Richards and other British officials were satisfied with what they saw in East Africa: a commercial industry dominated by British firms.[4]

What follows moves back and forth between the publishers' activities and Richards's personal reflections as he recorded them decades later. Whether speaking about the CMS Bookshop, the East African Literature Bureau (EALB), or Oxford University Press, these publishing outfits exerted great control over the types of writing that were produced and distributed widely. Inside each of the agencies, British publishers determined the criteria through which they would evaluate and decide to publish a title. Their decision-making reveals their changing priorities, including the increasing attention they put toward measuring and responding to market forces. Even when a publishing entity such as the CMS Bookshop or the EALB presented its interests as other than economic profit, economic calculations still crept into their decision-making.[5] This compares with how Richards painted what he described as his lifework of bringing the book to Africans. Richards was especially proud of his role in East African publishing because he assumed that commercial publishing was an obvious path for encouraging African authorship. Like the missionaries who came before him as well as the British publishers who would come after him, Richards believed very deeply in the power of British publishing structures to unlock African creativity and uplift African communities—as long as it was in conjunction with Britain's other political and economic aims.

"A GREAT CIVILISING AGENT": THE CMS BOOKSHOP

To hear Charles Richards tell it, the story of publishing books in East Africa began as part of the older history of European missionaries going to Africa to spread the word of the gospel. It was in fact one such missionary organization, the British Church Missionary Society (CMS), that brought Richards to East Africa in the first place. A group of activist evangelical Christians founded CMS in Britain in 1799 as part of their commitment to abolish the British slave trade. They started overseas mission work a few years later and steadily extended their activities into Africa and Asia throughout the nineteenth century. CMS missionaries began to work in East Africa in the 1870s, and by the end of the century the society had established itself as one of the most active missions in the region. In many areas of colonial Africa, the book publishing industry appeared to follow the pattern set by the newspaper industry—at least initially—beginning with mission presses (and then later colonial governments) seizing upon the technology of print.[6] One item the CMS missionaries set up inside their operation was a small printing press, intended to run off their newsletter and some pamphlets. Indeed, during this time, the printing press was becoming a common item inside Christian mission stations across sub-Saharan Africa, reflecting missionaries' belief that the printed word would reinforce their teachings and shape Africans' daily behavior through the habit of reading. Correspondingly, another key part of CMS's work in East Africa involved printed volumes, such as Bibles and hymnbooks that they had translated into vernacular languages—and those they imported from the metropole.[7]

When Charles Richards arrived in Kenya in the end of 1935, the CMS Bookshop was still a relatively small operation. Its stock was limited to materials that were directly related to the society's work, and consisted mainly of Bibles, prayer books, and portions of scripture in English and East African vernaculars. There was also a small amount of religious literature and educational books from local school syllabi, but nothing that Richards deemed general literature.[8] Although some of the other evangelical missions in the region had begun to experiment with local printing, all of the books on the CMS Bookshop shelves still came from overseas. When they wanted to publish materials in vernaculars, such as, for example, a book of hymns in the Dholuo language, CMS missionaries in Kenya would translate the work and then send the manuscript to their London office. The book would be published in London, often through the Society for Promoting Christian Knowledge or the British and Foreign Bible Society, printed in either London or Plymouth, and then shipped back to East Africa. It was a slow system, and not one designed for large-scale production of any sort.

But Charles Richards envisioned something much larger in East Africa. As he described later, even before arriving to the region he was confident that more Christian writing could play a central part in the development of African society.

During the 1930s there were not enough funds for the bookshop to begin a publishing operation, so Richards focused on widening the store's range of books instead. He was especially concerned about marketing materials to the educated African population in the colony. Richards's particular motivation stemmed back to sentiments of the International Committee on Christian Literature, which published a survey in 1934 that stated, "The few who demand good literature will assuredly multiply. They will need good literature both in the vernaculars and in European languages. If they cannot get good literature they will read bad."[9] Trusting the colonial government's stated commitment to education, Richards expected educated Africans were going to start reaching for materials to read, and he wanted to make sure those books continued to teach the Christian faith throughout all stages of life. For the rest of the decade his bookshop concentrated on broadening its stock to attract Africans across the literacy spectrum.[10] Richards was happy to report that as the CMS enterprise expanded, it also began to have influence on the stock of local commercial bookshops. For example, in the late 1930s a few of the Asian bookshop owners in Nairobi came and bought from CMS at a small discount, then restocked directly from the publishers if the titles sold well. By the end of the decade the CMS Bookshop had also become the agent for a number of British publishing firms, including Cambridge University Press, Oxford University Press, and Nelsons, who all showed interest in the region but did not yet want to invest their own resources there.

The circumstances of the Second World War prompted the CMS Bookshop to shift its operations from merely book selling over to book publishing. The bookshop saw an increase in sales in the beginning of the war, but also struggled with often considerable delays between shipments of books from Britain.[11] Charles Richards started to fear the shipping delays were standing in the way of Africans having access to reading material, and he appealed to the Society for Promoting Christian Knowledge for permission to publish some of its titles locally. Richards then used the profits from the local reprints to establish a publishing fund, which he applied toward producing new titles.[12]

Under Richards's leadership, the bookshop began producing titles under two imprints. First it had the CMS Bookshop, Nairobi imprint, under which the missionaries published books of religious instruction and devotion. One of the first works that came out under this imprint was by Richards himself: a booklet in Swahili titled *Sala Zangu* (My prayers), which he described as a devotional companion to the service of the Holy Communion.[13] The CMS missionaries in Nairobi started their second imprint, Ndia Kuu Press, a few years later for books of a more secular nature. The name Ndia Kuu was a translation of CMS London's Highway Press imprint into the dialect of Swahili spoken in Mombasa. Despite it being the more secular press, the missionaries used a biblical verse for the colophon, saying it would always remind them that the gospel remained their first priority.[14] CMS began publishing Ndia Kuu titles in 1944 with the series *The Peoples of Kenya*, a number of short books in English on the different ethnic groups in the colony. To write the series, the CMS publishers turned to people whom they thought of as the most qualified experts on the subject: members of the white missionary community in Kenya. The second series from Ndia Kuu was a set of six nature guides on the geography, flora, and fauna in the region. CMS went on to translate a few of these titles into African languages, but once again, all of the authors and most of the translators were European. For the rest of the decade the CMS Bookshop in Nairobi published books at an average rate of one new title a month. Although more and more of its publications were in a language other than English—either Swahili or one of the less common vernaculars—the authors and translators were almost always European.

When Richards described his work at the CMS Bookshop years later, he focused on his role in professionalizing local publishing in Kenya. Richards described the bookshop's first locally published titles as "horrible productions," amateur, and "not at all exciting."[15] He believed a lot of this was due to the fact there were no local printers who had experience in printing books at the time because Nairobi printers only ever produced newspapers and stationary. Therefore, Richards explained, he treated the early CMS Bookshop publications as trial runs, and over the ensuing years he worked with the printers to set up more professional operations. He described this work as having a broad range, from creating different layout options to establishing precedents for the printer-publisher relationship.[16] By the end of the war, Richards believed his clear vision and thorough work had turned the CMS Bookshop into what he had always known it could be. Through the bookshop, he proclaimed, he had created one of Kenya's "greatest civilising agents."[17]

In 1949 the CMS mission in East Africa formalized its publishing business a step further by setting up its own publishing department and forming a publishing advisory committee to oversee editorial decisions. By this point, Charles Richards was no longer working at the CMS Bookshop because he had been seconded to the new East African Literature Bureau, which was formed the year before. CMS retained his publishing expertise through the advisory committee, of which he was a vital member. One of the chief aims for Richards and the other members of the committee was to keep the price of CMS books low so Africans could afford to purchase them. With this aim they were very careful to avoid overprinting, even when it meant an exceedingly slow process to bring a manuscript to publication. Once they decided to publish, the publishing department would get estimates from local printers, such as Boyd's and Patel's, so it could determine the retail price. The advisers would forward the estimates to their territorial bookshops in Dar es Salaam, Dodoma, and Kampala, asking for their interest. With those responses, the advisers would go back to the printers for new estimates, then back again to the territorial bookshops for confirmation, until they could finally agree upon a print order.[18]

As slow as the system was, it seemed to be successful at bringing new titles to publication, though not necessarily in large numbers. At its peak in the early 1950s CMS published an average of two books per month, including reprints. The price of the titles ranged from 20 cents to 6/- (East African shillings), but the average price was 1/-, and the average price of non-English books was even lower.[19] One way they kept the price of vernacular books down was to print with newsprint instead of machine-finished paper, but the publishers felt it was still important to keep a good, bright, and attractive cover because they believed it would attract African consumers.[20] Still, although they aimed to keep prices low, the CMS publishers did not print many of their titles on a large scale. The typical print order for books that were not on educational syllabi rarely exceeded fifteen hundred to two thousand copies, even in the more widely read languages of English and Swahili.[21]

As forerunners in a new industry, the CMS publishers struggled to learn the demand for their publications and the factors that went into that demand. The publishing department began to track its sales by language during the 1950s. They soon observed that the largest share of sales—over 40 percent—came from books in Kikuyu, even though they had only a small number of Kikuyu titles on their active list.[22] Almost all the Kikuyu sales occurred during January and February, which was the busiest book-buying time because of the beginning of the school term. When the publishers examined the trend more carefully, they saw a dramatic difference between school-approved and non-school titles in the vernaculars. For example, by 1951 CMS had sold 38,200 copies of its first Kikuyu reader and 27,500 copies of its second Kikuyu reader; however, non-school readers such as the Kikuyu translation of *Pilgrim's Progress* and the biography of Samuel Adjai Crowther had sold only around 400 copies each.[23] From these numbers, the publishers realized their book sales in the vernaculars occurred almost entirely for schools; therefore, placement on an educational syllabus was the single factor behind a guaranteed demand.

More importantly, once the publishers could read market conditions, they began to make publishing decisions based on their data. Once the CMS publishers realized non-school books in Kikuyu were not selling, they became very reluctant to publish new titles of that type. For example, at the publishing advisory meeting where they recognized the sales pattern of Kikuyu titles, the advisers immediately rejected the three non-school books in Kikuyu that were under their consideration. The new publishing strategy came at the expense of developing the areas where readership was the lowest. The more the CMS publishers oriented themselves toward the market over the following years, the more they moved away from their initial purpose of reaching broad portions of the African population.

It was a priority shift that would have resounding effects for the shape of East Africa's book market in later years.

The early 1950s were the years when the CMS Bookshop was at its peak as a publishing and bookselling business. This was because it was still one of the only local publishers in the entire region: there were no other Kikuyu school readers available, so CMS held the entire market. But not long after, CMS's sales figures started to slip. A few years after its establishment in 1948, the East African Literature Bureau started publishing school readers in the vernaculars, cutting into the largest source of the mission press's profits. Soon thereafter, many metropolitan publishing houses such as Oxford University Press and Nelsons set up their own offices in Nairobi, which meant they no longer used CMS as their bookselling agent. Before long, new enterprises in Nairobi passed the CMS Bookshop in both volume and geographic reach, even in the area of religious literature.[24]

At this point, facing the options of "change and compete" or "stay the same and fade," the CMS missionaries ultimately opted for the latter. For several years during the early 1950s, Richards and other members of the publishing advisory committee reacted to the increased competition by trying to be more competitive themselves. This meant putting most of their attention toward educational and general interest titles because those offered larger sales. However, at the same time, other CMS individuals began voicing concern that their publications were moving too far afield from what was meant to be their main purpose: Christian works. One quarterly report from 1951 showed that of the twenty-nine books the press published over the past fifteen years, only eleven could be considered religious. The CMS Bookshop manager expressed disbelief that religious titles were no longer even half of the press's projects.[25] The manager was not the only one who noticed: the 1952 annual report revealed that a mere 15 percent of the books sold that year were titles with a definite Christian message. Over the next few years, increasing numbers of CMS missionaries expressed concern their bookshop was losing its identity as a Christian enterprise.[26] In particular, the missionaries felt the publishing staff had let the business component of publishing distract them from their calling to serve Africans and spread Christianity.[27] The tension of trying to survive in the increasingly competitive world while remaining true to its evangelical background became too much for the CMS Bookshop to maintain. In 1957 the missionary society negotiated the sale of all its Kenyan bookshops to a British school stationary company.

The departure of the CMS Bookshop from the publishing and bookselling world in East Africa was not the sign of a failing industry but of a growing one, as it had found it increasingly difficult to compete with the more commercially oriented ventures. The second section of this chapter will describe the East African Literature Bureau (EALB), one of the ventures that started to take over CMS sales during the early 1950s. The EALB was a British colonial development project that had the specific purpose of jump-starting a publishing industry in East Africa. As will be seen, the EALB's development-oriented practices reflected strong strands of the evangelizing aims of the mission presses it displaced.

"WHEN SPEED AND CHEAPNESS ARE ESSENTIAL": THE EAST AFRICAN LITERATURE BUREAU

As the Second World War came to an end, British colonial officials in both London and the colonies started to speak about a literature gap in Africa. They were alarmed that there was no pipeline supplying the African colonies with what they deemed "suitable literature." Furthermore, they anticipated the gap was about to become much more serious, as both demobilization and the spread of primary education generated greater numbers of Africans who would be reaching for something to read. Therefore, in October 1945 the governors of Kenya, Uganda, Tanganyika, and Zanzibar invited the journalist Elspeth Huxley to tour East Africa and study the literature gap, especially whether existing commercial firms and services might be able to meet future needs.[28] The governors selected Huxley because she was a familiar figure to them, in large part through publications such as *White Man's Country: Lord Delamere and the Making of Kenya*, which defended European settlers' claims to own land and govern in Kenya.[29] They also figured that as a journalist who had spent part of her childhood in East Africa, she was qualified to make an adept assessment. Huxley's findings confirmed there was an unfulfilled gap in literature provision, which she described as a threat to everything that colonial development and welfare might achieve. It was absolutely essential, she maintained, that something be done soon to provide sufficient good and desirable material to meet the skyrocketing demand. Otherwise, the British would suffer the consequences: East African readers who had been educated at the public expense would either relapse into illiteracy or, what she viewed as worse, turn in desperation to bad and undesirable literature, thus granting it space to enter the public domain.[30]

Huxley believed that literature, if used correctly, would play a central role in Britain's overall mission to shatter the apathy of the African. The benefits literature had over other media such as broadcasting, film, and still pictures were its cheapness and its relative permanence. In her words, literature therefore would "undoubtedly remain one of the most important means of enlightenment and persuasion."[31] Yet, when she studied the production and distribution of books in East Africa, she was alarmed that there was no way supply would ever meet growing demand. That was because at that point the private sector did not think it could make money in East African books. In the eyes of potential investors, the vast number of languages that were spoken in the region meant there was an extremely limited market for publications in any particular vernacular; however, vernacular titles had to be priced cheaply, or else African consumers could not afford them. Also, although literacy rates were increasing, it was not yet clear whether this would translate into a reading public. In other words, private publishing firms did not believe Africans would be willing to purchase books they did not have to. Therefore, as Huxley concluded in her report, the colonial governments needed to step in and subsidize publishing activities.

This happened in 1948 with the establishment of the East African Literature Bureau, a service under the new regional government, the East African High Commission.[32] To direct the new organization the colonial governors looked for a man who had practical experience in East African publishing and who was willing to cooperate with British commercial publishers.[33] They landed on Charles Richards. When the governors contacted CMS to ask whether it would release Richards, the missionary organization readily agreed, determining it was to its advantage that one of its own men—and a man with Christian conviction and vision—oversaw the new venture.[34] As for Richards, he realized the resources of the intergovernmental department allowed far more scope to do the work he wanted to. In a letter to the CMS regional secretary, Richards described the literature bureau "not as a deviation from the purpose for which I joined CMS in 1935, but as a development from it."[35] Even while at the government bureau, Richards kept a foot in the missionary community; along with sitting on the CMS publishing advisory committee, he also remained chairman of the literature committee of the Christian Council of Kenya.[36]

As a long-term, multifaceted, interterritorial development scheme, the East African Literature Bureau was an example of the Colonial Office's attempts to consolidate colonial government in the postwar period. The bureau began its activities in 1948, which was the same year as the setting up of the East African High Commission. The latter was an administrative device responsible for services that were common to the territories of Kenya, Uganda, Tanganyika, and Zanzibar. Along with the literature bureau, these services included customs and excise, the postal service, railways and harbors, and the desert locust control. As EALB director, Richards was responsible to the High Commission instead of any one colonial government. In addition, the bureau's funding was from the regional allotment of Colonial Development and Welfare monies instead of any particular colony's development plans. Over its first eight years the bureau received over £275,000 from the Colonial Development and Welfare Fund, which was more than 95 percent of its running costs. The East African governments also put money into establishing the bureau, namely, the £25,000 working capital for a publishing fund in 1948. After 1956, however, the burden of funding the bureau shifted from the metropole to the colonies. From 1956 to 1960, Her Majesty's Government provided one-third of the £157,634 budget and the East African governments two-thirds, and from 1960 to 1964 the Colonial Development and Welfare Fund share was even smaller.[37] By that point the bureau had begun looking to other sources of funding, particularly the large American foundations known to be active in its area of work. For example, the bureau made appeals to the Carnegie Corporation for assistance with its library activities and to the Rockefeller Foundation for support in encouraging African authorship.

Though it had been designed within a framework of regional cooperation, the bureau had to constantly balance the variations in publishing needs across the territories. Like the CMS Bookshop, the EALB had its headquarters in Nairobi and branches in Tanganyika and Uganda. This setup reflected practical considerations; at the time, Nairobi was the only place in the entire region with adequate printing facilities. It would be another decade before facilities in Uganda and Tanganyika improved to the point the bureau was able to print there.[38] From Nairobi, Charles Richards and his staff struggled to find the right balance between centralized efficiency and attention to the branches' particular needs. The staff tried to be mindful of the differences between the territories, their languages, and their education systems, but continued to hear the criticism that they remained too oriented toward Kenya.[39] As a government agency, the EALB was expected to jump over the infrastructure and language barriers that stood in the way of private investment. Instead, the EALB ran straight into several of those barriers and thus had to look for other ways to encourage commercial publishing in colonial East Africa.

Under Richards, the East African Literature Bureau developed a little differently than Huxley's proposal. Her report expected the bureau to obtain its own press and publish all of its own books, thus filling the literature gap in the quickest way possible.[40] However, British colonial officials took issue with that part of her proposal because they feared the bureau would start to compete with private enterprise. Therefore, they instructed Charles Richards to adopt a more long-term vision, where the bureau's overall purpose was to *support* the system, not *become* the system.[41] Coming from missionary publishing, Richards endorsed this view quite readily, believing that while government did have a place in literature provision, it was important government have neither too much control nor too much power.[42] Therefore, Richards defined the bureau's primary function as being to help other agencies—missionary or commercial—bring manuscripts to press by streamlining some of the work, such as translation and copyediting. In addition, Richards believed a publishing fund would allow the bureau to accept some types of books commercial firms would reject outright, as well as allow for some experimental publishing to measure a title or genre's success.[43] The catchall role of the bureau was encapsulated in its annual reports, which explained that it acted "in the several capacities of critic, literary agent, editor, financier and publisher." Added to that were the tasks of translator, illustrator, sales rep, and even author, since a number of EALB books were written by staff members themselves.

The early publications of the East African Literature Bureau reflected its missionary publishing roots and the government's new interest in colonial development and welfare. In its first year the EALB published nineteen titles in nine languages under its Eagle Press imprint.[44] Many of the vernacular titles were on topics that bridged the civilizing mission and colonial development. For example, there was a Meru story that taught morals and sex to girls and a Kikuyu pamphlet on cleanliness in the home.[45] With the latter, the bureau immediately started to prepare translations in other languages, and within two years there were versions available in English, Swahili, and Meru. The exceptions to vernacular publishing were a few English-language titles that were technical manuals on subjects such as soil conservation and health. The bureau prepared these with the Soil Conservation Service and the Red Cross respectively and showcased them to demonstrate how government publishing complemented other British development projects.

Charles Richards would later say that of all the titles the bureau published that year, the one he was most eager to see had an African author. He was speaking about the Swahili work *Uhuru wa Watumwa*, or *The Freeing of the Slaves*, by James Mbotela. The book was an account of Mbotela's father who had been a slave in the Indian Ocean slave trade. A British anti-slavery patrol liberated him in the late nineteenth century, and he settled in the Church Missionary Society's freed slaves' community near Mombasa. In 1934 Sheldon Press in London published Mbotela's book in English for the CMS Bookshop, and it was the first book written by a Kenyan that Charles Richards ever read.[46] By the late 1940s Mbotela's book was out of print; however, as soon as he had settled in as EALB director, Richards set about obtaining the rights. *Uhuru wa Watumwa* became one of the more successful titles from the bureau's early book list, and after reprints in 1951 and 1956 the bureau sold off the Swahili-language and English-language rights to private British firms.[47] In Richards's eyes this book served as a model for the bureau's work in East Africa in terms of building a competitive industry and fostering African authorship.

Richards declared he would always prefer to see a title come out through the normal publishing trade, even when it meant passing the bureau's successful titles to private firms for successive reprints.[48] Ultimately this did end up happening in several cases: Evans and Nelsons picked up *Uhuru wa Watumwa*, and Macmillan and Oxford University Press each picked up several EALB titles during the late 1950s and early 1960s. Overall, however, local publishing did not grow as quickly during the 1950s as Richards wanted. He explained in a Nairobi newspaper, "Publishing is done where possible through commercial firms, but when speed and cheapness are essential the Bureau's own Publishing Fund is used, and the books then appear under the Bureau's own imprint."[49] For the first ten years, over three-quarters of the bureau's production list were published under the Eagle Press imprint and funded out of its publishing fund. The bureau continued to operate along this model into the 1960s, despite the increasing number of complaints from government officials about its unprofitability.

The EALB played an important role in the practice of colonial development through its impressive production of educational and instructional works. After ten years of publishing, the bureau's 1959 catalog listed 420 active titles in twenty-two different languages. It did not focus on vernacular publishing as much as the CMS Bookshop; therefore, titles in English and Swahili comprised over half the book list. The larger vernacular languages of Luganda and Kikuyu were also represented accordingly, and then there were very small numbers of titles in eighteen other languages.[50] Among this final group the titles in a given language were typically one or two school readers and one or two books about domestic life and civics. Yet, after the departure of the missionary presses, the East African Literature Bureau was still doing more vernacular publishing than almost anyone else. One Kenyan publisher remembered how as a child in the 1950s he had grown up reading books in his mother tongue through the bureau's children's titles. Although limited, he felt the East African Literature Bureau did more for the mother tongue than anyone else at the time.[51] Finally, the bureau's entire book list reflected Britain's new focus on colonial development and welfare. Over a quarter of the active titles in 1959 were categorized under education and subcategorized as adult literacy or general education. The other substantial categories were books on health, agriculture, and administration, all areas of other British development projects in East Africa.

Although they only produced a handful of titles in most of their languages, the bureau's officials often pointed to the less-published languages as visible evidence of their commitment to uplifting and modernizing Africans' lives. With the aim of making the corresponding illustrations authentic and the books more personalized, British colonial officials reduced Kenyan populations to archetypes throughout the process of bringing a single educational work to publication. This was on display throughout the bureau's process of publishing an adult literacy primer in Maasai during the late 1950s. After deciding it would produce such a work, the bureau sent its staff artist, Ruth Yudelowitz, on a research trip to a village near Kajiado, about fifty miles from Nairobi. Accompanying Yudelowitz on the trip were an adult literacy officer and an information officer, who photographed scenes of her examining Maasai women's jewelry and making sketches for the book's illustrations, all part of her expressed aim to ensure her illustrations were accurate (figure 4). For the trip, Yudelowitz also brought sample copies of a separate EALB publication—a Swahili-language reader—so she could show Maasai individuals what the final product would look like and get them excited. The information officer captured this scene as well. When he returned to Nairobi, the Kenya Information Office developed his photographs under the series heading "The Masai learn to read," and included them in the bureau's next annual report.[52] Moreover,

FIGURE 4. Village children watch the East African Literature Bureau staff artist, Ruth Yudelowitz, make preliminary sketches for an adult literary primer in the Maasai language. The National Archives, Kew, United Kingdom, INF 10/159/93 (c. 1958).

as similar photographs from the early 1960s demonstrate, depictions of Maasai individuals examining books and learning to read became a common way that the EALB illustrated its work (figure 5). Such images, which both the Kenyan colonial government and the London office used for public relations publications, served as typological photographs of a civilizing encounter and reflected the consistent message behind the colonial publishing endeavor.[53]

Charles Richards stated that encouraging African authorship was one of his primary goals, and although he did not do much while at CMS, he was excited by the prospect of doing it at the EALB. At CMS, Richards and other publishers solicited manuscripts primarily from their friends in the missionary community and other European settlers in the region. Once Richards moved to the EALB, however, he incorporated African authorship into his longer-term vision for the development of publishing in Africa. In a 1950 interview with the *East African Standard*, Richards said that if the bureau was going to make Africans book minded, it needed to stimulate a native literature. He felt that already the diverse backgrounds of the bureau's authors said a lot, and he described the publications as everything from the "'mzee,' narrating oral tradition for recording

FIGURE 5. Maasai women looking at East African Literature
Bureau books during an adult literacy class. The National
Archives, Kew, United Kingdom, INF 10/159/50 (1963).

and publishing in the *Treasury of East African Literature*, to the Government
officer or missionary writing a textbook or handbook on subjects which range
from intestinal parasites to an explanation of the working of the 'rule of law.'"[54]
But Richards was perhaps speaking too soon, as it ended up being far more of the
latter (the government official or the missionary) than the former. After a decade
of publishing, only one-third of the titles on the East African Literature Bureau's
book list were written by Africans.[55] Nevertheless, to hear Richards describe it,
the East African Literature Bureau was poised to help develop civil society in
Kenya because it would not place limits on either the types of publications or the
background of authors it considered.

The one category where African authorship was more prominent was in the
general literature section of the bureau's book list: fiction, poetry, and plays. This

was a small part of the total list—only 52 of the 420 titles—but more than half of the works had African authors. Literature titles were also what the EALB was most often able to see published through the normal publishing trade. Half of the bureau's 52 literature titles were later published by British commercial firms such as Macmillan, Longmans, Nelsons, and Oxford University Press, all of which had become more active in the area by the late 1950s.

In his memoir, which he wrote in 1980, Richards explained how one particular example encapsulated the bureau's role in fostering African literature. He described a writing contest the East African Literature Bureau started in the middle of the 1950s through a grant it obtained from the Rockefeller Foundation. The bureau would arrange to publish the winning submissions, determined each year from a panel of judges the publishers selected. The 1961 competition was for a novel in English, and the winner out of forty-seven submissions was a Makerere University student named James Ngugi. Charles Richards later stated that he recognized immediately how much Ngugi's manuscript stood apart from other East African writing. It was so special, Richards felt, it deserved to be published by a firm with an international audience.[56] Instead of merely publishing it himself, Richards explained how he passed the manuscript to Heinemann, which made *The River Between* one of the early titles in its well-known African Writers Series.[57] Richards ended his telling of how he discovered Ngugi with that. He did not go on to describe how Ngugi (later Ngũgĩ wa Thiong'o) became one of the most outspoken critics of the British cultural project later in the 1960s. Chapter 5 in this volume will return to Ngũgĩ wa Thiong'o, Heinemann's African Writers Series, and the international market for African literature. In the meantime, the final section of this chapter will describe the next stage in the development of a publishing industry in East Africa.

As a civil servant Charles Richards was expected to retire when he turned fifty-five, which was in 1963, after Tanganyikan and Ugandan independence and a few months before Kenyan independence. The East African Common Services Organization replaced Richards with a Kenyan from the bureau's staff, and over the next decade the EALB staff was fully Africanized. The EALB continued to operate as a department of the East African regional government until 1977, when the bureau split into national organizations that got folded into the different ministries of education. There is still a Kenya Literature Bureau today that is mostly involved with textbook production.

But back in 1963, Charles Richards was not ready to retire from publishing. He took up an offer from Oxford University Press (OUP), which expected him to develop its one-man office in Nairobi into a full-fledged branch of the press. Richards ended up staying at Oxford for only two years, before he moved to be the director of the World Council of Churches' Christian Literature Fund. However, this chapter will stay with Oxford University Press, an example of a British commercial firm with designs in East Africa, and examine how the business organized itself to capture African markets.

"VAST OPPORTUNITIES":
OXFORD UNIVERSITY PRESS IN EAST AFRICA

Decades earlier, during the late 1920s, Oxford University Press sent an editor from its new Overseas Education Department to southern and eastern Africa to evaluate commercial opportunities. The editor wrote back about what he saw, and more importantly what he imagined. "I have a vision . . . of Oxford African Primers in the hands of these squatting boys, in mission schools, in town and village, in bush schools far out in the blue where native teachers, only a little less heathen than their pupils, are struggling to make a greater Africa. This is not only 'uplift,' it is also a sound business proposition, because each book will be paid for!"[58] The editor, Eric Parnwell, clearly shared the conviction that publishing and book reading had an integral place in Britain's civilizing mission in Africa. But the real consequence of Parnwell's assessment was that he spoke of uplift and profits in the same breath—and that was what caught attention back in London. Over the following decades, OUP publishers started to develop their strategy for expanding into colonial Africa. In particular, they saw an enormous untapped market for school textbooks and were eager to grab a share of it before their competitors—other British firms such as Longmans and Macmillan—secured it first.

As one of several British firms eying African markets, Oxford University Press was a direct beneficiary of the historical developments that are traced above. The specific manner in which the book publishing industry developed during these decades gave British presses considerable time to learn about the market without much risk. First, OUP developed regional sales through the CMS Bookshop, which acted as the press's local bookselling agent until 1954. In that year, OUP publishers decided the region was a large enough market to send their own representative. (This was hardly a full break with the CMS Bookshop; in fact, CMS and OUP shared an office for the next several years.)[59] Over the next nine years the Oxford man in Nairobi was responsible for promoting forthcoming titles and running the warehouse, but since it was not a full OUP branch, he did not do local publishing. Sometimes, if he became aware of a manuscript that would sell well in the region, such as one the East African Literature Bureau recommended, the OUP representative would pass the title to London, which might take up the rights and then export the publications back to East Africa. What this all meant was that over the late colonial period, Oxford University Press gained familiarity with and became a known entity to populations in East Africa at very little risk to its bottom line.

OUP was not the only publisher that saw potential in Britain's new approach to colonial education. Throughout the 1940s, publishers large and small cited the Colonial Development and Welfare Act as a reason to investigate possibilities in East and West Africa.[60] In addition, all British firms knew they could count on support from their government; in addition to local projects like the EALB, the Colonial Office was also eager to aid any firms that expressed interest in exporting to the colonies. When a British publisher sought information or advice about African markets or a colony's educational system, the Colonial Office was one of its first queries. For instance, Evans Brothers editors contacted the Colonial Office with their idea of a Basic English course for African schools, and OUP contacted it when they sought authoritative authors for their new *African Welfare* series.[61] From London, the Colonial Office put British publishers into contact with colonial governments, who could make local arrangements for any publishing representative's tour to examine conditions in person. More significantly, the Colonial Office also endorsed certain authorships over others. For example, in 1947 a Longmans publisher wrote to the Colonial Office asking for suggestions for someone who could edit a volume on African writing, saying they wanted specifically someone "with a fairly wide and sympathetic knowledge of African (and negro) authors."[62] In response, a colonial education adviser recalled the name of a Methodist reverend who had retired to Cornwall, saying that although the reverend might not have knowledge of African authors, he could certainly acquire it. The Colonial Office official added, "On the whole I doubt if I would recommend having an African editor; I doubt if an African would have the necessary detachment just yet, though twenty years hence he might have."[63] If a British publisher wanted a reason to encourage African authorship, it was not going to come from the British government.

From OUP's vantage, one of the most important competitions for colonial markets during this era was in the field of English-language course books. During the 1920s and early 1930s, OUP's overseas editors such as Eric Parnwell expressed frustration over the powerful hold that Longmans had on this particular field—especially given how large the potential profits could be. After that same tour to southern Africa, where he saw that neither pupils nor teachers had books, Parnwell concluded, "Evidently there were vast opportunities for the publisher if he could find the man to write the books that were so badly needed."[64] Parnwell soon found his man: Laurence Faucett, whose prior experience working with Protestant missionaries in East Asia fueled a personal interest in English-language teaching. Faucett dedicated the following years to writing down his methods, and in 1933, OUP announced its arrival to the English-language teaching market with the publication of the *Oxford English Course*.

With this course, OUP launched not only a set of textbooks, but a full-on pedagogy for teaching English overseas. OUP boasted that the selling point of Faucett's course was that it was much more comprehensive than Longmans' *New Methods* course because it tackled all language skills (reading, writing, speaking, and listening) together. Faucett and Oxford University Press quickly developed an entire course package that came to include a graded sequence of six textbooks, companion readers, teachers' handbooks, and teaching aids, such as a picture dictionary and reading cards.[65] One of the ways Faucett linked all the materials together was through graduated vocabulary levels. He stipulated that pupils should build their English-language vocabularies in five-hundred-word steps as they advanced through the course, so that by the time they finished Book Four, they knew fifteen hundred English words, Book Five was two thousand English words, etcetera. Contemporary critics of Basic English found Faucett's system of graduated but not limited vocabulary learning acceptable, since it did not impose a ceiling on students' learning. For his publisher, it was an extremely marketable way for showing schoolmasters and teachers how the pieces of the Oxford course worked together.

Through the *Oxford English Course*, OUP's Overseas Education Department branded "Oxford English" worldwide. The press of course had already staked its authority in English-language reference materials and was starting to use the term "Oxford English" with increasing frequency. (For example, as Richard Smith points out, the *Oxford English Dictionary* was published under that title for the first time in the same year, 1933.)[66] Although Faucett's health declined later in the 1930s, OUP's Overseas Education Department ensured his English course flourished. In the late 1930s, OUP arranged for Frederick George French and Isabelle Frémont to develop the *Oxford English Course* further, including a graded series of *Oxford English Readers for Africa*. French and Frémont designed these to reinforce vocabulary and reading skills through stories they considered to be entertaining, informative, and tailored for colonial students. A sampling of Book Four, for instance, included the lesson "Children of the World," which contained lines such as "English, French, and German children look very much alike. Some of them have blue eyes and some of them have brown eyes. . . . The children who live in North Africa have brown skins, brown eyes, and dark hair."[67] The piece went on from there to describe not only physical characteristics, but also behaviors—Chinese students eat rice, American children like baseball—that conveyed both the intended vocabulary and reductive thinking. Not known for missing an opportunity, the Oxford readers also contained informative pieces about British life and British culture. Later in that same volume, for instance, there was a lesson titled "London" that described the city's major features, including Big Ben and the BBC Empire Service. If African students advanced to Book Six, they read summaries of Shakespeare dramas like *Julius Caesar* and *The Merchant of Venice*. The *Oxford English Readers for Africa* became another piece of OUP's English-language catalog for Africa and continued to be reprinted and sold in the African colonies during the 1940s and early 1950s.[68] Pupils were struck by the fact that they were learning *Oxford* English as well—a category of content as much as a standard for the language. Ngũgĩ wa Thiong'o, the Kenyan writer Charles Richards claimed to have discovered, described his colonial-era education by saying, "Before I knew the names of any other towns in Kenya, I already knew about a town called Oxford."[69]

As Oxford University Press opened new offices around the world, such as the Nairobi office it opened in 1954, it fell to its local representatives to get titles like the *Oxford English Course* into schools. Depending on the colony, this was often a combination of formal and informal connections. Take colonial Kenya, for example, where there was no colony-wide curriculum, meaning different secondary schools could follow different English courses and use different set texts if they wished. But, despite the chance of variety, the colonial inspectorate nevertheless aligned its directives and suggestions with only one course: Oxford's. This preference showed through in a myriad of small instances, such as the way the chief inspector categorized classroom library purchases according to where pupils were in the Oxford progression.[70] Or, if teachers sought books related to teaching, colonial officials only recommended those with techniques for using the Oxford course.[71] In other words—and in a manner that greatly assisted OUP's efforts to monopolize the field—the comprehensive approach and graduated vocabulary levels Faucett first proposed in the 1930s now stood as the de facto way to teach and measure English-language abilities.

During the mid-1950s, Oxford University Press's Overseas Education Department adopted a slightly different model for revising its English-language coursebooks. This once again fell to Frederick George French, and over the next decade he tailored versions of the course to specific markets. For example, there was a *New Oxford English Course* for southern Africa, another for India, another for Malaya, and another for the Gold Coast (Ghana on covers printed after 1957), just to name a few. In East Africa, French devised a course series for African schools and another series for Asian schools. The contents of all these courses were virtually the same, with only superficial differences that French assumed made the material more familiar to students. Therefore, while schoolchildren in Ghana read about Kwesi, Kofi, and Ama, schoolchildren in India read about Hari, Sita, and Abdul.[72] In addition, the illustrations also differed from version to version, changing the characters' dress and the setting to depict West Africa and South Asia respectively. Although French updated several parts of the original pedagogy, other elements remained the same. There was still the gradual vocabulary, where the words reflected what French believed African and Asian students should know. Students learned "ink" in book 1, "insect" in 2, "island" in 3, and "ice" in book 4. French wanted students to gain other content alongside their English lessons, so the students practiced reading and speaking about the queen in book 1, and learned the words for Christian mission, Parliament, and policeman by the end of book 4.[73]

When OUP released the first book of the *New Oxford English Course: East Africa* in 1956, the colonial government in Kenya recommended that schools begin replacing older coursebooks. However, Kenyan teachers were confused that OUP had not consulted them before developing a course supposedly tailored to East Africa. As the principal of the teacher training college in Thika explained to the inspectorate, "This is such an important part of a student's training . . . we would have appreciated being given some chance on reporting on a few of our difficulties. Now we have to start off again interpreting Mr. French to our students. I shall be glad to know he has made himself a bit clearer."[74] He was also upset that OUP had not even given schools advance notice that a revised course was in the works, stating that schools across the region had fully stocked themselves with the original Oxford course just two years earlier and would have waited if they had known a new edition was coming.[75] Even colonial officials in Nairobi were not entirely sure how OUP had put together the *New Oxford English Course: East Africa*. While they assumed the publishers had gathered feedback at some stage, they admitted they did not know whether there had been any effort to consult local schools or teachers.[76]

Oxford University Press reprinted the *New Oxford English Course: East Africa* during the early 1960s, and this time the imprint looked different. Instead of being published from London, the books came out of the new OUP branch in Nairobi. After setting up a representative and an office in 1954, OUP had seen its sales grow, especially in textbooks. In 1963, on the eve of Kenya's independence, the press converted the office into an OUP Eastern Africa branch that would do its own local publishing. This practice—setting up an office in the 1940s and 1950s, and then turning it into a branch in the 1960s—was central to OUP's Africa strategy, as the publishers also expanded to Nigeria, Ghana, Zambia, and Ethiopia during the same period. In his history of the press, Peter Sutcliffe described the pattern: "As the old Empire dissolved, the Overseas Education Department set out to build a new one."[77] Part of the thinking behind the pattern was efficiency. After a period of gaining familiarity with the market and developing titles, now an OUP branch could publish titles directly for that nation's schools. But there was a political impetus for the pattern as well.

During the 1940s and 1950s OUP's overseas expansion was primarily to the empire. This was logical, as the press could count on information and endorsements from the Colonial Office and local colonial governments that ensured British books did well in British colonies. But the press recognized that after independence it would be operating in a new political environment. There was always a possibility that new national governments could dramatically change their primary and secondary education system or could enact policies that were drastically unfriendly to foreign companies. It would remain to be seen whether British presses such as OUP felt a need to change their publishing strategies in response.

What about non-English works? When it started publishing locally in 1963, OUP Eastern Africa made it sound like they would also publish in African languages. One of the first publications Oxford obtained print estimates for was an anthology of four plays written in Luganda that the publishers thought could be appropriate for junior secondary schools. The OUP publishers first heard about the plays from Richards's replacement at the East African Literature Bureau, who continued Richards's policies of aiding British firms with local publishing in any way he could.[78] After receiving the estimates, OUP also consulted with Uganda's Ministry of Education to determine whether the publication would find a market in schools.[79] The publishers did not hear back from the ministry for eighteen months, at which point the Ugandan government said it would appreciate the title. The delay turned out to be significant because in that time OUP Eastern Africa had determined that a Luganda-language text (or other vernacular title) did not have a broad enough market to support publication. Their development and editorial process was oriented almost entirely around English-language books, as their efforts to produce a Swahili-language title came to show.

For that, it is worth looking at how the OUP Eastern Africa branch brought its first Swahili-language title to press. Outside the highly profitable textbook market, Oxford also pursued titles that had other indications for high sales, especially when they judged the material as meeting the high standards of the OUP imprint. In 1962 the OUP representative had a meeting with Julius Nyerere, then prime minister of Tanganyika, to discuss the national curriculum. During the meeting, Nyerere mentioned he had been working on translating Shakespeare's *Julius Caesar* into Swahili. The OUP rep was very excited to hear this and he eagerly wrote to London about the economic possibilities for such a book, especially given there was very little available for secondary schools in Swahili.[80] In addition, they could be certain the work would be in line with the high standards of the Oxford name; Nyerere was reputed to have excellent Swahili, and the original story was Shakespeare. While the prime minister finished the translation and an introduction about the book's role in East Africa, the publishers negotiated with his office about how they would produce the translation. This would be one of the first works to come out under the new OUP Eastern Africa imprint, and the publishers expected to edit it in Nairobi, print it in Dar es Salaam, and distribute it through their warehouses in the three commercial capitals. They believed the main value would be in secondary schools and they expected to price the book accordingly.[81] Nyerere's representatives responded that they wanted the book to be done well but it was more important the price was as cheap as possible.[82]

In all their communication with Dar es Salaam, the OUP Eastern Africa editors did not indicate any preferences for the translation itself, which granted the prime minister a great deal of latitude with regard to how to render Shakespearean English into Swahili. In his introduction, Nyerere stated that this was easier said than done, given that—as he described it—English was a language meant to be read, while Swahili was meant to be sung.[83] Therefore, to stay true to the Swahili language, he found himself prioritizing how passages sounded aloud. Even then, there were words such as the names "Cassius" and "Brutus" that he knew Swahili speakers would find jarring. Nyerere kept with the original in that he wrote in blank verse; however, he also ensured the finished product abided by certain rules of Swahili poetry that his readers could recognize and appreciate.[84] One such reader, the Kenyan scholar John Mbiti, lavished praise upon Nyerere for retaining a familiar underlying rhythm in the passages and giving alliterative qualities to the text. It was in Mbiti's eyes a beautiful handling of the Swahili language and one that stood as proof of what African languages could do for literary masterpieces. "Through this and similar translations," Mbiti declared, "we are able to examine how far African languages can sustain and express concepts and ideas which may not be so familiar to African people."[85] Both Nyerere's interest in producing such a translation and reviews like Mbiti's, appeared to confirm what proponents of British cultural outreach had been insisting upon—that British culture was welcome in postcolonial Africa because it could shape how Africans understood humanity.

What British authorities did not hear—or at least did not acknowledge—was the underlying critique that lay within Nyerere's translation. When Nyerere spoke about the knowledge and use of Swahili, he asserted that Swahili needed to be promoted in its own right and did not need foreign content to be relevant. The prime minister seized the opportunity of the introduction to his translation to defend the knowledge and use of the Swahili language. He couched his remarks in humility, expressing hope that upon reading his amateur translation, real Swahili experts would be spurred to offer better publications. "Swahili is a sweet and broad language," Nyerere concluded, "but its sweetness and breadth should be used more."[86] Nyerere agreed with his British publishers that education was key to Tanganyika's future—but what students really needed for their futures, he declared, were books in Swahili, not English.

Although they considered the Swahili Shakespeare an absolute top priority, the OUP staff lacked the in-house expertise to take it through to publication. When the full manuscript arrived at the office in the end of 1962, OUP did not yet employ a Swahili proofreader or even have a fluent Swahili speaker in the office. The publishers scrambled to send the proofs to expert linguists they had heard of in the area. The next year it ended up being the party secretary of Nyerere's TANU party in Tanganyika who assembled the final proofs. As she was working, OUP contacted her to request that she also translate the back of the title page, including the information about the copyright and performance rights.[87] Despite these issues and delays, the book finally went to print in June 1963 with an initial order of ten thousand copies.[88] The play sold relatively well, and the branch ordered reprints throughout the 1960s and 1970s.

The sale figures reflected what the OUP editors had presumed—that this was a work that would generate attention. During the rest of the decade, numerous groups performed the translation in both formal and informal settings and across different media forms. Upon hearing about the work, for example, the BBC African Service quickly decided to record it in their London studio as a two-part series to air during their Swahili-language broadcasts. When Nyerere, who was now president, learned about this, he requested three hundred copies to distribute to secondary schools in his nation. The BBC was eager to accommodate, but reminded Tanzanian authorities that it would charge them for the recordings.[89] Meanwhile, in a very different setting, the Makerere Free Travelling Theatre brought Nyerere's Shakespeare on their 1964 tour throughout Kenya and eastern Uganda. Speaking from the perspective of an onlooker, the group's expatriate director expressed that audiences took in the rhetoric eagerly and with awe, and that as the only African-language performance that was not a light comedy, it contributed a significant weight and body to his group's repertoire. "This was a worldly venture compared to most of our plays: I do not think it could have been a popular success, as it was, if we had performed it in English."[90] However, despite the star power of both the author and the translator and the broad promotion and acclaim the work received, Oxford University Press ended up carrying a loss on *Julius Caezar*. This was due to the remarkably low price of 2/75 that it had finally agreed upon with Nyerere, who thought unaffordable books were not compatible with his socialist program.

The publication of *Julius Caezar* was one example where the publishers at OUP Eastern Africa did not make their decision solely based on sales. It was also an exception. In the coming years, the branch did publish more titles in the literature and drama fields, but it was always with the school market in mind. The cover blurb for OUP Eastern Africa's New Drama from Africa titles advertised that the series was meant to provide schools with "good, mature and relevant scripts" for informal reading and formal performances.[91] One of the titles that could have fit into this series was the second of President Nyerere's Swahili translations of Shakespeare, and another case where OUP expected symbolic capital to convert eventually into economic capital. During the first years of his presidency Nyerere continued to translate Shakespeare in his spare time, and this time it was *The Merchant of Venice*. While Nyerere had not explained why he was so interested in *Julius Caesar*, he made clear that his attraction to *The Merchant of Venice* was based on the underlying message about the dangers of capitalism. By 1968, Oxford University Press had published other works by Nyerere, such as his writings on freedom and socialism. They were the first publisher he went to with his latest translation, which had the working title *Tajiri wa Venisi* (Wealthy person of Venice). However, as the publishers prepared to go to press, the president contacted them to say he wanted it changed to *Mabepari wa Venisi*, a much more antagonistic title that referred to the capitalists or imperialists of Venice. Nyerere realized that this was not a direct translation of Shakespeare's title, but he thought it was an appropriate one.[92] The change did not resonate with several of the Oxford staff in Nairobi, who felt it was important to do a faithful rendering of the original.[93] However, as the translator, Nyerere got his way—on that point at least. When Nyerere first sent OUP the manuscript he asked if they could get the price down to 2/-, which was even less than *Julius Caezar*. He explained, "I do realise that prices have gone up since 'Julius Caesar' was first published, but unfortunately incomes in Tanzania have not gone up in proportion!"[94] This time, feeling they should learn from their prior mistake, the publishers held to their principles and priced the translation at 4/-, an amount that could at least put them in the black. Thus, while Nyerere was incorporating Shakespeare's texts into his vision of African socialism, his foreign publishers continued to dominate the regional book industry.

THE OUTCOME OF COMMERCIAL TRADE

The outcome of this history—a commercial publishing industry in East Africa dominated by British companies—was not so surprising given how the earlier initiatives directed themselves toward that outcome. The missionary presses did not criticize the commercial market, even as they removed themselves from it, while the government-led development initiative made it a priority to support private enterprise in every way it could. Moreover, when British publishers such as OUP expanded their work into British colonies, they could rely on support from the Colonial Office in London and from local colonial administrators. The publishers at OUP's new Eastern Africa branch recognized that much of their formal support would disappear after political independence, but still expressed confidence that their investment in Africa would pay dividends, especially if they were politically savvy.

The commercial firms that took up the mantle of the publishing industry inherited two main criteria for assessing a potential title. First, educational books were the only titles that sold in large numbers. This was a point the publishing advisers to the CMS Bookshop discovered as soon as they started tracking sales figures, and the EALB realized that educational titles were not the works it needed to subsidize through the Publishing Fund. Although both the CMS missionaries and the EALB government officials aimed to develop a reading public, private publishers who came after them did not discern any noneducational market to publish for. Second, within the educational field, the place where real profits could be made was in English or (only sometimes) Swahili. At the Church Missionary Society, publishing in the vernaculars had been a crucial—though unprofitable—part of the mission to bring enlightenment to semi-literate Africans. The East African Literature Bureau was also able to publish in the vernaculars, but those had been the titles ordinarily subsidized by the government. Oxford University Press was a strictly commercial venture, and each branch was expected to show a profit every year. Therefore, the Oxford publishers in Nairobi went after the most broad-based market, which they believed lay in English-language textbook series. During the colonial period, commercial firms such as OUP could be inflexible about their publications to a certain degree. However, starting immediately after African independence, OUP and other British firms began signaling to state officials in Kenya and other nations that if the national curricula changed, they were more than willing to change their catalog in response.

Even when the book publishing industry in East Africa was still in earlier stages, there were already signs of critique that would become resoundingly loud during the postcolonial period. For instance, the colonial governments set up the East African Literature Bureau as something that would serve all of East Africa; yet, once it was in operation, bureau officials struggled to balance all the different spoken languages and local needs with centralized efficiency. For all three publishing agencies, there was a question of the degree to which publishers should consult with the audience they claimed to serve. It was a telling moment in 1956, for example, when OUP announced the publication of *The New Oxford English Course: East Africa* and teachers in East Africa asked why they were never consulted. As a result, the teachers felt clearly the expectation that they were to conform their teaching to the textbook, not the other way around. Whether this would change after British companies adopted more of a contractor-client approach to their business model remained to be seen.

By the early 1960s, it was already clear that there would be different ways of telling the history of publishing in colonial East Africa. When Charles Richards looked back on his career, he took great pride in what he had accomplished. He felt his legacy in Kenya was what he had created, an industry modeled after Britain's that carried forward the mission to civilize. But African publishers who followed Richards portrayed his legacy in a very different light. One who began working in the 1970s looked back and wrote, "However well intentioned Charles Richards may have been, he lost a major opportunity to leave a national monument behind after 30 years of credible service to Kenya, unleashing instead a multinational ogre that was to dominate the post-independence publishing scene for many years."[95] When this volume returns to the publishing industry in chapter 5, it will examine those "multinational ogres" and the strategies they devised in response to their critics.

3

"This Is London . . ."

BBC Broadcasting to Colonial Africa

As an institution that transmitted the English language, British entertainment, and British news to sites all over the world, the British Broadcasting Corporation (BBC) was an obvious part of the cultural project of the late empire. The BBC started domestic broadcasting in the 1920s and inaugurated its external broadcasting arm, then named the Empire Service, in the early 1930s. The latter was built on shortwave, a relatively new discovery that allowed broadcasters to transmit over long distances cheaply. As the technology improved over the next decades, British officials envisaged it solving several issues in the empire all at once. They spoke of the medium as a means to forge cultural ties over long distances, as an avenue for education and development, and as a tool of government control. In the span of one day, they could transmit a radio adaptation of *Othello*, a lesson on English grammar, a lecture on soil erosion, and information about a new government ordinance. The convergence of technology and content made the BBC an important player in how Britain communicated with its empire in the period right before the empire disintegrated.

This chapter is about the growth of British external broadcasting from its beginning in the late 1920s until African decolonization in the early 1960s. Although parts of this history have been told many times over, in scholarly treatments and individual memoirs, studies of the BBC external services in this period rarely mention, let alone focus on, Africa.[1] The authors of those studies would say that was due to Africa being one of the lowest priorities for the BBC—and they would be right. The original conception of the Empire Service was to serve white audiences in the British world, at the exclusion of nonwhite colonial subjects. Then, as the BBC became increasingly specialized to reflect Britain's strategic priorities, Africa still did not make the list. Yet, even if the BBC did not address itself to Africa during this period, Africans did hear the BBC. The chapter describes the British programs Africans heard on the radio during the late colonial period, whether they came from the general worldwide service in English or were among the handful of specific programs designed just for Africa. For reasons of technology and accessibility, most African listening occurred through the colonial broadcasting stations that each British colonial government ran. To design and operate such a system, colonial officials called upon the best broadcasting experts they could think of— namely, the BBC. During the 1940s and 1950s especially, the BBC offered guidance and manpower to ensure that colonial authorities could add broadcasting to their methods of colonial rule. British assistance was not limited to schemes and personnel—it also arrived through the British broadcasts themselves. Colonial stations did not have the resources to create full program schedules; therefore, they drew heavily from what was on offer from Britain.

What all of this adds up to is that BBC broadcasts were a known entity to African audiences during the late colonial period, even though British broadcasters took their African audiences for granted. Britain did not prioritize African listeners until it was on the verge of losing them. During the late 1950s, Britain reacted to the Suez Crisis and impending decolonization by directing itself for the first time toward audiences in East and West Africa. With African independence, however, the BBC lost its privileged position vis-à-vis the state, and correspondingly lost its monopoly for audience attention. British broadcasters found themselves having to compete for postcolonial listeners at the very moment that this audience had become the most crucial.

IMPERIAL BROADCASTING

It was not long after the formation of the British Broadcasting Corporation that its officials started to speak about using the new technology for the empire. The first general manager (later director-general), John Reith, was a high modernist who had emphasized the national role and reach of broadcasting earlier in the 1920s in order to secure the BBC's position in Britain. By the end of the decade, Reith's rhetoric shifted from the national community to the imperial community, where broadcasting had the means to connect and coordinate between the different parts of the British world.[2] It would also require a different technology: shortwaves, which were seen as largely unreliable. On the other hand, as physicists and engineers explained, there also were some advantages to shortwave communications—namely, they required relatively low amounts of power and could travel long distances.[3]

The potential of these developments for the British Empire were just being understood in 1927, when the Colonial Conference discussed wireless broadcasting for the first time. Altogether, the conference identified several strategic benefits to imperial broadcasting, beginning with Reith who spoke positively about how this seemingly limitless medium would generate emotional ties within a cohesive empire. While Reith presented an abstract vision of cultural ties, officials in the British government described the potential payout in more specific political and economic terms. The Colonial Office and Dominions Office representatives underscored that other nations' broadcasts were already starting to reach British territories—a warning that Britain needed to act soon before the chance disappeared.[4] Meanwhile, the Overseas Trade Department, Empire Marketing Board, and Treasury representatives spoke enthusiastically about imperial broadcasting but focused on the economic trade that could grow out of cultural and sentimental connections.[5] Initial discussions around imperial broadcasting demonstrated that from its start, British imperial broadcasting was meant to foster cohesive identity, combat international competition, and strengthen the metropolitan economy.

All discussions over external broadcasting ran into the same unresolved issue: Who should pay for external broadcasting? Reith sought assurance that external broadcasting was a public good and was categorically different from domestic broadcasting, which was funded by license revenues. He explained that those same funds could not go toward an external service that United Kingdom license holders could not hear. But it was quickly apparent that what he wanted to see—a structure that the wider British world felt invested in—was unlikely to be funded by the intended listeners. The dominion governments made it clear they preferred to put their resources toward developing their own national systems, while dominion listeners would not want to pay for British programs that would never be as interesting or as clear as their own.[6] As for the colonies, the Colonial Office took issue with the current expectation that the BBC service was only for white listeners.[7] Although imperial broadcasting had been billed as a public good, its public was still somewhat nebulous. The matter was finally resolved during the economic crisis of the following year, when the British government made clear it could not afford the Empire Service and the BBC had to fund it or risk losing it altogether.[8]

Although the funding arrangement for British external broadcasting changed before the end of the decade, the dispute forced the BBC to think carefully about what its service would sound like and who its listeners would be. British overseas broadcasters quickly began to distinguish between two distinct audiences: the direct listener who tuned his set to the signal from Britain, and local broadcasting stations who might rebroadcast BBC content. Officials in London wanted to devote most of their attention to individual direct listeners, whom they envisaged as the "lonely listener in the bush."[9] These were British expatriates who lived in remote parts of the tropical empire and owned a shortwave set, but did not have anything else to listen to, or sometimes even a newspaper to read. The Empire Service, the BBC asserted, would serve as these individuals' only source of news and their only connection to British civilization.[10] The image of the isolated Briton—characterized by his race, language, and nostalgia for Britain—resonated powerfully in the overseas broadcasting mission in the 1930s.

But for more practical reasons, BBC broadcasters quickly realized that rebroadcasting was going to be crucial if they were to reach listeners in the dominions.[11] This was due in part to the inadequacies of shortwave technology. Despite recent advancements, long-distance transmissions in the 1930s were still characterized by distortions, interference, and fading, all of which made intelligibility difficult. Listeners who tuned in directly did so for the novelty and nostalgia associated with listening to Britain, but there was not a general demand for daily programs.[12] If British programming was to be heard by greater numbers of people in these places, the BBC's best strategy was to schedule its transmissions at times convenient for local stations' high-powered receivers to pick them up and relay or rebroadcast the output over their medium-wave networks. With rebroadcasting, the BBC's targeted audience was not the Canadian or Australian who listened to CBC or ABC, but rather the broadcasting station deciding if and when it would relay British programs. In parts of the world where ownership of high-powered sets was rare, such as Britain's African colonies, the BBC's reliance on local broadcasting stations was all the more consequential.

British broadcasting used the diverse locations of its listeners to demonstrate its worldwide reach and drew on its common programming to cultivate what it saw as a shared identity. After initiating the Empire Service, British broadcasters quickly realized that just as they could not predict ideal reception conditions in different parts of the world, they also could not anticipate their listeners' preferred listening times. They therefore abandoned their geographically based schedule in favor of one where time alone determined a program's potential audience.[13] The new schedule capitalized on the capability of a single transmission to attract audiences from several parts of the world simultaneously. For example, transmission 3, which was between 1400 and 1700 GMT, was an evening listening time for South Asia, an afternoon interval for the Middle East and Mediterranean, and a morning program for parts of North America. The program output therefore needed to serve all of these audiences at all of these times of day—no easy task for BBC producers.[14] What resulted from this model was that broadcasters at the BBC began to conflate the simultaneous character of the broadcasting medium with a universal, not targeted, approach to programming.

But just how universal was it? Since the BBC designed its Empire Service to speak to white English-speaking populations living in the British dominions and colonies, this audience determined most of the BBC's programming choices. Therefore, Empire Service producers selected items from the home services that they thought would prompt nostalgia for Britain.[15] Whether it was an orchestra concert, advice about English gardening, or the religious service on Sundays, their program lineup spoke to the old audiences they knew, not new audiences they might draw in. The corporation justified its programming by explaining that regardless of how the service was set up, nonwhite populations would not be interested in European-style programs. Colonial needs, the BBC asserted, should be served by colonial stations.[16] British broadcasters were fixated on the white British world and did not anticipate the multitude of ways colonial broadcasting would start to develop in Britain's colonies and territories.

COLONIAL BROADCASTING

During the 1930s and 1940s broadcasting systems varied greatly across British Africa, and therefore, so did the amount of BBC content that reached African listeners. In the absence of clear direction from London, individual colonial governments each pursued their own arrangements depending on how they assessed their information needs as well as what they were willing to finance. The result was a wide array of technologies, programs, and mindsets about the provision of public broadcasting. For starters, as anathematic to the BBC model as it may have been, several colonial governments saw reason to encourage commercial provision of broadcasting. One such colony was Kenya, where during the mid-1920s the colonial government granted the company Cable and Wireless Ltd. a thirty-year contract to operate a wireless service. Cable and Wireless based its service out of Nairobi and generated its revenue through the sale of wireless licenses. License sales steadily increased over the next decade, but radio sets were almost exclusively in the hands of the colony's European and Asian populations. Although license figures are an imperfect measure, the following figure is telling: in 1943, Cable and Wireless issued 4,045 private licenses to Europeans, 1,136 to Asians, and 4 to Africans.[17] From London, BBC and Colonial Office officials expressed their strong preference for public service broadcasting, although their justification centered around noncommercial principle more than any mention of broad access. At the same time, London officials regarded commercial provision in certain colonies as a necessary evil if colonial broadcasting was to be anything close to self-supporting.[18] BBC officials also had another reason to begrudgingly accept commercialization. Any overseas broadcaster, commercial or not, was a potential rebroadcaster that they could try to convince to take British programming. But in this, British broadcasters were soon disappointed by the service in colonial Kenya. After a decade on the air, the Nairobi station had built a schedule of twenty-six hours each week, but rarely relayed any BBC material.[19]

As it would turn out, however, Kenya was an exception more than the rule in Britain's African colonies, and early colonial broadcasting stations usually developed around what was on offer to them from Britain. In contrast to the commercial station in Kenya, broadcasting in the Gold Coast was a government service that aimed to reach a larger portion of the African population. The Gold Coast service commenced in 1935 through a system of wired broadcasting or rediffusion. In this system, the colonial government relayed overseas radio programs and local entertainment through an overhead line network that radiated outward from local stations. For a nominal monthly fee, subscribers rented a receiving set that was essentially a small loudspeaker connected to the network by a long wire.[20] Although the Gold Coast government also began operating a wireless transmitter in 1940, rediffusion remained an important means through which the African population received broadcasts. The technology had many advantages in that it was a low-cost service and did not require the listener to have access to electricity. Colonial—and later Ghanaian—authorities recognized one additional advantage to rediffusion: the subscriber could not tune to any other station.[21] The only station the majority of Gold Coast listeners received was their local one—and in the colonial period almost all of its content came from the BBC.

As different as they were from one another, early systems such as those in Kenya and the Gold Coast demonstrated to the Colonial Office how broadcasting policy related to other long-term plans for economic and political development. In 1936 the British government appointed a committee under Lord Plymouth to evaluate the different manners in which broadcasting was and could be used in colonial settings. By then, several British colonies in Asia and the Caribbean were seriously considering the commercial route to establish services in their territories, citing that lack of funds gave them no other choice. However, the Plymouth Committee's report highlighted the Gold Coast system, in part because of the state's ability to control content and deny listeners access to objectionable outside broadcasts.[22] Most significantly, the report underscored that broadcasting was for more than just the Europeans and educated groups in colonial territories. Instead, what the Plymouth Committee envisaged was the development of an "instrument of advanced administration, an instrument, not only and perhaps not even primarily for the entertainment but rather for the enlightenment and education of the more backward sections of the population and for their instruction in public health, agriculture, etc."[23] The pairing of language that spoke to the need for an "instrument of advanced administration" with rhetorical references to the older aims of the civilizing mission showed how much the committee rooted its ideas about broadcasting in evolving aims of colonial development.[24] The committee connected these aims to another set of pervasive ideas about empire, which was the sense of an imperial network around the British world.[25] Therefore, the Plymouth Committee stressed to colonial broadcasters, whether commercial or state controlled, that they should distribute British programs at all opportunities and should think of the BBC news bulletin as mandatory.[26] By this point it had become a given that the development of colonial broadcasting services would be a joint project between the Colonial Office and the BBC, which offered technical expertise and training facilities in addition to its transmissions. This arrangement, however, presupposed that the BBC Empire Service was aligned with the imperatives of colonial governance.

In a letter to the Colonial Office in 1937, the governor of the Gold Coast demanded, "Can't anything be done to censor broadcast news to the West African colonies?" He elaborated on the enormous risk at play. "It is the worst possible propaganda for the people to hear all about the Trinidad strikes, especially if the strikers are successful. As you know we have our share of professional agitators. At present they are quiescent but they are bound to say to the workers here 'Go then and do likewise!'"[27] The broadcasts to which the governor referred were the daily bulletins on the BBC Empire Service. The BBC had only introduced news to its overseas broadcasts a few years earlier, but the news bulletin quickly became an essential feature of every Empire Service transmission. Each bulletin aimed to cover the important events that had taken place in the empire and the world during the past twenty-four hours.[28] The BBC designed these bulletins specifically for the "lonely listeners"; they assumed diasporic Britons near population centers already received the news. However, when a colonial broadcasting station relayed what it received from Britain—as was the case in the Gold Coast—then the Empire Service news reached thousands of colonial subjects.[29]

The Gold Coast governor's demand to censor particular news in particular places was difficult on both technical and principled grounds. The Empire Service was designed for reception throughout the world, and its transmission schedule made special censorship from the point of view of each colony virtually impossible. Therefore, as the Colonial Office explained, any censoring would have to be done at the West African end. To do this, Gold Coast broadcasting authorities would have to take down the news from the BBC transmission, make their omissions, which would come across as gaps, and then rebroadcast it over their wired system. The Colonial Office left this option open to the governor, but implied that it was a drastic solution for what appeared to be a relatively minor problem. More significantly, the Colonial Office went on to caution that such an action might hurt Britain's long-term mission of linking up the different parts of the empire.[30]

The Gold Coast governor's complaint had thus exposed the clash between the liberal vision of British worldwide broadcasting and the illiberal methods of colonial rule. The governor's letter set off a debate within the Colonial Office about the short-term drawbacks versus long-term gains for cultivating trust through uncensored news. Some of the Colonial Office officials who reviewed the issue asserted that control of information was a crucial factor in maintaining colonial rule; here, the content of the BBC news bulletin was a tool at the state's disposal. But many other London officials spoke of the BBC's value in different terms. They repeatedly pointed out that the principal object of the British broadcast was consistently reporting a complete version of the news. They trusted the BBC to compile its bulletins with strict attention to objectivity and comprehensiveness; therefore, by extension, it was imperative that local administrations did not tinker with or disassemble them.[31] Moreover, they professed that the BBC's honest and impartial approach made Britain stand out among its foreign counterparts. As one Whitehall official noted, "There is something to be said for broadcasting British versions of untoward events in the Colonies etc. to counteract any distorted or exaggerated versions which would no doubt reach the Colonies from other sources."[32] As revealed in the Colonial Office's cautionary reply to the Gold Coast, the central question about the overarching aims of broadcasting in the colonies thus remained unresolved. British officials both in London and the colonies continued to voice concerns about the short-term effects of uncensored bulletins while—sometimes in the same breath—speaking of the BBC news in positive terms and equating it with liberal values in general. Nor would the tension disappear. Whether it was the "war of words" against Goebbels in the 1940s or the Suez Crisis in the 1950s, BBC external broadcasters and the British government would return to this critical issue again and again in the future.

British overseas broadcasting began as a means for Britain to cultivate cultural ties with the English-speaking world. The BBC produced and transmitted the Empire Service from the metropole, thus reinforcing Britain's position in the center of the imperial network. A BBC postcard from 1936 showed that British broadcasters drew the world that way, putting themselves in the center and their transmissions radiating outward to all parts of the empire.[33] But the imperial network was quite a lot looser than the BBC wished to acknowledge, and the places where the contradictions between imperial and colonial aims were most visible were the colonies. That is because in most parts of the colonial empire, colonial governments fit broadcasting into the rubric of development, where broadcasts were a tool of control just as much as they were an avenue for education. Correspondingly, colonial states set up systems that met their immediate needs and concerns without much regard to the liberal vision that initially propelled British imperial broadcasting. Finally, the introduction of newscasts raised new questions about how Britain should present itself and other parts of the world to different broadcast audiences. The issues and questions raised in the 1930s would not go away in the 1940s, when wartime circumstances brought fundamental changes to British external broadcasting.

"THIS IS LONDON":
BROADCASTING DURING THE WAR

During the Second World War, British external broadcasting took on a size and importance that was previously unimaginable. The total number of BBC employees more than doubled, BBC program output tripled, and BBC transmitter power nearly quadrupled. The transformation was most obvious in the overseas services, where the size of the staff increased almost sixfold during the first two years of the war.[34] The rapid transformation would have numerous profound effects on BBC external broadcasting through to the postwar period, whether it was the introduction of foreign-language services or its hesitant editorial independence. Yet, as much as the BBC grew during the war and began targeting its languages and programs to certain audiences, the BBC devoted only a small amount of attention to colonial Africa. When it did try to tailor its programs for Africans, it immediately sparked a three-way contest between the BBC, the Colonial Office in London, and the colonial governments about what it was exactly they were trying to achieve through broadcasting. Although the war years were the period when many populations in British Africa began hearing BBC content, it was not always in the way that British broadcasters wanted.

The first transformation to overseas broadcasting—moving away from an imperial approach and introducing foreign-language services—actually predated the war. Four years after the beginning of the Empire Service, a committee chaired by Lord Ullswater reviewed the BBC charter. Its report recommended, "in the interest of British prestige and influence in world affairs," that the BBC should expand the Empire Service, including the appropriate addition of foreign languages.[35] The recommendation came in reaction to what Britain's European competitors, including the Germans, Italians, and Soviets, had started doing in foreign-language broadcasting. But BBC officials had thus far held the outlook that broadcasting was an imperial medium, not an international one. As they explained, they designed the English-language programs and news to strengthen Britain's imperial community; if other populations chose to listen in, that was merely an added benefit. Were the BBC to begin foreign-language broadcasting, it would be leaving the confines of the British world and targeting audiences that were, by definition, not British. Furthermore, BBC officials believed their competitors' propaganda polluted the airwaves and they did not want any suspicions to spread to them. John Reith explained, "It is more in British interests—and also a subtle form of propaganda for the British point of view—to avoid any action that might lead listeners, who have turned to British bulletins as a reliable source of information, to think that we too were joining in the babel of broadcast nationalist propaganda."[36] He captured what would become a common refrain among British external broadcasters—namely, British prestige and its reputation for integrity arose from the fact that the BBC was *different* from what other countries did.[37]

Despite these reservations, BBC officials felt pressure from Westminster to look at the technical and administrative requirements to transmit in other languages. It was clear the transmissions would have to come from the Empire Service's station at Daventry, as that was the only high-powered station equipped to transmit short-waves.[38] The larger question was what languages, in what transmissions, and in what form—whether it should be just news, or talks and other programs too. As British officials considered the possible uses of non-English broadcasts, they also triaged languages according to their divergent priorities. In weighing their options, British officials explained that if the overarching objective was to strengthen the hold over the British Empire, they should use the established languages of the dominions, such as French for Canada and Afrikaans for South Africa, and non-European languages for the rest of the empire, such as Hindi, Malay, and Swahili. On the other hand, if the real aim was to improve the British position in diplomatically strategic locations, the corporation should begin broadcasting in Spanish and Portuguese for South America and Arabic for the Middle East.[39] When the BBC finally began to broadcast in other languages in 1938, the first languages were indeed Spanish, Portuguese, and Arabic, indicating that geostrategic concerns now trumped a desire to strengthen the imperial community. The pattern held fast during the war. During the next seven years, the number of languages Britain broadcast in reached forty-five—a figure that was still less than the Germans' fifty-two—but more than half were European languages, and the only language for sub-Saharan Africa was Afrikaans. (It was briefly floated in 1940 that the BBC start short programs in Hausa and Swahili, but when the BBC and the British government realized the limitations of Britain's transmitters, they cut those two languages. The BBC did not broadcast in African languages until 1957, the year the first black African nation received independence.)[40] Foreign-language broadcasting had become core to the BBC's role overseas and would continue to act as a measure of the audiences and regions British foreign policy makers deemed most important to their interests.

The BBC's wartime expansion all but ignored colonial Africa; however, Africans became a significant unintended audience nonetheless during this period. Although the vast majority of British broadcasting resources went toward audiences in Europe, the BBC did make some approaches to its listeners in Africa. During one of the internal reorganizations that took place during the war, the corporation created a small section under John Grenfell Williams to produce programs for Africa and the Caribbean.[41] As a white South African, Grenfell Williams was familiar with the primary audience the African programming was meant for—namely, white listeners in southern Africa. At the same time, Grenfell Williams recognized that he could not completely ignore the non-settler colonies, and that made him one of the first BBC officials who tried to think specifically about programming for African listeners. Grenfell Williams's problem, however, was that he did not have anyone on hand at the BBC whom he could speak with about living or broadcasting in colonial Africa. (This stood in contrast to many of the other regions of the world, where the BBC's translators, announcers, and producers in the language services also served as sources of information.)[42] This meant Grenfell Williams had to rely upon colonial authorities, both in London and in the colonies, to collect and report any on-the-spot knowledge.

As the BBC was to learn, there was no single mind behind British colonialism in Africa. In London the Colonial Office stressed long-term economic and political development, while in Africa the colonial governments prioritized programs that would pacify resistance and make it easier to maintain control. In 1939, right after the war began, the colonial secretary, Malcolm MacDonald, met with BBC officials to discuss British broadcasting in the empire. He was particularly concerned that they make both the European and colonial populations feel they were Britain's partners in the present war. The importance of this, MacDonald urged, was so the types of nationalist protest several colonies had experienced during the late 1930s would not derail Britain's war efforts. But as MacDonald and the broadcasters discussed how Britain would convey war news to colonial subjects, they began to detail what they saw as the deficiencies of the native listener. They concluded the BBC did not have enough time to fully explain the historical, political, and geographical context to listeners who had no background; therefore, they should not try to tailor their broadcasts to uneducated audiences. Furthermore, they agreed it was not feasible for the BBC to broadcast in hundreds of local languages. By the end of the meeting, the colonial secretary and the broadcasters agreed that for financial and practical reasons the BBC could only focus on speaking to the population of educated Africans who understood English and owned their own wireless sets.[43]

Although MacDonald and the BBC acknowledged this was not a large portion of the African population, they likely did not realize just how tiny it was. Many of Kenya's rural districts would not receive their first wireless set until the next decade. Nigeria estimated there were about three thousand wireless sets in the colony by 1950, distributed among a population of twenty-five million. For those who did have access to the wireless, it was often because there was a set in a public space such as a market or a social hall. Similar to the Gold Coast, there was also a wired rediffusion system in many of Nigeria's large towns and cities that broadcast through loudspeakers in public spaces as well as homes.[44] What this meant was that during the 1940s, radio listening among Africans was more likely to occur in urban and educated or semi-educated parts of society than elsewhere, but it was largely in noisy spaces. This was at odds with the model of the individual listener that the BBC designed its overseas programming around.

In addition, as the BBC would soon hear through feedback from the colonies, the Colonial Office did not always share the same views about broadcasting with its officials on the ground. In 1941, in consultation with the Colonial Office and the Ministry of Information, the BBC proposed that it start a weekly fifteen-minute newsletter for West Africans. This was one of the BBC's first programs specific to black African audiences, and its planning exposed some of the problems that would plague the African Service in future decades. First, although the program was only meant for one region, it proved difficult to find an evening time slot that could work for a geographically dispersed audience. There was a two-hour time difference between Nigeria and the Gold Coast, and colonial officials reported that Africans tended to go to bed early. Forced essentially to choose between the two colonies, the broadcasters went ahead with the best time for the Gold Coast because the slot fit better with the BBC's other overseas schedules.[45] The more significant issue was the matter of content. For the first three programs, the BBC and Colonial Office arranged for Kofi Abrefa Busia—then a student at Oxford—to do a series of talks. Although officials in Britain praised the series wildly, the response from their counterparts in West Africa was quite different. The governments of Nigeria, the Gold Coast, and Sierra Leone all reported Busia's talks were "confined to lengthy and repetitive expositions of views of Intelligentsia to which it is not necessary to give publicity."[46] Then, the West African governors tried to help the BBC out by suggesting the programs they would rather hear instead. The governors' chief aim was to use the opportunity to head off colonial subjects' complaints. For example, the governors suggested one program on "wartime life in Great Britain, with varied illustrations of war effort and attitude with special reference to high taxation cheerfully borne," and another on the "comparison between present conditions in British West African Colonies and those in countries which directly or indirectly have come under German control." So not to be too obvious, the governors also stressed to Britain that "news not views" should predominate in programming, and propaganda must be carefully concealed.[47]

A year later, the feedback from West Africa showed BBC programs were still missing their mark. London broadcasters had tried to incorporate the request for locally oriented programs, but their method for doing so was to run talks on dull topics like the role of West African exports in the war effort.[48] Meanwhile, the colonial governors explained that African populations would welcome more light music and dance music, instead of talks and more talks. They further recommended the BBC follow the German example and do a more skillful job of interspersing talks with music.[49] In the governors' minds, the best BBC material by far was when the producers occasionally brought Africans in Britain to the microphone to send messages to friends and relatives at home. The governors felt a regular "Africans in London" feature could arouse a lot of interest, particularly if it was set to music.[50] What the colonial governors described was a series similar to the BBC program *Calling the West Indies*, a highly popular magazine program of interviews, literary discussions, and music.[51] While officials at the BBC celebrated the success their programs had in the Caribbean, they did not feel they could do the same for somewhere like West Africa. One of the factors that made programs such as *Calling the West Indies* viable, they explained, was the number of West Indians in Britain whom the BBC could call upon for segments and material. They felt it would be near impossible to fill a regular weekly program for West Africa.[52]

In an effort to reproduce the model that worked for Caribbean audiences, the BBC soon introduced *Calling West Africa*, a fifteen-minute program on the

African Service two evenings a week.[53] They were dismayed *Calling West Africa* did not gain the same following as its Caribbean counterpart. The broadcasters in London attempted to find personalities that would appeal to West African audiences, but—like most of the African Service programming—they continued to hear the complaint that their programs contained far too much talk.[54] At the BBC, broadcasters were incredulous that a large number of their listeners truly felt this, but they did agree to compromise a little more often in their West African programs and from time to time give listeners the things they asked for.[55] Therefore, *Calling West Africa* evolved into a more varied biweekly program, with poetry readings, illustrated talks on music, and even a few musical items sandwiched in between the topical talks on education and nutrition. The additional variety—however limited—made the program an exception in the early days of BBC broadcasting to Africa. The other regional programs on the African Service, such as *Calling East Africa* and *Calling Southern Rhodesia*, were almost entirely topical talks, as were many of other features on the BBC's African transmissions.[56]

While the BBC showed reluctance to adjust to listeners' tastes, it was more willing to adjust to what it perceived as listeners' needs. Early on during the war, government officials and BBC broadcasters were concerned about how to simplify the language of the news bulletins and provide the right amount of geographical and political background so a good portion of Africans could understand them. Their motivations were a combination of wanting to promote the war effort and paternalism toward colonial populations. (There were a lot of references to "simple minds" going around the BBC in this period.) Thus, the corporation instructed its *Calling West Africa* announcers that they needed to speak considerably slower here than they did in the pieces for European audiences. As one BBC memo commented, "If [West Africans] miss the opening and closing announcements they are apt to get the whole programme wrong, and we get the most extraordinary summaries of what they think they have heard!"[57] Once again, however, British broadcasters had to defer to local colonial officials, who emphasized the dangers of moving too far from a formal style because then listeners would feel patronized. It was a complicated act, as one recommendation from Lagos revealed: "Talks by Africans should be 'gossipy,' typical, objective and factual with accounts of personal experiences. Abstract theorizing should be avoided, as also any tendency to 'talk down to' listeners."[58] After the war, the BBC continued struggling to find a tone and content both it and local authorities could agree upon.

The BBC programs that targeted particular overseas audiences were shaped by the presence of international competition. However, during the second part of the war, the BBC found that it was also competing against itself. This gets to the second and more impactful way that African audiences benefitted from the BBC's wartime expansion. The other British transmission that could be heard in sub-Saharan Africa was the BBC General Forces Programme, programming for

British troops that ran twenty-one hours each day over the worldwide General Overseas Service (GOS).[59] The General Forces Programme was unique for the BBC for two reasons. First, as a link between servicemembers and their families, it was one of the few times a program was heard by audiences both overseas and at home in Britain. Second, because the General Forces Programme was meant to entertain British servicemembers, it prioritized light music and variety programs over the types of educational and informational material found on other British programs. The BBC produced these lighter programs with all types of servicemembers in mind, regardless of their national or regional identities.[60]

The introduction of the General Forces Programme was a relief to the British producers responsible for Africa because it took off some of the pressure to provide something for everyone in their vast region. Until that point, the broadcasters had felt a need to include some lighter programs for the military forces in Africa, which came at the expense of the more serious material they believed their primary audience most wanted.[61] Now, as the African Service director explained, they were free to return to their primary functions of supplying news and information.[62] The BBC did not anticipate that as the war wore on, the programs meant for servicemembers would also attract a considerable civilian audience overseas. In West Africa, direct listeners followed the light music and variety programs over to the lighter world service. African listeners preferred the forces programming because they felt it was much better balanced. This stood in contrast to the African Service, where, as one report explained, "There appears to be far too much talking on the African Service—we are being instructed instead of entertained!"[63] Meanwhile, British colonial officials' preferences were evident by their choices about what to rebroadcast over their colonial systems. They frequently chose to relay the forces programming instead of the less-relevant African Service programming.[64] The enormous expansion of British overseas broadcasting during the Second World War did touch African audiences eventually—although, they were almost always an unintended audience. When Africans were the intended audience, British broadcasters in London showed reluctance to move too far from their rigid ideas about which information colonial subjects should receive. Going into the postwar period and facing a new series of demands from the British government, colonial officials, and local audiences, the BBC African Service had to confront the question of how it could keep an African audience listening.

SEEKING BALANCE

British broadcasters continued to discount African audiences until the middle of the 1950s. This was not only because the BBC did not view them as a priority—it was also because the BBC did not value Africans' preferences. Beginning in 1947, the BBC restored the title of General Overseas Service (GOS) for the whole of the

English-language output on its worldwide network so the name no longer refer-
enced "forces" specifically. In part, the move reflected Britain's demobilization,
but it also signaled that the broadcaster was going to pivot away from the types of
light programming it had done during the war. The shift prompted alarm inside
colonial territories like the Gold Coast, where officials had taken advantage of the
BBC's lighter fare and wanted assurances it would continue.[65] In response, they
heard that the BBC would maintain a worldwide English service but would be
making changes to its content. A BBC official explained, "Obviously, the gradual
decline of a Forces audience will mean more concentration on the needs of civilian listeners, but I imagine that there will always be good material for your purposes."[66] Of course, what the BBC thought was good material was not always what
the colonial stations—let alone their audiences—wanted to hear. For example, the
director of the GOS aimed to cut back the music request program *Forces Favourites*, despite it being by far the most popular program on the service. Colonial
systems like the Gold Coast, which had organized itself around what was on offer
from Britain, were left turning to other ways to get the BBC to recognize its black
African audiences.

During this time, all the audience reports the BBC received about West Africa
came by means of the colonial governments. In 1946, the Gold Coast government
took the initiative of comprehensively surveying the habits and preferences of its
listening audience. At the time, the Gold Coast relayed British programs for an
average of eight hours each day (one to two hours of Africa-specific programming
and six to seven hours of the worldwide English-language GOS), spread across
morning, midday, and evening periods. In between those periods, the colonial
system transmitted government broadcasts in English and West African vernaculars and played gramophone records.[67] Through its survey, the government was
interested in learning what listeners thought about all the transmissions, both
British and local. Therefore, the broadcasting department sent a questionnaire to
over six thousand wired diffusion subscribers in the colony and then used the staff
at the rediffusion stations to follow up. The result was the first broadly sampled
audience report from West Africa, although it was still skewed toward the European population in the colony.[68]

When the Gold Coast forwarded its audience survey results to London, BBC
officials had to confront the ways their programs were unappealing. One piece
of revealing information was that the program *Calling West Africa* only ranked
fourth for BBC programs that listeners in the Gold Coast enjoyed. Colonial
administrators in the Gold Coast explained, "Listeners definitely want this programme, but complain that it does not serve its purposes."[69] The primary reason for this, the officials described, was that most of the program content did not
appeal to West Africans. For the program's music segment, for example, listeners
had once enjoyed broadcasts by Fela Sowande, a Nigerian composer who worked

in the classical European tradition. Gold Coast listeners remembered enjoying Sowande's program because he focused on using simple language and analogies when he introduced musical works—that, coupled with his Nigerian background. However, when Sowande became unavailable, the BBC switched to a man named Scott Goddard, whose descriptions of abstract musical concepts failed to interest West Africans.[70] The colonial administrators added that there were several other ways that Gold Coast listeners did not feel the British had thought enough about what made enjoyable programming. For instance, another program segment was Victor Silvester's ballroom dancing lessons, which were extremely popular in Britain, but had almost no appeal in West Africa. Explained one Gold Coast official, the Silvester lessons might have been acceptable on the regular BBC service, which was oriented toward Europeans and elite Africans, but it certainly did not belong on anything titled *Calling West Africa*.[71]

BBC authorities said they welcomed the audience report, which they called a major step for Britain's outreach to West Africa. Some of the information was not a surprise to them, including the criticism leveled at *Calling West Africa*. The head of the African Service also heard negative feedback from Nigeria, Sierra Leone, and Gambia, which he took to mean the BBC could not hope to serve four different colonies with a single program.[72] But other aspects of the Gold Coast report surprised British broadcasters, especially the clear preference to rebroadcast programs specifically designed for the forces in lieu of the African Service.[73] Although the BBC transmitted the African Service for five and a half hours a day, the Gold Coast Broadcasting Department only relayed a small portion of this content to its listeners. The 1946 Gold Coast audience report and the number of forces programs the colony chose to carry demonstrated the continued disconnect between the African programming that was planned in London and what was actually heard and enjoyed in West Africa.

At the same time, BBC officials in the mid-1940s used the feedback from West Africa as further validation that connecting with nonwhite colonial subjects was not their primary purpose. Given that they continued to design the majority of their African programs for white listeners in southern Africa, they gave themselves permission to disregard much of the feedback from West Africa. This remained the case until 1950, when the South African Broadcasting Corporation stopped its daily rebroadcast, prompting a precipitous drop to the BBC's white audience in Africa.[74] Although some South Africans continued to listen directly, after that moment, BBC producers started making more references to "balance" in their scheduling discussions, signaling an interest in speaking to audiences both black and white.[75] For example, one report in 1955 explained, "The GOS cannot hope to please all its listeners all the time. It has to try and provide a balanced diet for many different palates and at the same time make sure that each of them has a share of its favourite dish."[76] It was a different sentiment from the earlier era of imperial broadcasting, when British broadcasters were uninterested in serving populations they did not think would appreciate their content.

Nevertheless, the BBC's attitude shifted at a very slow pace over the 1950s, and British broadcasters still found reasons to discount their West African listeners. One of the ways the BBC tried to measure audience engagement was through the number of listener letters that Bush House received each year. Among audiences in Africa, West African listeners sent by far the greatest number—three thousand letters a year—to the BBC during the mid-1950s. But rather than reward West Africans for their engagement, British producers took exception to the fact that the majority of the letters were to *Listener's Choice*, a popular music request program that had replaced *Forces Favourites*. The producers at the General Overseas Service regarded *Listener's Choice* to be one of the compromises that they had to make in the schedule for their worldwide service and stated there would not be more like it. Their disregard for the program extended to the audiences who appeared to demand it. The same 1955 report that advocated for balance and variety also made clear that there were still audiences the BBC did not care to attract. "For those who required a unvaried diet of light entertainment," the report continued, "the GOS cannot appeal, and there are plenty of commercial radio stations in the world to satisfy them."[77] Although their audience had become increasingly diverse, British broadcasters continued to apply a hierarchy of cultural standards to their program output. With regard to colonial Africa, they still did not think they should produce programs specific to local demand.[78] Well into the 1950s, therefore, African audiences did not figure into either the universal or the targeted types of programming Britain offered.

THE PROVISION OF WORLD NEWS

There was a noticeable omission from the Gold Coast audience survey, and it was the output British authorities attached the greatest power to: the news. From the war, BBC officials had already seen how external newscasts served as a programmatic compromise between their softer aim to forge cultural affinities and the demands for more overtly propagandist influence being made by some members of the government. Therefore, it was not surprising to hear the director-general state immediately after the war that the top priority of overseas broadcasting remained the provision of what he described as "an accurate, impartial and dispassionate flow of news."[79] He was repeating the corporation's stated commitment to the liberal principle that unmediated provision of balanced information was essential for critical, rational debate to take place—both between citizens in a nation and between nations themselves. By this reasoning, if the BBC wanted to fulfil the role it saw for itself, the broadcaster needed to do all it could to remove barriers to access its version of the world news. During the 1940s and 1950s, British authorities went about this in a manner that had long-term implications not only for the authority of the BBC world news but also for communications infrastructures within many African nations.

British broadcasters instituted forms and conventions that made BBC newscasts recognizable and authoritative. By this point, the regular news bulletins were fixed points around which all of the other programs on the overseas services were planned; broadcasters at the BBC considered them "focal points round the clock."[80] During the mid-1950s, BBC producers transmitted eleven GOS world news broadcasts each day. These bulletins lasted nine minutes and fifteen seconds each, which included the time announcement that consisted of either the Greenwich time signal or the chimes of Big Ben followed by the news items in order of their importance. The rest of the nine-minute time slot featured either British home news, an expert commentary, or a sports roundup, depending on the time of day.[81] Also depending on the time of day was how many people were listening, and where they all lived. Some of the GOS bulletins, such as the 1100 and 1300 GMT broadcasts, transmitted at a time when a huge part of the global population was awake, and stations from Jamaica to Nigeria to India to Singapore relayed the BBC news simultaneously.[82] More than anything else, these bulletins were Britain's best opportunity to use a synchronous technology to connect disparate parts of the world.

Presentation was also crucial for constructing effective and credible news. By the 1950s, the overseas presenters at the BBC were more conscious than ever of their global reach and the importance of maintaining a certain conduct on the air. A 1955 handbook reminded the announcers on the General Overseas Service that they served as important ambassadors, particularly because many listeners did not recognize the BBC's independence and regarded it as a department of the British government. For the qualities of an on-air persona, the handbook described, "His cardinal virtues must be authority, courtesy, precision, presence-of-mind, confidence, alertness, and omniscience. There is only one deadly sin—carelessness."[83] What followed was a list of general rules and helpful hints the corporation implied it had accumulated over the past decades. Some of the hints referred to grammatical particularities and etiquette, such as the point that it was more correct to say "The United States *is*" instead of "The United States *are*" as well as the reminder not to fade out in the middle of "The Star-Spangled Banner" because it was a national anthem. The handbook also supplied a long list of offensive words and phrases that broadcasters needed to avoid using on air so as not to offend certain ethnic and religious groups. Finally, BBC presenters were reminded once again that they were meant to form bonds with many different parts of the world at once. In contrast to the 1940s handbooks, which explained that the British Commonwealth referred only to the dominions, the 1950s handbook instructed broadcasters to "Be careful" when using the words "Colony,"

"Commonwealth," and "Empire." Last, announcers were instructed to "Assume you are talking to friends, and do it in a common idiom which does not imply the background peculiar to prosperous Englishmen."[84] Whether the guidelines were minute or substantial they alluded to vast experience and knowledge that British broadcasters used to claim authority over style, rhetoric, and delivery of the world news.

The BBC's self-concept of its expertise and credibility was reinforced further by colonial broadcasting stations, which relied almost exclusively on the British corporation for world news. During the decade after the war there were still gaping differences between Britain's colonies with commercial stations, such as Kenya, and those with government stations, such as the Gold Coast. However, the broadcast news was one area where almost all the British colonies in Africa followed a similar formula. For example, although the service in Kenya did not take up much other British programming, it did rebroadcast the BBC news three times a day. After each world bulletin the Nairobi station presented a fifteen-minute local newscast, which was supplied by material from the *East African Standard* and the government Information Office.[85] Meanwhile, the Gold Coast Broadcasting System was different from that in Kenya in a large number of ways, but its approach to the news was almost identical. Gold Coast authorities designed their entire service around the programs they received from Britain and relayed between four and six BBC news bulletins each day during the late 1940s. In addition, public relations officials also prepared local news bulletins in English and five West African vernaculars that contained items from sports and social clubs, trading companies, and colonial government departments.[86] Despite their different approaches to other aspects of broadcasting, broadcasters in both Kenya and the Gold Coast agreed that short but regular news bulletins were a central feature of a broadcast schedule. They also adhered to a formula where world and regional news came from Britain and local news came from the colony. Finally, they did not believe local news should be kept independent from government control; instead, the information office or department provided most of the local content.

After so much discussion about the British world news during the postwar decades, it becomes necessary to question how broad the BBC coverage truly was. Despite its cultivated reputation as authorities for delivering world news, the BBC still had difficulty collecting pieces from outside Britain and Europe. For example, during a twelve-month period in the late 1940s, the BBC ran only 113 programs on its home services that had any relation to the colonial empire.[87] Broadcasting officials had begun to realize this ran contrary to the shifting attitude toward the Commonwealth they were tasked to promote. In 1949 the head of the overseas services explained, "It was the BBC's constant aim to try and develop in its broadcasts the real meaning of the Commonwealth and to explain to Colonial listeners that they were regarded as part of the family."[88] Therefore, British broadcasters began to look at ways to record and transmit more material from what they described as far-flung areas such as sub-Saharan Africa. One way they could do this was to directly pick up local broadcasts. This would depend upon London receiving a strong enough signal from the colonial station. One of the first times the BBC attempted this was in 1946, when the Gold Coast opened its new Legislative Council, under an African majority for the first time.[89] The signal from Accra was strong enough for the BBC to record and rebroadcast later in its *Radio Newsreel*; however, the process required such a large amount of coordination between Britain and the Gold Coast that British producers expressed reluctance to make it a common practice.

During the early 1950s, the BBC began looking to sub-Saharan Africa as a site for international stories, particularly stories about development. In 1950, the corporation was not yet prepared to post a permanent correspondent there, but stated that a well-planned short trip could be just as effective. That year, the BBC sent two members of the European Services to West and East Africa respectively. The correspondents' producers instructed them to record enough actuality material that they could edit at least twelve feature pieces plus another twelve to twenty-four talks from these two trips alone. In addition, British officials reasoned, upon the reporters' return, the external services would have two more speakers with on-the-ground experience of African conditions and could thus cover new topics as they arose.[90] The BBC wove material from the correspondents' short trips in 1950 into its external output for more than two years. Whether describing economic planning in West Africa, mass education in Somalia, or the groundnuts scheme in Tanganyika, the pieces focused overwhelmingly on colonial development. That was because both the correspondents and their producers back in London felt the subject of development would most effectively dissipate British and European audiences' general ignorance about this part of Britain's empire. At the same time, British broadcasters realized that the topic of development could be tricky, thus they had to tread somewhat carefully in the way they described it. But even with this statement, the BBC was not thinking about its colonial audiences who might get offended. Instead, one of the reporters explained, British broadcasters did not want to come across as smug or self-congratulatory in their development stories because it could lead overseas listeners, especially those in Eastern Europe, to be less apt to believe them.[91] Though the BBC thought of its European audiences foremost when collecting pieces from Africa, it is important to remember that colonial audiences around the world heard the BBC newscasts too. Until the mid-1950s, the majority of broadcasts that African audiences heard from their continent were filtered through this context: meant to explain the setting and conditions in Africa to audiences in other parts of the world.

THE DEMOCRATIC FUNCTION OF BROADCASTING

The division of world and local news remained firmly in place during the 1950s, despite a significant policy shift regarding the development of broadcasting in the colonies. The Plymouth Report of 1936 remained a key document in the development of colonial broadcasting after the Second World War. Its description of broadcasting as a tool of advanced administration aligned with the British government's postwar ambitions to establish a new form of modernizing trusteeship in the colonial empire.[92] It also helped secure in 1949 a central allocation of £1 million specifically for broadcasting under the Colonial Development and Welfare Act.[93] As it did with other colonial development schemes, the Colonial Office rationalized that broadcasting services in the colonies would bring both economic and political returns. For the former, for instance, colonial authorities acting under the BBC's advice purchased their new materials and equipment from British companies, such as the Gold Coast's new 20 kW national transmitter and generating plant from Marconi (figure 6). But London civil servants made clear that whatever the economic calculus might be, the far more consequential concern—and the one that justified the expenditure—was political.

The extra funds and attention toward colonial broadcasting showed a pivotal shift in the BBC's imperial designs. Since the inception of overseas broadcasting, the BBC had sharply distinguished between the needs of the empire and the needs of individual colonies. London officials designed the worldwide English-language service to fulfill the imperial function of British broadcasting and left it to individual colonial governments to build infrastructures and schedules that served their local information needs. However, after the Second World War, British civil servants expressed increasing levels of concern about the ferocity of popular politics in sub-Saharan Africa, be it nationalist or communist in nature. Their alarm was punctuated by specific disturbances in Britain's African territories, such as the labor strikes in Mombasa in 1947 and the riots in Accra in 1948.[94] In response, colonial governors continued what they had been doing since the beginning of the decade, which was to formalize and expand the powers of their public relations or information departments. When the governors looked to Whitehall for support, they often found it—or at least, they encountered little resistance.[95] But by the late 1940s, the impulse to censor and control was matched by an appeal for a different and more broad-minded approach. When read in a different light, as some Colonial Office administrators began to do, the reports from the African colonies revealed a paucity of a public sphere that could mitigate forceful demands for political change. To these officials, such reports were a warning sign not to censor but to commit to building stronger political institutions in Britain's soon-to-be-independent empire.

FIGURE 6. Installing the new 20 kW transmitter and generator at the Gold Coast Broadcasting Service in Accra in 1955. The words "Marconi England" appear prominently on the front of the equipment. The National Archives, Kew, United Kingdom, INF 10/122/13 (1955).

Commit Britain did—and while the government's £1 million allocation for broadcasting addressed urgent information needs in certain colonies, it stressed longer-term institution building in most others. When the colonial secretary explained how the broadcasting funds would be divvied up, his top priorities were to improve listening facilities in Malaya, where British forces were in the midst of the Malayan Emergency, and to establish a reliable service in Cyprus to ease constitutional reforms. After those needs, however, he assessed the next priority regions were, in order, West Africa (£295,000) and East Africa (£178,000), which together received almost half the total allotment. The colonial secretary's assessment reflected the political urgency that British civil servants increasingly assigned to building durable liberal institutions in their African colonies. For the specifics, the Colonial Office turned to the BBC, thus putting the independent corporation in a strong position to attempt to impart its public service principles to the colonial empire.

In the course of a few years, a series of BBC experts visited West Africa to survey and advise a plan of action. Although these individuals' expertise stemmed from production and technical sides of broadcasting, they nonetheless couched their recommendations to the Colonial Office in political terms. After a tour in the middle of 1948, John Grenfell Williams cautioned that if the colonial systems continued to rely too heavily on British content, it risked their capacity to develop into fully fledged services in which West African publics were invested. In his report, Grenfell Williams went so far as to label the political atmosphere in colonies like the Gold Coast as dangerous.[96] The following year, two British engineers traveled to West Africa to conduct a more comprehensive survey. Their recommendations were somewhat typical of the Colonial Office's development planning at the time, in that they envisioned an interterritorial West African Broadcasting Corporation that was an extension of the BBC's administrative operation in London.[97] The scheme did not materialize for a series of reasons, including lack of cooperation among the respective West African colonies, but it had a lasting significance in the question it raised about the future of state-controlled broadcasting. Going into the 1950s, proponents of British broadcasting practices articulated that if Britain truly aimed to impart liberal principles to its colonies, colonial authorities needed to relinquish some of their control.

During the first half of the 1950s, the BBC and the Colonial Office made it clear their aim was to develop colonial broadcasting stations into miniature versions of the BBC. Their offers of assistance and directives took two main forms: first, professional training, and second, organizational independence. Between the two, BBC officials expressed far more confidence in how to accomplish the first. The government's £1 million allocation earmarked a portion of funds to go to the BBC's staff training department so it could train visiting broadcasters from the colonies. At first, this comprised setting aside slots in the BBC's general staff training courses, which the corporation ran for its own employees. By the mid-1950s, however, BBC administrators had created a separate ten-week curriculum that they felt was more tailored to the needs of broadcasters from the developing world. To fill the courses, London officials invited colonial administrators to nominate mid-level broadcasting staff who showed potential for future management and had a mastery of English.[98] The trainees traveled to London, where they spent their first two weeks in an "Introduction to British Life" course run by the British Council. The colonial broadcasters then moved to the BBC, where they received a catch-all of lectures and demonstrations from across the corporation, including production, presentation, studio management, educational broadcasting, and news.[99] Over the following decade, the BBC trained an average of thirty broadcasters from Britain's colonies in Africa, Asia, and the Caribbean each year through these short-term courses. Nevertheless, London officials were well aware they only made a dent in colonies' demands for more training. On occasion, if British officials felt the need was urgent enough, the BBC dispatched a staff member overseas for a few months to instruct a larger group of students from a single colony (figure 7). This was the case in Nigeria in 1959, after British

FIGURE 7. A former BBC staff member leads a class on microphone characteristics as part of a program operations training course at the Nigerian Broadcasting Corporation. The National Archives, Kew, United Kingdom, INF 10/245/9 (1959).

administrators and broadcasters alike panicked that Nigerian broadcasters were drastically ill-prepared for the next year's independence.[100] For the most part, however, the BBC held fast that the most effective means for teaching British techniques and professional standards was through total immersion—and that could only occur in the metropole.

When the BBC trained colonial broadcasters, it did so under the assumption that the trainees' organizations would one day resemble the parent corporation. In 1953 the Gold Coast government requested that another commission of BBC experts visit the colony and recommend how to develop its broadcasting services. The commission—led by John Grenfell Williams—recommended the government form a separate entity, the Gold Coast Broadcasting System, to take over the existing services in the government information department. The commission understood the colonial government would retain some control over the broadcasting service, at least for a few years, but stated that authorities' control should be as light as possible so the body and its staff could foster a spirit of independence.[101] This model—a version of gradual independence—came to stand for the BBC standard recommendations for how a colonial state could build an independent public system. That was seen two years later, when a similar commission from London prepared a similar set of recommendations for Kenya that detailed a progressive changeover from commercial broadcasting to a colonial government service to an independent corporation. Although British officials framed their recommendations in the language of gradual self-government and institution building, they could not fully hide their political fears. West African colonies like the Gold Coast were now on an accelerated path toward self-rule, but British onlookers expressed alarm at the way political elites such as Kwame Nkrumah were using the power of print media to control debate.[102] If Britain could impart a professional, independent broadcasting tradition, they expressed, it would be able to correct the imbalance so that rational, critical debate could emerge.

Meanwhile in Kenya, Britain's proposals to cement a liberal tradition might seem jarring, given that the colonial state was at that very moment denying thousands of Kenyans their rights and property in a protracted and violent counterinsurgency campaign. Although the state of emergency occupied an enormous part of Britain's attention in Kenya, British officials were also trying to quickly lay a foundation for a constitutionally minded multiracial society.[103] Thus, they claimed that if they wanted to control the pace and nature of Kenyan political change, they needed to institute a noncommercial, non-state broadcaster that would ease the way for controlled decolonization. Over the 1950s, aims to use broadcasting as primarily a system of control had been replaced by a great amount of discussion about the democratic function of broadcasting and how it facilitated other British practices and institutions, such as the critical, rational debate within a healthy parliamentary democracy. But a gap remained between the theory and the reality; as many of Britain's colonies moved toward self-government, their broadcasting systems were still in the hands of the colonial government and were helmed by British expatriates on secondment from the BBC.

Finally, as often as British experts proclaimed their intentions to establish a full-fledged broadcasting organization in each colony, they assumed there was one key way these organizations would always be satellites to the parent corporation in Britain. That was the provision of world news. Although the plans for the Gold Coast and Kenya both detailed the establishment of news sections staffed by professional journalists, the journalists' responsibilities did not extend beyond events of regional significance. British broadcasting experts did not help African stations plan for international news operations because they assumed the stations would continue to take the BBC world news.[104] At the eve of African independence British officials continued to imagine and impose a metropolitan/colonial division of labor between world and local news.

LOSING THE COLD WAR AND FINDING
THE AFRICAN AUDIENCE

The dramatic expansion in British overseas broadcasting during the war forced London civil servants to fix a new arrangement for external broadcasting policy and financing in the postwar period.[105] In 1946, a white paper on broadcasting proposed a relationship whereby the corporation had editorial independence, but was expected to operate under the guidance of the government "as will permit it to plan its programmes in the national interest."[106] By the following year this language had become a key part of the BBC license agreement. Because "the national interest" was a purposely vague concept, each year the Foreign Office, Commonwealth Relations Office, and Colonial Office negotiated with the Treasury which services and for how many hours per week the BBC would transmit overseas. As the controllers of the purse strings, the prescribing offices and the Treasury had enormous leverage over the BBC during these negotiations, and they wanted to see clear evidence of what they were paying for. So began a new phase in the relationship between the BBC Overseas Service (renamed the External Services in 1948) and the British government, one marked by successive reviews and cutbacks.

As the successive reviews and cutbacks continued into the mid-1950s, the BBC found itself grouped with the British Council, the Central Office of Information, and the departmental information offices under the broad label of overseas information work. All the organizations and departments pointed to the escalating Cold War and Britain's declining prestige as urgent reasons to increase the overall resources given to the information effort. But the austerity climate also pitted the different organizations against one another, fighting over portions of a diminishing public diplomacy pie. The BBC drew heavily on its ability to reach mass audiences whenever it found itself arguing against the British Council and the Information Office, which each focused on reaching the influential few instead. During the middle of the 1950s the annual grant-in-aid to the BBC external services was a little over £5 million out of the total £12 million Britain spent on information services each year.[107] Whether this was the correct amount and whether it was distributed the most effective way was the subject of study for the committee appointed under Lord Drogheda in 1952. Chapter 1 described how the Drogheda committee recommended the British Council shift its emphasis from cultural to educational work and from more developed to less developed parts of the world. The recommendations for the BBC external services fell along the same lines. When the committee first met in the early 1950s, British external broadcasting still retained much of the shape it acquired during the Second World War, albeit in a diminished capacity. The Drogheda committee heard the corporation's anxiety about how out of date its transmitting network had become. The committee recommended a large-scale capital investment program, to the tune of £500,000 per year for at least five years, for Britain to modernize its equipment and install high-powered relays in new parts of the world where the British signal was being crowded out. To find the funds, the Drogheda committee recommended the BBC drop seven foreign-language services: French, Italian, Portuguese, Dutch, Danish, Norwegian, and Swedish.[108] Just as it had with the British Council, the Drogheda committee tried to move the BBC away from its old-fashioned orientation toward Western Europe so it could pay attention to the rest of the world.

The Drogheda committee certainly had good reason to issue its recommendations, as signs were everywhere that Britain was losing the information war badly. In the broadcasting field, the United States and the USSR passed Britain in external output in the late 1940s and early 1950s; both superpowers continued to grow their services while the British tried just to maintain what they had. China came onto the external broadcasting scene very quickly in the later part of the decade and would also pass Britain in output by 1960. Britain had to pay attention to regional powers as well. For example, Radio Cairo—one of the strongest signals to reach the East African colonies—tripled its output between 1950 and 1956 and added broadcasts in Swahili, Somali, and Amharic. Throughout the decade, Radio Cairo broadcast a consistently virulent anticolonial interpretation of world events, often using vivid and memorable language whenever it mentioned Britain.[109] The sudden explosion in external broadcasting worldwide was in anticipation of the transistor radio revolution in the developing world. What British officials observed overseas was later confirmed by statistics: during the decade between 1955 and 1965, radio set ownership increased by a factor of five in the Middle East, a factor of six in China, and a factor of twelve in Africa and India.[110] But despite mounting evidence that Britain needed to remodel its approach to external broadcasting, the British government ignored the Drogheda committee's recommendations for broadcasting in the middle of the 1950s. This meant that British broadcasting was in an even weaker relative position at the end of 1956 when the crisis over Suez occurred.

In BBC lore, the Suez Crisis stands as a pivotal moment for the corporation, one in which the broadcasters' conduct was nothing short of exemplary. That telling refers to the BBC's decision to transmit Opposition leader Hugh Gaitskell's statement over the GOS and the Arabic Service. What the broadcasters felt was a test for their journalistic integrity prompted enormous outcry from the Foreign Office and parts of the Conservative cabinet, which proclaimed that the BBC had undercut the national interest. The cabinet was already looking to make cuts to the BBC's grant-in-aid and threatened to defund external broadcasting even further, if not take it over completely.[111] But, by the next year, it became clear that neither action would take place, leaving the Suez Crisis to appear in the corporation's history as a moment when it successfully defended its principles against government pressure.

The Suez Crisis is significant in the history of British external broadcasting in another, much more important manner. The events of Suez revealed a global order where Britain was no longer near the top. It proved definitively what the Drogheda and other review committees had been saying for years, which was that Britain was fighting the Cold War in all the wrong places. The year after the crisis, the British government appointed another review of its overseas information activities and finally adopted several recommendations that had been pending since the early 1950s. The government committed to a long-term program of replacing and modernizing the BBC's transmission equipment around the world. It also agreed to double the Arabic Service output to more than nine hours a day and restore the General Overseas Service to twenty-four hours a day. Last, the government acceded to the BBC starting new foreign-language services in Hausa, Swahili, and Somali. Although the BBC broadcast in over forty languages during the 1950s, this would be the first time it would transmit material in an African language. To offset the costs of the additional services, the BBC was forced to reduce or eliminate several of its Western European languages.[112] Seeking to recover its global position in the late 1950s, Britain ended its focus on Europe and turned toward the developing world.

If Suez was the first indicator that the British needed to put more of their broadcasting resources into the developing world, the second was the wave of African independence that started in 1957 with Ghana and accelerated after 1960. That meant that the BBC recognized African audiences as a priority just as Britain was losing its African colonies. The British corporation introduced its half-hour broadcast in Hausa in March 1957, one week after Ghana had become independent. It added Somali and Swahili transmissions to its schedule a few months later. Officials in the Colonial Office had raised the idea for African-language transmissions the year before while preparing for Ghana's independence. They were looking for ways to demonstrate Britain's interest in Ghanaian affairs and thought they could do so with a half-hour cultural magazine once a week.[113] When the idea reached Bush House, broadcasters pushed for it to be a daily show that focused on world news instead. As more African colonies became independent, Britain continued to expand its program offerings for African audiences through a revamped African Service. During the early 1960s the BBC doubled its transmission time in both Hausa and Swahili to an hour each day, including an evening program. It also broadcast the world news twice a day and added a special "News of the African World" segment.[114] Also during the early 1960s, the BBC started a new French service for West and Equatorial Africa, where the programs differed in content and accent from the French for Europe service. And the BBC introduced a full series of English programs specific for African audiences. The

English for Africa service continued to grow over the rest of the decade; among a few of the programs it contained were *Focus on Africa*, *Good Morning Africa*, and *African Theatre*.

Was it too little too late? When Ghana became independent on 6 March 1957, its broadcasting station was relaying five BBC news bulletins a day. One week later, the Ghanaian cabinet ordered the Ghana Broadcasting System (GBS) to drop all but one of the relays immediately and replace them with bulletins from their own news department. At that time, in a carry-over from the late colonial period, both the director of broadcasting and the head of news at GBS were BBC employees who had been seconded to Ghana from 1955 to 1960. The two men were horrified by the cabinet's order, particularly because they did not feel the GBS news section could handle the responsibility of both home and world coverage.[115] When news of Ghana's decision reached Britain it prompted another set of reactions, starting with the BBC head of external broadcasting, J. B. Clark, who had worked at the BBC since the very beginnings of the Empire Service. Clark declared it was a completely arbitrary action, a slap in the face that abetted a decaying diplomatic relationship.[116] Others at the corporation characterized that the move had come out of the fervor of nationalism, but that would eventually pass and then sense in Ghana would prevail.[117] Meanwhile, officials at the Commonwealth Relations Office took the news in a different direction. They reassured each other that Ghanaian broadcasters would need to obtain material for their newscasts somewhere and would presumably do it by monitoring the BBC and Reuters. Although the newscasts themselves were not BBC, at least the content would still be British.[118]

But Ghana's decision to drop the BBC bulletins marked the beginning of the end for Britain's monopoly on broadcasting to Africa. Within a few years it had become obvious that British outlets were only a few of the international sources Ghana looked to for news. In addition to the BBC and Reuters, the Voice of America, Radio Brazzaville, and Tass (the Soviet news agency) stories were also prominent in Ghana's newscasts. Furthermore, in other British colonies in Africa, nationalist parties and listeners appeared ready to follow Ghana's example. By the late 1950s Nigerians were fed up with the section of the BBC broadcast that began, "And now for some home news from Britain." As one listener explained to the *Daily Times*, "Just how this idea of London comes to be regarded as the 'home' of Nigerians beats the imagination of all right thinking people."[119] Officials at the Nigerian Broadcasting Corporation were already under pressure to drop the British news altogether, and they pleaded with the BBC to change the introduction.[120] The "Home news" remained in the bulletin, though, and was one of the reasons that so many of Nigeria's regional stations dropped the BBC following independence in 1960.[121] After Ghana and Nigeria, other new nations such as Tanganyika, Zambia, and Kenya also used independence as the moment to reduce drastically or drop altogether the amount of British output they transmitted over national airwaves.

African governments' decision to drop the BBC was a real threat to the British cultural project in Africa. Until that point, British broadcasters had enjoyed a broadcast environment with very little competition because they relied on colonial stations to relay their programs. In several places, the colonial government had control over the receiving end of broadcasting as well as the transmitting end. Private set ownership in the African colonies remained very low, even in the mid-1950s. The number of receiving sets in the Gold Coast tripled between 1950 and 1955, but there were still only nine sets for every one thousand people in the colony in 1955. That was one of the highest amounts for sub-Saharan Africa; in Kenya it was less than three and in Nigeria it was less than two. Of course, more than half the sets in the Gold Coast in the mid-1950s were government-provided wired loudspeakers.[122] Those listeners had no choice over the station they listened to. They could only receive the government station, and in the colonial period that meant they heard a lot of BBC. When he took power in 1957, however, Kwame Nkrumah recognized the same benefits to wired rediffusion that colonial officials had seen. The Ghanaian government continued to build the wired diffusion system and doubled the number of wired sets by the end of the decade.[123] What all of this meant was that when the Ghana Broadcasting System decided to drop the BBC, it took thousands of African listeners out of the BBC audience.

The wired rediffusion system in the Gold Coast was a bit unique, but in other colonies the colonial government found ways to control the stations that African populations heard. Kenya estimated there were thirteen thousand wireless sets in the colony in 1950, but almost all of them were in the hands of the colony's European and Asian populations. African populations in many rural districts in Kenya received their first or second wireless set in 1953, as part of a gift scheme connected to the coronation of Queen Elizabeth II. The set was either placed in the African District Welfare Hall or put in the hands of a local chief, which meant listening was public and/or outside. (See figure 8 in the next chapter, showing a crowd listening to a set outdoors.) The sets were "saucepan radios" that operated on dry batteries; they were precursors of the transistor radios that would appear all over East Africa a decade later.[124] The Information Office in Nairobi hoped the sets would mean more Africans would hear its broadcasts, particularly the announcements and propaganda related to the state of emergency.[125] As the provincial commissioner in the Rift Valley distributed the allotment, he instructed recipients that they were only permitted to tune to broadcasts by the Kenyan government or the BBC. If the government suspected they were not observing the rule, local officials would immediately remove the set.[126] Kenya was another colony where the BBC relied on the support it received from the colonial government to reach the African listeners that it did. What British broadcasters now realized, though, was that after independence, it could no longer take those listeners' attention for granted.

The BBC lost its privileged position in African broadcasting over the late 1950s and early 1960s—just as the transistor revolution started to reach the continent. The rate at which Nkrumah's government in Ghana added wired loudspeakers to the system was still less than the number of new wireless sets Ghanaians purchased. By 1959, sixty-eight thousand of the one hundred nine thousand receiving sets in Ghana were wireless.[127] Over the 1960s Africans across the continent gained access to wireless sets that they could tune to the stations of their choosing. Among their choices were their national broadcaster or one of the growing numbers of foreign broadcasters trying to reach Africa. The next chapter will show how the BBC tried to find ways to stand out amid all the competition it faced. African audiences represented a new market for broadcasters all over the world, and British broadcasting in the postcolonial period was clearly going to be different.

LOSING ITS REACH OR STRENGTHENING ITS VOICE?

In contrast to older forms of cultural exchange, such as drama and books, radio was a new technology for British authorities, and they were still learning all the ways they could use it. They first started using the technology in their empire during the 1930s, but throughout the late colonial period—the 1940s, 1950s, and early 1960s—British officials continually brought up new ways that broadcasting could serve their different imperial interests all at once. When British officials spoke of the potential of broadcasting, they moved between three interconnected features: the content, the technology, and the expertise. British broadcasting was therefore not unlike other colonial development fields where colonial regimes tapped into new funds for development, built new infrastructures, and dispatched technical experts into the territories—all during this very same period.[128] Broadcasting not only followed the same pattern, but it also complemented other development fields through its capacity to package and distribute expertise. Broadcasting was not the only cultural technology that Britain deployed for this purpose; like the books described in chapter 2, or like colonial development films that began to appear during the same era, British colonial development aims hinged on the ability to spread messages across a vast space cheaply.[129]

One of the threads throughout this discussion, however, is that there were many occasions when Britain's imperial and colonial interests were at odds with one another. The development of colonial broadcasting in British Africa was the joint effort of three bodies—the BBC, the Colonial Office, and the colonial governments—but officials in these bodies imagined quite different futures for the relationship between Britain and Africa. Although officials in Britain did not think broadcasting to Africa was a priority in this period, officials in Africa did. Colonial governments incorporated the BBC worldwide service into their colonial development plans, and for decades African audiences heard the BBC through an instrument of colonial rule. This held true during most of the 1950s; although Britain started to speak of a new commitment to public service broadcasting, systems almost invariably remained under control of the government. That meant that broadcasts from Britain, whether it was a talk or a newscast, were always interspersed with the aims and messages of the colonial regime—to the extent that African listeners did not make a distinction. Though African listeners were not the BBC's intended audience, they were among its audience, and their perception of British broadcasting from this period would impact their decision about whether to listen to it later. Part of their decision would rest on how the BBC represented news from other parts of Africa as well as other parts of the world.

Was British culture an inclusive or exclusive project? The institutions introduced over the earlier chapters each grappled with this question in their own way, deciding which audiences they sought to reach or in which languages they chose to publish. With broadcasting, the question returns, this time through a technology that offered both possibilities and constraints for exclusion. Across all three, Britain did not reach out to African audiences until it was losing its empire because African audiences were not on top of Britain's imperial and international concerns. British cultural agencies found themselves having to compete for postcolonial listeners at the very moment that that audience had become crucial for Britain's revised position in the world. British broadcasters recognized that if they were to continue having an influence in the former empire, they needed to reconfigure the context and the content of their broadcasts. They were not alone: British Council officers and British publishers also saw the need to rethink how they designed their aims and activities in postcolonial Africa. The second part of this book examines the first decades of the postcolonial period and looks at how the BBC and other British agencies attempted to fit their work into a different strategic context: that of the decolonized world.

PART TWO

Cultural Imperialism
after Empire

4

"... Calling Africa"

Capturing the Cold War Audience

As the previous chapter explained, the BBC was a familiar entity to African listeners. During the colonial era, radio listeners in Britain's colonies became accustomed to hearing British voices coming through the scratchy static of their own or (often more likely) their community's bulky dry-battery wireless sets. Oftentimes what listeners were hearing was not a direct transmission from London, but instead a rebroadcast relayed through the colonial government's local transmitters. Colonial broadcasters—whether they worked within the colonial government's information office or were a semi-autonomous body—typically integrated BBC content such as the GOS news among their own local news and programs that were designed to enhance the colonial government's authority. Given how closely associated the BBC sound was with the colonial government, it might be assumed that after independence Africans would definitively reject listening to or trusting British broadcasts. And yet, as this chapter will describe, a portion of African listeners continued to tune into British broadcasts nonetheless. The fact the BBC continued to reach African audiences propels the question this chapter will answer: After independence, why did Africans want to continue hearing from Britain?

British broadcasters' answer to that question was simple: because the BBC was undeniably the best. Whether for its reputed truthfulness or its worldwide news coverage, they reasoned, Africans who sought the highest-quality news and programs sought the BBC. British broadcasters rooted their thinking in the way they understood their institutional history, where moments such as the Suez Crisis demonstrated the unshakeable journalistic principles they believed were at the heart of their work.[1] By extension, they portrayed their overseas audience as an empowered public that could discern those principles in action. As part of this chapter shows, British broadcasters had some reason to think this way: their repeated demonstrations to British politicians about the BBC's impact, combined with the process by which the BBC solicited audience feedback, and further combined with their understanding of the corporation's history, all continually reinforced one another. Academic studies of the BBC also contain some of the same faith in the BBC brand. Even when academics conduct them, institutional studies of the BBC World Service rely on the corporation's records to find evidence of overseas listenership, thus reinforcing how the BBC viewed and defended itself.[2]

This chapter, which examines Britain's efforts to woo African audiences through the different offerings of the BBC African Service, is going to take a somewhat different approach. Beginning in the 1960s, the BBC competed for African audiences against dozens of other broadcasters. The British faced competition from other international powers, whether they were the Voice of America, Radio Moscow, or another, and the British also now competed against the African national services that took over the colonial-era infrastructure. Given how crowded the broadcasting field became by the end of the 1960s, it is logical not only to examine the content of BBC programs, but more importantly to position British broadcasts against what was on offer from other stations. The chapter thus compares the BBC newscast against national newscasts, such as those from the Voice of Kenya, and other international newscasts, such as those of the Voice of America. When looked at in this light, it shows that African audiences who chose to continue listening to Britain after independence did so because they found relative value in it. In particular, BBC listeners found newscasts that resembled the style they were used to, contained more information than those of their national stations, and presented that information in a more objective-sounding package than other international stations. In other words, for these listeners, the BBC was not the standalone best, it was simply better than the other options.

Across all the avenues in which Britain maintained a cultural presence in Africa, broadcasting is one that reflects the Cold War backdrop very clearly.[3] The Cold War pushes in on the history of the BBC African Service in numerous ways, beginning with the fact that Britain faced a very large field in the competition for African listeners. But it was more than just a matter of developing an attractive and influential program lineup. Like during the colonial era, Cold War–era broadcasting in Africa was just as much about technology and training as it was about program content. Here too, Britain faced a growing amount of competition. African national states that sought to modernize their broadcasting technology did not have to purchase Marconi or other British equipment any longer. Now, they could entertain offers from any international purveyor, including the Soviets and the Czechs, as Ghana and Kenya did. In the area of training, the BBC's short-term courses in London were reputed to be the best. However, the British could only offer a certain number of slots each year, and it was not anywhere near the demand. Facing heavy pressure to Africanize their staff as quickly as possible, therefore, African officials also accepted offers from other nations—whether the United States, Australia, or China—to take in and train African broadcasters.

The period under study in this chapter is the 1960s, a decade that a *BBC Handbook* described as the "Decade of Africa." Over this period, British broadcasters expanded their African language schedules and introduced a wide range of French- and English-language programs oriented around African needs and interests. Within all the different content that comprised the BBC African Service, most of what follows focuses on the most utilitarian and ubiquitous programming: the news. It does this to explain some of the differences in the news that audiences heard when they compared the BBC with its competition. In particular, this discussion examines the procedures behind news gathering, editing, and reading, under the assumption that the presentation of news had power. After explaining when and why African listeners tuned to the BBC for news, the final part of the chapter considers a very different type of BBC programming: a radio play series called *African Theatre*. Through cultural programs such as this one, BBC producers strove to provide some balance to their transmissions and to show a whole other way that British broadcasting served Africa. The BBC thus claimed that in addition to delivering information about the broader world, British broadcasting encouraged creativity and helped Africans connect to one another.

Even though most of the discussion here does not look at what British broadcasters categorized as their "cultural content" for Africa, culture is prevalent throughout the chapter in the cultural values that shaped news collection and compilation and that were then conveyed through newscasts.[4] I show how British broadcasters acted upon information differently than their Kenyan counterparts and their American counterparts, with each group selecting, refining, and delivering information for audiences in their own way. British broadcasters were fully aware of the cultural values and ideology that went into a newscast. That became why the crowded field they faced after African independence was not just about the BBC topping its rivals, it was about Britain continuing to teach its values. In British minds, it worked the other way around as well. When British broadcasters found evidence that there was still a BBC listenership in Africa, they interpreted it to mean there was a demand from Africa for British cultural values more broadly.

A NEW CHALLENGE

The end of formal colonialism presented a technical challenge to British broadcasters who hoped to speak to African publics. With political handover, the network of local transmitters in each former colony passed into the control of the national government. Just as was seen with Ghana, within a short period after independence, most national broadcasters reduced drastically the amount of British content they rebroadcast over the national system. The short-term effect this had varied, depending whether there were other nearby stations that continued to rebroadcast British news and programs. For example, after the Nigerian Broadcasting Corporation dropped many BBC programs, some of the commercial stations in Nigeria continued to carry them, which British broadcasters happily described as offsetting potential damage.[5] In Tanganyika, which became independent in 1961, listeners could still hear the BBC through the colonial station in Kenya, at least until Kenyan independence in 1963. Then, for the following year, the British Forces Station outside Nairobi continued to broadcast the BBC GOS news until the end of 1964, when Britain withdrew its troops and closed the station. It was at that point that British observers remarked with more finality that British material was disappearing from the region. From Britain, the *Daily Telegraph* rued, "Many listeners are now faced with the alternatives of buying more powerful receivers or losing the BBC news altogether."[6] From this point forward, Britain's main means of speaking to Africans was through the direct signal from London.

Here, proponents of British broadcasting saw developments that worked in their favor, most particularly the "transistor revolution" that engulfed Africa during the 1960s. Compared to just one decade earlier, when the colonial government in Kenya gifted many rural districts their first wireless receiver set so they could tune into the queen's coronation, by the 1960s international broadcasting to Africa flourished in part because of private set ownership. At the beginning of 1964, a survey by the United States Information Agency (USIA) estimated that the number of radio transmitters in Africa had increased by 19 percent over the past year—making it by far the fastest growing listenership in the world.[7] Not only were the new radios smaller and cheaper, they were also more likely to be capable of picking up long-distance shortwave transmissions. The new prevalence of radio sets also affected how African audiences listened to the radio. By the end of the decade, the BBC's audience surveys showed that the vast majority of their listeners in Africa had a set in their home, to which they would listen with friends or family members—that is, smaller clusters than the public listening that occurred during the colonial era, as shown in figure 8.[8] While the political climate meant listeners had a far greater number of choices about what to tune into, changes to the setting in which they listened gave many individuals more opportunity to pursue their personal preferences. The BBC's new challenge, therefore, was to offer content that African listeners would choose over their other options.

FINDING THE "INFLUENTIAL FEW"

Before describing how the BBC designed its African Service programs during the 1960s, it is first important to remember that the African Service, like all the

FIGURE 8. A crowd in Uganda gathers around a wireless set to listen to the news. The information office's caption describes, "The Uganda Broadcasting Service broadcasts daily in 5 languages. . . . Switch on in the open air and a crowd soon gathers to listen." The National Archives, Kew, United Kingdom, INF 10/368/11 (1955).

external services, was funded by the British Treasury. The BBC's functional relationship with the British government went unchanged in this period; the Treasury controlled the external services' funds, the foreign offices prescribed the broadcast languages, and the BBC determined the program lineup and content. The Treasury's grant-in-aid to the BBC for external broadcasting rose steadily during the decade, with the funds for operating expenses going from £6.3 million in 1961 to over £12 million by 1970. In addition, during that period the Treasury also approved significant capital expenditures, such as a major push to modernize British transmitters and relays around the world.[9] As their recurring discussions reflected, British government officials sought several things all at once from British external broadcasting. The first and most often cited was its political function, namely, that through the broadcasting medium, Britain could speak to and sway audiences all over the world, especially those who were hard to reach otherwise. That was coupled with the expectation that Britain would see returns on investment for the publicity provided to British industries, British products, British universities, etcetera. Whenever British broadcasters had an opportunity to speak about their contributions, they did—and their message almost always underscored that the government must resist the temptation to interfere in their content. For example, when BBC officials described their relevance to British foreign policy in Eastern Europe, they emphasized that their reputation stemmed from the appearance of disinterestedness.[10] The British government's relationship and continued funding of the BBC during the 1960s reflected the clear thinking that broadcasting was one of the primary ways Britain would fight the Cold War. Although it granted the BBC a great amount of control in certain areas, such as program content, the British government determined the overall shape of British external broadcasting because it controlled how much the BBC broadcast and in what languages.

Government funding meant that the BBC external services were frequently subject to government funding reviews, sometimes alone but more often as part of a larger investigation into all of Britain's overseas information services. With regard to the BBC external services, different reviews made different recommendations, as two consecutive reports from the late 1960s showed. In 1967, a report by Sir Harold Beeley found that too much emphasis on English-language broadcasts risked "narrow casting" or missing influence on audiences who could not understand English. However, two years later a different inquiry by Sir Val Duncan made a different set of conclusions, finding that Britain needed to concentrate its resources in English-language broadcasting at the expense of other languages because that was where the BBC could have the greatest impact.[11] As opposite as the two reports might have seemed on the surface, together they reveal quite a lot about how the government viewed the BBC's target audience. Both the Beeley and Duncan reports defined the BBC's primary audience as "the influential few," namely, the educated and professional populations. (While the Beeley Report stated that widely spoken languages such as Hausa and Swahili were the most obvious guarantee this audience could access the BBC, the Duncan Report took the stance that English was an obvious marker of an influential individual.) The government's emphasis on a relatively small audience was a consistent message, as that had also been one of the messages behind the Drogheda Report during the mid-1950s.

Even when a report's recommendations did not go into effect, the consistent emphasis on influential, educated audiences set the terms by which the Foreign and Commonwealth Office (FCO) and the BBC measured the BBC's audience and its success. The Duncan Report prompted the FCO to demand quantitative evidence of an "influential listenership" for each of the foreign language services, threatening to cut any language where such evidence could not be proven.[12] The BBC did push back, but it was only to make a point that qualitative measures were also important. "What has to be examined in each instance is a case history rather than a table," the managing director of external broadcasting explained.[13]

Overall, the BBC's main goal was to detail that it did indeed influence the influencers, while at the same time showing that the overall size of its audience was also substantial. British broadcasters were in full agreement with the government over "the influential," and they also wanted to show they reached many more than just "the few."[14]

During the 1960s and 1970s, British ministers expected to see measurable returns on their overseas investment—but the BBC was not equipped to provide such definitive evidence. In a study such as this that examines how British broadcasting fared against international competition, one expects a slew of audience figures, describing how many people listened to the BBC, who they were, and how often. Yet, even though the British government invested increasing amounts of funding into external broadcasting to Africa, the BBC did not attempt to collect audience data at such a detailed level. The corporation believed that conducting such a scientifically designed survey in Africa was neither cost effective nor practical, given the vastness of the area.[15] During the late 1960s, the corporation's external services audience research department started conducting surveys of its African listeners, but it did so through listener panels, not randomized samples. The listener panels were comprised of individuals who had already contacted the BBC through one form or another. For example, the BBC's most popular Swahili program after the news was *Maarifa Club*, a listener question program. (In Swahili, *maarifa* translates to "knowledge.") Each Sunday evening, BBC broadcasters would read aloud letters from listeners and answer their questions on subjects ranging from science to politics to BBC operations. During the program, the hosts invited their listeners to become members of the Maarifa Club by sending their address to Bush House, which would mail them a membership card.[16] Then, when the corporation's audience research department decided to do a listener survey of the BBC Swahili transmissions, it mailed questionnaires to the members of the Maarifa Club. In addition, whenever Bush House received a letter from a listener in Africa, the African Service producers forwarded the letter to the audience research department so it could mail questionnaires to those listeners as well.[17] As had been the case during the colonial era, British broadcasters still showed more concern with the content of their programs than accurate evidence of how many people tuned in.

In place of conducting a randomized survey, the BBC's audience research in Africa was primarily among listeners it already knew had access to high-powered sets and were literate, experienced at tuning in to BBC frequencies, and highly interested in British broadcasts. In one way, the practice was in line with the British government's identification of its primary audience; in other words, this audience research was just a check that they were still influencing the influential few. At the same time, though, these methods of audience research had a powerful effect of reinforcing what British broadcasters already thought about their broadcasts. When the audience research department reported in 1972 that over three-quarters of its Swahili listener panel tuned to the BBC every day and that 92 percent heard the BBC world news at least once a week, it confirmed to British broadcasters that their African-language broadcasts played an essential role in Africans' lives. When the survey asked listeners why they listened to the BBC news and allowed them to choose as many options as they liked, 91 percent selected "For world news," 70 percent selected "For African news," 66 percent selected "Because it is first with the news," and 65 percent selected "Because it is impartial."[18] The reports also contained excerpts of respondents' comments that buttressed these explanations all the more. For example, the 1972 report quoted an Islamic teacher in Uganda who wrote, "It is the most truthful broadcasting service in the world and broadcasts without bias," and a policeman in Kenya who explained, "We hear news from London long before our local station broadcasts it."[19] Through figures about how frequently they listened and a sample of respondents' quotes, British broadcasters presented their audience as highly engaged, discerning, and empowered.

Although the BBC did not attempt to survey mass audiences in Africa, the data the BBC did collect and publish were still telling. While British broadcasters showed more interest in hearing and considering audience feedback from Africa than they had during the colonial era, their methods of listening to audiences during the 1960s and 1970s were not designed to hear negative comment. However, what does come through in these surveys is what it was that these African listeners—self-selected as they were—believed they heard when they tuned to the BBC. Among the comments that the BBC published in its audience reports, many spoke of the BBC news in relative terms: "the *most* truthful," "*before* our local station," and so on. Although British broadcasters spoke of their disinterestedness, coverage, and immediacy in absolute terms, African audience feedback revealed how listeners usually described these qualities relative to their other options— namely, the other national and international services they could tune to. Therefore, before examining how the British set out to capture African audiences, it is worth describing what they were competing against, beginning with the national stations that took over British colonial infrastructure.

COMPETITION: NATIONAL

In most of their former colonies, British broadcasters had to watch while African national governments integrated broadcasting into their larger nation-building agendas.[20] Many governing parties set out to achieve this by praising the technology but disavowing colonial-era content. In Kenya, for example, Jomo Kenyatta's KANU party was quick to cite the "colonial attitude" inherent in Kenya's system and to call for "a number of adjustments, both technical and psychological" so that broadcasting could serve the needs of the new nation.[21] Then, during the first year of his national government, Kenyatta announced the nationalization of broadcasting services. The government moved the semiautonomous Kenya Broadcasting Corporation—which British colonial officials had imagined as a miniature BBC— under direct control of the government's ministry of information and renamed it the Voice of Kenya. Over the following years, Kenyan government ministers made a show of rooting out what they described as the vestiges of colonial broadcasting. Government ministers castigated producers, editors, and other broadcasting staff who they felt were not doing enough to support the government's efforts to "de-colonialize the minds of the people."[22] An official from the ministry of information and broadcasting elaborated that for the Voice of Kenya, this meant developing programs and selecting music that would "give our radio its own original African cultural image, as opposed to [the] colonial image which portrayed radio as something absolutely western."[23] Among former British colonies, Kenya was by no means alone in terms of how its new government spoke about and sought to use the broadcast medium. African politicians in other nations such as Tanganyika and Ghana expressed similar attitudes and language when describing how they wanted to shape national broadcasting.[24]

For many African states, one key step toward decolonizing broadcasting was to Africanize fully the broadcasting staff. In most former British colonies, the BBC staff who had been seconded to the colonial broadcasting station stayed on for months or sometimes years after independence because there was not yet an experienced African staff member who could take over the position. Kenyan and Tanganyikan officials who felt pressure to accelerate Africanization built their expectations around overseas training opportunities. They did not limit themselves to the BBC; instead, East African broadcasters, editors, and engineers variously traveled to the United States, Canada, Australia, West Germany, and Israel, among others, on short- and medium-term training schemes.[25] Although African officials who oversaw broadcasting tried to take advantage of training courses wherever possible, they also acknowledged that Africanization might mean a drop in the quality of their broadcasts—at least for the short term.[26] But British onlookers sometimes interpreted much more serious stakes in personnel changes. When the Ghana Broadcasting System announced three years after independence that it had replaced its BBC secondments, the UK Information officer in Accra phrased the decision in dire terms. "Thus, Radio Ghana has now been completely taken over by the C.P.P. diehards, who will have no hesitation in using the G.B.S. as an instrument of ideological warfare," he wrote about Kwame Nkrumah's Convention People's Party.[27] He ended the note with a plea that the BBC improve its direct signal strength to West Africa. To British onlookers, the area where African-run stations most gravely abused the power of broadcasting was the news.

Just like in most other African nations, Kenyan politicians saw broadcasting as a powerful instrument they could use to control the spread of information and reinforce a favorable image of the united nation. When Kenyatta announced nationalization in 1964, he tried to assure Kenyans that his government still valued freedom of expression—and then hinted that dissent would not be tolerated.[28] The Ministry of Information, Broadcasting, and Tourism translated Kenyatta's sentiment into VOK policies that always began with a token statement that of course they aimed to deliver all the news to the public. Then, the ministry's permanent secretary, P. J. Gachathi, moved to remind the newsroom of what he called their greater responsibility to their nation. He explained that the primary purpose of broadcast news was to portray "the harmonious and constructive side of life in Kenya and the world" and that "items which tend to have any other effect should be played down at times and be ignored completely if they are likely to create or encourage any feeling which would not be for the welfare of the country."[29] Gachathi's instructions took on different meanings depending on whether a news piece was domestic or international. Indeed, in that and future instructions— since the ministry reminded the newsroom of these policies regularly—most of the government's attention went toward domestic news, and particularly whether political and cultural stories confirmed the creed of Harambee, which directed that the nation's people work together harmoniously. The newsroom had permission to cover speeches where a speaker made "reasonable" suggestions to the government—giving news editors great difficulty in discerning what, if anything, fell into the category of reasonable critique—but could not grant publicity to anything more severe.[30] While the intention of these memos came through clearly, it was always framed in an appearance of impartiality. "We must avoid appearing to favour one area as against another," read one memo that reviewed the reasons to censor criticism.[31]

The Kenyan government's emphasis on the appearance of impartiality also applied to international news. Here, the government imposed a policy of "positive non-alignment" where news pieces could not appear to favor either East or West. More significantly, the policy also stated that Kenyan news could never appear to *condemn* East or West either, since, it was reasoned, that would make it appear Kenya was taking a side. Kenyan broadcasting officials quickly realized that individuals in the government could interpret the policy to an extreme. For example, in February 1964, the minister of information, broadcasting, and tourism relayed complaints about a KBC reporter's interview with an American from the United States Information Service. The complaints issued that even by asking about the man's work, the interviewer revealed the station's "cold war attitude" and eagerness to provoke.[32]

One of the reasons Kenya's international news bulletins frequently came under the government's scrutiny was the source of the news. When British broadcasters built colonial services such as that in Kenya, they assumed the BBC would provide all regional and international news. In contrast to local and national news, where there was at least some news-gathering structure in place, the Voice of Kenya was starting from scratch if it wanted to include international news in its broadcasts. The VOK quickly determined it did not have funds for international correspondents, not even in the neighboring capitals. Therefore, Kenyan state media relied upon two news services—Reuters and Tass—for all of its international stories.[33] However, when Kenyan news editors applied the government's standards for non-partisanship, they found almost none of the Tass output was usable.[34] This was actually a common conclusion among postcolonial African states that sought balance by taking from both Western and communist media. For example, in Tanzania—another nation with a stated policy of nonalignment—newsroom staff looked over the material they received from Soviet and Czech sources but decided they could not use it.[35] (One Tanzanian news editor explained they also received material from the Chinese News Agency, "but it goes straight in the bin.")[36] In both Tanzania and Kenya then, the newsroom staff found themselves relying almost entirely on Reuters, despite the frequent accusations of holding on to colonial tendencies.[37]

The news editors in these newsrooms sometimes found it very difficult to navigate between their governments' sometimes contradictory, often changing, political aims. The news editors recognized that in general they must not cover news of successful coups or secessionism, but most news was not as straightforward, such as the unfolding crisis in the Congo.[38] During the middle of the 1960s, Kenyan ministers sent a slew of conflicting instructions to the Voice of Kenya about how to cover the Congo. In 1964, for example, the government instructed that no matter what Reuters releases might say, Kenyan news should not call the forces fighting the Congolese government "rebels" and instead needed to call them "nationalist forces" in English and "majeshi wananchi" in Swahili.[39] But then, after Mobutu Sese Seko seized power in 1965, the government reversed itself; now, it instructed, forces fighting the Congolese government were indeed "rebels."[40] Yet, as another set of instructions the next year explained, while it was perfectly in order to condemn the rebels, the broadcasters also needed to ensure they did not go too far, or Kenyan listeners might become inflamed.[41] By then, the Voice of Kenya editors had taken to checking with their director about *any* story on the Congo, rather than try to keep it straight.[42] After independence, African governments such as those in Kenya and Tanzania aimed to control the spread of information. But to the journalists who worked for the state, the ever-changing directives went against their training about how to prepare balanced and consistent news reports.[43] As the director-general of Radio Tanzania explained, "Politicians make demands, and they have no real idea about broadcasting. We have to maintain our professional ethics, and at the same time to compromise with the demands of politicians. This can be awfully difficult!"[44] (He was speaking with a British graduate student at the time.) While African broadcasters rooted their objectives in their journalistic ethics, they also expressed that the state risked seeing its broadcast policies backfire. They explained that there was the risk their citizens would be able to pick out the misrepresentations and discrepancies and that this would affect general attitudes toward the state-run broadcasting in general.

As much as the Kenyan government wanted to control the spread of information, it had difficulty doing so, in part because the Kenyan public saw good reason to seek out broadcasts from alternative sources. When he announced nationalization in 1964, Kenyatta asserted that one benefit of integrating broadcasting into the government was that the Voice of Kenya could now procure a greater amount of provincial material from the information officers already in place around the country.[45] Yet, as his government's protocol took effect, listeners quickly recognized a tedious pattern to each day's national news. Regardless of what else may have occurred that day, the newscast always led with President Kenyatta's activities—sometimes newsworthy, but also sometimes mundane. Next were the vice president's activities. Then, the news started working down the ministers, then (time permitting) members of parliament, provincial commissioners, and so on.[46] In the words of an information officer, this meant the Voice of Kenya news was really the "Voice of Ministers."[47] In addition, since broadcasters' language was supposed to remain impartial, broadcasts often left out specific names and details. For example, a virulent speech in parliament might be reported as, "The speaker attacked the attitude of several leading politicians," without saying anything more.[48] In accord with government protocol, the Voice of Kenya provided listeners with information about what the government was doing—and almost nothing else.

In addition to finding it boring, listeners also found the national service to be bad. Throughout the second half of the 1960s, listeners flooded the Voice of Kenya with complaints about errors they heard, whether they were mistakes about Kenyan geography or naming the wrong government minister.[49] Exasperated listeners regularly wrote to the station when they heard their national broadcaster carelessly translate English-language copy for the Swahili news—as was the case, for example, when a news story about light showers turned into "mvua nyembamba," or skinny rain.[50] Their frustration mounted when they accused the Voice of Kenya of running stale news, and not even disguising it well at that, which happened whenever newsreaders began an old story with "Today . . .".[51] Among all the complaints leveled at the service, news reading was the subject of some of the most virulent criticism. Here, the criticism came from all sources, including the public, angry government ministers, and officials and advisers inside the Voice of Kenya. Different complaints targeted different aspects of the news presentation. For example, an American observer explained he was willing to overlook small mispronunciations and mistakes with the language but he could not excuse the "dull, uninteresting, and unvaried delivery" because it was difficult to follow the broadcast.[52] Government ministers, on the other hand, criticized the inexperience and unprofessionalism they heard on air because they thought it hurt the entire effort of projecting a single voice of Kenya.[53] In sum, Kenyan listeners knew the Voice of Kenya news for its mundane information, incomplete coverage, unnecessary repetition of news items, and poor editing and delivery. To listeners, this stood in stark contrast with what else they could pick up through their radio dial.

COMPETITION: INTERNATIONAL

After independence, British broadcasters believed their real competition for African audiences was not national stations, but other international broadcasters. When Nigeria was about to become independent, the colonial government pinned heavy consequences on the BBC losing its monopoly over the airwaves: "At best the Americans might come in. And there are others far less desirable who might clamour for a place."[54] It was an understatement of sorts—by the end of the decade African listeners were the targets of news bulletins from around the world and in a selection of languages. The USSR, which was the largest external broadcaster in the world, tripled its transmission hours to Africa in the early 1960s, and by the end of the decade it transmitted in twelve African languages.[55] (The BBC, in comparison, broadcast in only three.) During the late 1960s, Swahili speakers in Tanzania could choose among forty-seven foreign stations that broadcast to their country.[56] Foreign broadcasters, whether coming from London, Washington, Moscow, Peking, or Cairo, all sought the same thing. They hoped African audiences were not satisfied with what they got from their national service and would thus look to outside sources for news and information about the world.

When British officials surveyed the increasingly competitive field of broadcasting in Africa, they distinguished between the African stations that had begun external broadcasting and other foreign broadcasters, whom they defined as their true competition. British officials acknowledged African citizens often tuned to other nearby national stations, whether it was to hear regional news or music. Therefore, the BBC Swahili Service producers were not too worried when they learned, for example, that over half their listeners in Tanzania tuned regularly to the Voice of Kenya and vice versa.[57] British broadcasters registered more concern about another trend they witnessed in African broadcasting during the 1960s: the rise of African external broadcasting. One of the nations that stood out in this regard was Ghana, which viewed external broadcasting as an integral component of broader Pan-African unity. In 1961, Ghana started broadcasting to West and Central Africa in six languages: English, French, Portuguese, Arabic, Hausa, and Swahili. Ghana's Ministry of Information pointedly stated these broadcasts were necessary in order to present the news "from an African point of view . . . without concealment or distortion."[58] Ghana used four 100 kW transmitters to broadcast for one hundred hours each week during the first half of the 1960s and double that for the second half of the decade—far more than the weekly output of the BBC African Service. Even so, while the BBC continued to monitor African external broadcasts, British officials did not view African stations like Ghana as their real rivals in international broadcasting. For instance, after reviewing an externally conducted audience report in 1968 that showed only one-tenth of Ghanaian adults listened to the BBC in English, British officials emphasized they still came out on top among non-African broadcasters.[59] In their minds, the true competition for influence in Africa occurred among the main Cold War powers—both East and West—that outpaced them in duration and strength.

During the postcolonial period, broadcasting was clearly a domain of the Cold War, and, in technological terms at least, the British were losing. During the early 1960s, Cold War powers built their direct transmissions to Africa around a two-pronged attack: first, generate hundreds of hours of content each week, and second, build high-powered transmitters that cheap transistors could pick up. Although Britain was somewhat competitive in the first, it was drastically outpaced in the second. That meant that while the United States constructed a 250 kW relay in Liberia to transmit the Voice of America, and West Germany opened the same in Rwanda for its Deutsch Welle service, the BBC still relied upon a World War II–era infrastructure to transmit its new African Service programs. Not only was the BBC clamoring among a growing number of choices, but it was also clamoring to be *heard*, literally, because other stronger transmissions congested the wavebands.[60] During the 1960s, the British Treasury started to grant funds for a major program of relay transmitter construction, including a new transmission station at Ascension Island in the South Atlantic and new transmitters in the East Mediterranean. The new relays improved the BBC's reception exponentially in West and Central Africa. However, Britain still did not have adequate coverage of East Africa, where listeners complained about the unreliable and weak signal all the way into the mid-1980s, when Britain finally invested in a transmitter in the Seychelles. But despite their lack of firepower, British broadcasters continually reassured themselves that there were other reasons African listeners heard their broadcasts. As one of the BBC's annual reports explained, "People will still search for it hardest because they believe in it most."[61]

That the British news had this reputation did not go unnoticed by the BBC's rivals. Just like it was worth comparing how the BBC's news style compared to that of African national stations, it is also valuable to draw a comparison with one of its main international rivals, the Voice of America (VOA). Since its start during the Second World War, the VOA had boasted proudly that its services broadcast all news, regardless of whether it made the United States look good or bad.[62] Nevertheless, during the 1950s the VOA attracted a propagandist reputation that it had a lot of difficulty shaking. By the 1960s, the Kennedy administration made a big push to reform this reputation, beginning with the appointment of prominent broadcaster Edward R. Murrow as director of the United States Information Agency, which oversaw the VOA. Upon coming to the position, Murrow declared that a key way to convince overseas audiences of the VOA's impartiality was to model its news-gathering operation after that of the BBC. Therefore, Murrow followed what he knew about the BBC news protocol and imposed a two-source rule for all VOA news items.[63]

Murrow's early years at the USIA overlapped with the United States making a huge information push in Africa, one of two regions (the other being Latin America) that the State Department assigned a new "most crucial" status. As the agency's deputy director described in 1960, the USIA's outlook for Africa was quite straightforward: "Secure a foothold in every new country."[64] Just like their British counterparts, American officials identified radio broadcasting as one of the most effective media for countering other international activity in Africa; this was why the United States was currently spending $13 million to build its powerful relay station in Liberia. Murrow justified the transmitter as serving Africa just as much as it served American interests. As he explained in a testimony to the House subcommittee on Africa, "If we use these transmitters properly, I think they can be, in a sense, used to report Africa to a people who are trying to hammer out their own destiny while at the same time searching for their own history."[65] When the Liberia relay opened in 1964, the VOA immediately began its new program schedule for Africa. In addition to the VOA's worldwide English service, which the new transmitter relayed for seventy-seven hours per week, the VOA started broadcasting Africa-specific programs live from Liberia for another twenty-four hours per week. It also initiated a daily one-hour program in Swahili. On the face of it, the VOA schedule for Africa looked relatively similar to what the BBC African Service was developing: a mix of news, features, and entertainment, even if the Americans gave more time to the latter. With regard to the news, though, Murrow continued to stress that the VOA news was "straight"—it was not propaganda. Or, as a congressperson asked him in 1962, "You are really doing a BBC more or less at the moment, is that correct?" Murrow readily agreed.[66]

Although there were some similarities in the way that the VOA and the BBC sourced their news, their overseas audiences also discerned some important differences. The most significant difference was how each organization balanced its informational programming. The Voice of America took a counter-programming approach to its news, where it set out to combat what it viewed as misconceptions about America. During the early 1960s, American information officials believed that one reason African audiences viewed US activities with suspicion was because they heard so many stories about American racism and violence against civil rights protesters.[67] (The USIA was quick to put most of the blame for this on their Soviet and Chinese rivals, whom they accused of inflaming Africans' attitudes toward the United States by circulating "fake" pictures of police dogs, fire hoses, and lynchings.)[68] The agency adopted the line that the appropriate way to respond was not by hiding the truth, but rather by presenting a picture of "a society resolutely standing up to problems and staunchly seeking solutions."[69] In due course, therefore, the VOA gave enormous publicity to moments such as President Johnson's signing of the Civil Rights Act and the Supreme Court striking down segregation laws. The VOA's method for demonstrating that there was pervasive free debate in the United States was always to conduct interviews with both sides, pairing for instance, interviews with a southern Democratic senator and an NAACP leader. Overall, however, the fraught debate over civil rights received very little broadcast time in comparison to celebratory stories about the bipartisan support for the bill and the participation of both black and white students in the civil rights movement. The VOA's efforts to show what it deemed the "full civil rights story" overwhelmingly underscored a message of unity, progress, and correcting America's wrongs to the rest of the world.

This was not to say that the BBC did not care about presenting a palatable view of Britain—in fact, that was exactly the case the BBC made for government funding. The difference was only in the balance; the British put most of their promotional pieces in other feature programs and not in the news, which was the BBC program that drew the largest audiences.[70] It might seem slight, but BBC listeners cited it as reason to stick with what they knew instead of switching to one of the new international broadcasts. When the BBC surveyed its African listeners on why they tuned to the BBC news, the listeners responded that it was because it was the most truthful and the most balanced, compared to their other national and international options. BBC listeners' stated impression of news content was buttressed by the other components they heard in the broadcast, such as the quality of translation and news reading.

THE BBC'S DECADE FOR AFRICA

During the 1960s, the BBC set out to attract African listeners in a way it never had before. As chapter 3 established, before the wind of change swept the African continent, the BBC did not put much attention or resources into targeted programming for African audiences. However, the year of Macmillan's speech marked the beginning of the BBC's self-titled Decade of Africa. During the years that followed, British broadcasters expanded their output in Hausa, Swahili, and Somali, and developed programs under the new "French for Africa" and "English for Africa" labels.[71] Altogether, these comprised what was known as the BBC African Service—that is, targeted broadcasts to Africa—while the General Overseas Service (renamed the World Service in 1965) continued to transmit what the BBC thought of as universal material. Among all the programs on the BBC African Service, two types in particular stand out for the way they captured how British broadcasters sought to cultivate African interest. First, through new language services, British broadcasters set out to increase Africans' exposure to the British world news. Second, through cultural programs, they provided a venue for African writers and intellectuals to reach audiences across the continent. In both types, British officials sought to bolster the BBC brand as they understood it—namely, high-quality, professional broadcasts that connected different parts of the world.

To produce high-quality programs in African languages, the BBC relied on staff on secondment, or loan, from African stations. In contrast to their ten-week training programs, which they viewed as a form of aid, British officials promoted secondment as a reciprocal arrangement. The ways that secondment helped the BBC were obvious: British broadcasters needed a staff of at least six native speakers to transmit a foreign-language service for seven hours each week. BBC producers wanted these services to run efficiently and consistently; thus, they expected seconded staff to stay in residence in London for a period of two years. All that was left was convincing national stations to let some of their best people go. When the BBC requested an individual's secondment to London, it emphasized that African candidates would gain far more experience and BBC "know-how" than they ever could in a short-term course. When the system of secondment began, administrators in Africa spoke highly of its reciprocal benefits and planned around the absences. They assumed they could assign returning staff to senior administrative or training positions, which would have a multiplier effect and help fulfill the directive to Africanize. Indeed, some of the BBC's African-language newsreaders eventually became directors of national broadcasting in their home countries; that was the case, for instance, with David Wakati in Tanzania and James Kangwana in Kenya. However, problems between the British and African stations arose when the BBC expanded its African-language services and requested greater numbers of broadcasters for longer periods of time.[72] Colonial services such as the Kenya Broadcasting System and the Tanganyika Broadcasting Corporation complained that the BBC was essentially poaching their best men, thus depriving the African stations of the little professional experience that they had. "Our growing pains are of a more serious kind," the director of Kenya Broadcasting System protested to London, after the BBC offered East African secondments the chance to extend their stays from two to three years.[73] After independence, when many African stations dropped the BBC bulletins, the arrangement appeared even more one-sided.

Secondment from African stations explained in part how the BBC maintained a reputation for high quality, even while broadcasting in unfamiliar languages. The British were not alone in trying to figure out the best way to broadcast in African languages, and other international broadcasters from Moscow to Accra faced the same constraints. Different nations came up with different solutions.

The Soviets, for instance, started language courses in Swahili, Hausa, and Amharic at Leningrad, and then sent their graduates to East and West Africa to improve their skills further.[74] In contrast, Ghana arranged selection boards in France, the United Arab Republic, and Tanganyika to recruit French, Arabic, and Swahili speakers respectively.[75] British broadcasters, however, preferred secondment because attachments from Africa already had microphone experience and would stay the full length of their contracts. There was one more added value: these were individuals whose voices were already known and enjoyed by the targeted audience.[76] For example, one of the main voices heard on the BBC Swahili Service during the late 1950s was Stephen Kikumu, whose supervisors in Kenya had described as "a natural broadcaster and probably the most popular one in the whole of East Africa."[77] Announcers and translators of Kikumu's caliber gave the new BBC transmissions legitimacy. It was a difference great enough to give the BBC an edge in international broadcasting—or at least, that was what the BBC read into the self-selected feedback it received in its listener mail.

Furthermore, the British ensured that whatever language they broadcast in—English, Swahili, etcetera—they adhered to high linguistic standards. Before a man or (every so often) a woman could be attached to the BBC, he or she had to pass translation exercises and take voice tests, which were recorded and sent to London for British experts to review.[78] BBC officials stressed that emphasis on standards was vital for conveying professionalism. As evidence, they pointed to comments they received from listeners who compared the high caliber of British broadcasts to what they heard on other stations. For instance, one audience report quoted a trader in Nigeria who wrote, "When you come on the air I stop work so that customers at my market stall can listen to you. I would like to say that we are all highly appreciative of the standard of Hausa spoken by your broadcasters: it is better than that used in any other Hausa broadcasting service."[79] His sentiment was echoed in another BBC report by Swahili speakers in Kenya who declared that the Swahili spoken on the BBC was far better than that spoken on the Voice of Kenya.[80]

After independence, there was an awareness among some British broadcasters that the BBC might not be the first-choice station of postcolonial listeners who opted for their national station. The BBC's aim, therefore, was to be the second. By broadcasting in languages such as Hausa and Swahili, Britain joined numerous other international powers seeking to influence Africans by speaking to them in their own languages. Nor was the BBC alone in its reliance on secondments to deliver African-language materials; for example, Voice of America did as well.[81] Instead, Britain's "edge" in this area was a combination of some of the same factors that attracted postcolonial audiences to its English-language news: familiar style of news reporting, adherence to consistent, professional-sounding delivery, and the appearance of relative disinterestedness. Whether speaking to its

English- or African-language news bulletins, then, it is worth examining how the British world news in any language stood up against its competition.

BRITISH WORLD NEWS TO AFRICA

Within all the education, information, and entertainment the BBC produced for its worldwide audience, BBC officials agreed that the news was the most important element of British transmissions overseas. Broadcasters started referring to the news as the backbone of the external services in the early 1940s and they continued to do so in the postcolonial period. BBC news bulletins were uniform, utilitarian, and ubiquitous. Positioned at regular intervals throughout the twenty-four-hour transmission schedule, each bulletin was supposed to begin with the same tune and the same words every single day. These newscasts signposted the rest of the General Overseas Service (GOS) schedule and determined the basis for other programming and engineering decisions. When the BBC added African languages services in Hausa, Swahili, and Somali in the 1950s and then expanded those services in the early 1960s, every additional transmission included a timeslot for the news.

Whether in their summaries of listener letters or the questions in their audience research, BBC officials expressed confidence in the superiority of their news. They almost always rooted this confidence in a short list of criteria—namely, breadth of coverage, professionalism of delivery, and appearance of disinterestedness—and described these as absolutes that pulled listeners in. As much as British broadcasters worked in the early 1960s to improve their coverage and remove their Eurocentric focus, when it came to attracting African audiences they were helped considerably by the changes taking places within African state media. In other words, it was not so much that the British news was a pull, but more that the absence of news sometimes pushed African audiences to seek other sources of information. Still, it is worth examining how the external services news department strove to maintain the head start it attained during the colonial period.

During the 1960s, the BBC set out to improve its news gathering and reporting network around the whole world, but especially in Africa, where it had some of the biggest gaps to fill. In 1960, the BBC appointed its first correspondents to East and West Africa, bringing its total number of correspondents on the continent to four, when including Cairo and Cape Town. By the middle of the decade, however, the corporation stationed permanent correspondents in each geographical region of Africa and was considering a budget and staff to post additional reporters as breaking news developed. It was not a smooth operation by any means—Angus McDermid, the BBC's correspondent in the Congo and in Biafra, described how his bosses in London were usually surprised by breaking stories and then had to scramble to reassign him—but, nevertheless, the BBC was better equipped to cover African news than its competitors.[82] Illustrating this superiority is the fact that McDermid was one of two BBC correspondents who reported from West Africa during the late 1960s because as soon as the Biafran secession happened, the corporation had the resources and staff to send a second man. For the next several years, the BBC tried to keep one reporter in Lagos and another in Biafra, thus ensuring more complete coverage. The news stories that McDermid and his colleague Keith Carter were able to get past Nigerian censors informed audiences in Britain and all over the world about the developments and ramifications of the civil war. British officials were pleased to see evidence that even audiences in Northern Nigeria tuned to the BBC to hear breaking news of events taking place within their own borders.[83] As chaotic as some of McDermid's experiences with Bush House were, his reporting still stood apart from state broadcasters such as Voice of Kenya, which received all its news—even events in Uganda and Tanzania—through international services such as Reuters. This point was not lost on Kenya's press officers, such as one who pleaded to the government, "It looks very ironical for us here in Nairobi to wait for London to tell us what is happening in Tororo!!"[84] Having had decades to set up its international network and with greater resources at its disposal, the BBC's coverage of world news was vastly greater than African national stations. The BBC's African listener panels confirmed that this was an area where the BBC most outpaced its rivals, as 90 percent of its audience panels named "For world news" as the reason they tuned to the BBC.

As further proof that presentation of the news had power, British broadcasters ensured their news delivery conformed to the style that African audiences were accustomed to (at least, the audiences who had grown up listening to the BBC.) The BBC's protocol for turning copy from around the world into uniform, smoothly run newscasts had been in place since the Second World War. When the corporation started its African language services, the BBC accommodated them the same way as its dozens of other services. The presence of African broadcasters on secondment at Bush House made the task possible. Within the World Service news department, subeditors and translators collaborated in the preparation of news bulletins. The entire process was meticulously timed so that the news department could be confident its copy was as up-to-the-minute as possible, while still leaving room for translation. Meanwhile, to ensure all BBC bulletins were uniform in their format and length, the translator was responsible for instructing the news desk to adjust to particularities of a given language, such as the speed of spoken Swahili or Hausa compared to English.[85] As a final check, BBC administrators recorded transmissions from time to time and had other staff in the section check them for presentation and linguistic standards as well as translation and accuracy.[86] Whereas, in comparison, in Kenya the ministry that oversaw VOK repeatedly issued strict protocols for editing and reporting the news, but never stemmed the complaints and outcry from listeners. Inside VOK, advisers tried to diagnose the problem and usually arrived at the answer that the government oversight—seemingly inconsistent and strict at the same time—caused "dangerously low" morale among the staff.[87]

The final criteria—disinterestedness—is the one where it is most important to remember that the BBC only had to best its competitors in terms of probity and the degree to which it considered all viewpoints. Whether it was events in Suez or political representation in Kenya, the late colonial period saw the BBC external services broadcast several stories and positions that were critical of British imperial interests.[88] That did not go unnoticed by African audiences, even if they remained skeptical of the BBC's proclaimed objectivity. African listeners after independence faced an array of broadcasting options, including their national service, those of neighboring states, and a range of international broadcasters. It is not surprising, then, that African listeners switched around between these options, seeking out the content they wished to hear. For the group that tuned to the BBC news, they knew what they were getting—broader coverage but with a slight British slant. Meanwhile, the fact that postcolonial populations did not abandon the BBC on the whole resonated powerfully back in London, where British broadcasters became all the more convinced of their capacity to give Africa more than just news.

AFRICAN LITERATURE OVER THE BRITISH AIRWAVES

During its self-titled Decade of Africa, British broadcasters struggled to identify the right balance between targeting specific linguistic or national groups (through, for instance, the Swahili-language service or a program such as *Calling Nigeria*) versus programming designed for broader audiences. Over the 1960s, the BBC maintained its African-language programming so it did not lose ground against other foreign broadcasters. However, the portion of the African Service that truly grew in this period was the "English for Africa" programming. From London, BBC producers strove to create programs that had broad appeal and would attract English-speaking audiences in all parts of sub-Saharan Africa.[89] This had a political payoff in a few different ways, they reasoned, beginning with how audiences were less likely to worry they were targets of propaganda. In addition, British broadcasters and civil servants used wide-reaching programs to make the claim their work was with Africa's long-term development in mind; by broadcasting material out of one region to listeners in others, the BBC boasted it linked up African publics across the continent. Meanwhile, Britain retained a pivotal role in that relationship, as it provided the source of the link and the English language.

Cultural programming gave British broadcasters even more to boast about, which was that they (and by extension the British government) encouraged

African creative work. That was a message behind the monthly half-hour program *African Theatre* from its very beginning in 1962. The publicity around the new series—which broadcast radio plays by African authors—announced that it helped "foster a tradition of writing and acting among Africans interested in the present-day theatre," a strong echo of the language British publishers used when they announced African literary competitions during the same period.[90] *African Theatre*'s producers were still saying this eight years later, when the program was still on the air and had broadcast dozens of different plays. One producer proclaimed that in her view, the BBC provided a rare opportunity for African writers to experience their work being put on professionally and to reach wide audiences in all parts of Africa.[91] When she and others corresponded with the writers, they explained that in contrast to radio drama on African stations, the BBC gave writers access to a deep pool of acting talent in London, superior production facilities, a larger budget, and more experienced producers. This was a way to encourage authors to trust British authorities with their writing. In producers' minds, it also provided the BBC with another angle to eagerly promote what it offered Africa. Through their patronage of the arts, British broadcasters hope to generate goodwill and dispel any suspicions that their interests might be political.

To accomplish their aims, BBC producers sought out African writers whose reputations preceded them—usually because the authors were internationally published. The list of individuals who contributed at least one play to the program contains almost all the big names in the first generation of postcolonial African writing in English. The producers behind *African Theatre* made it clear that they wanted to have all the important names in their program, even if it meant a lot of extra work to prepare a piece for production. The producers correctly guessed that the investment would pay off in prominence, as other renowned authors would then want to be part of the program. This came through, for instance, when *African Theatre* producer Shirley Cordeaux enlisted a script from Ngũgĩ wa Thiong'o (then James Ngugi) in part by telling him Wole Soyinka, Cyprian Ekwensi, and Peter Nazareth had all already contributed plays to the BBC series.[92] The producers had no qualms either about broadcasting numerous plays by a single author such as Soyinka or Ekwensi, especially if they believed their name would draw in more listeners.

As a series designed around drama from Africa, the British employees in charge of *African Theatre* found themselves unexpectedly in a position of deciding what qualified a play—or playwright—as African. The first criterion they set out was that the radio plays should be written by black Africans. However, over the years this criterion was not always adhered to, particularly when Asians who lived in South Africa and East Africa wanted to participate. Sometimes the producers would pause and ask whether they should stick to their original policy, but usually they reasoned that those individuals such as Peter Nazareth or Kuldip Sondhi had experiences that allowed them to speak to African audiences successfully; there-fore, the African Service should broadcast the works. And then, over time, even white authorship—though not particularly encouraged—was not a bar, provided the producers found something in the material that made them think of Africa.[93] Being of African origin became of lesser importance than the producers' primary consideration, which was that the play was set in Africa and many of the main characters were Africans. In the producers' minds, this ensured the series stayed true to its purpose for the African Service.[94]

The BBC producers of *African Theatre* tried to convince their listeners and writers that they did not censor material because of its tone, topic, or politics. As evidence, they pointed to the enormous diversity of *African Theatre* plays that they broadcast, including soap operas, adventure tales, a few comedies, and many more tragedies. During a four-week span in 1969, for example, *African Theatre* ran a biblical story (*The Exodus* by Tom Omara), a play about intergenerational clash (*Sons and Daughters* by Joe de Graft), a portrayal of a prisoner's dilemma (*The Tortoise* by Femi Euba), and a comedy about "three ne'er-do-wells . . . trying their luck as Nairobi's answer to the Beatles" (*Top of the Pops* by John Storm Roberts).[95] During its long run, *African Theatre* did produce plays with political content, although the works were usually critical of current African states, not the colonial predecessors. Ngũgĩ's play *This Time Tomorrow* was a good example. The Kenyan writer composed the script specially for the BBC program and made it a drama set in Nairobi slums the government had targeted in an urbaniza-tion program. In his description to the producers, Ngũgĩ instructed, "They (the slums) are sort of self-contained, a world of their own, so their destruction is also a destruction of a world, a way of life. . . . In production, the actors should be made aware all the time that in fact slums are a creation of the main city and the whole socio-economic environment in present-day Africa."[96] As far as the producers were concerned, this was well in line with what they were looking for in their program.

It was the stated aim of its producers that *African Theatre* offer programs that the entire African Service listenership could enjoy. Therefore, producers did reject material that they deemed offensive to a portion of their audience. In a feature that ran on the BBC African Service, one of the producers explained that he had to ask an author to redesign what was otherwise a suitable play because, in his view, the author attacked traditionalism too violently. The producer explained, "It would have been better if the playwright had put both sides impartially and let the audience decide for themselves, rather than to force his own point of view down the listeners' throats."[97] His demand of a rewrite reflected just one of the instances producers' judgment shaped the content of their program; they also frequently provided feedback to writers on suitability for radio, writing style, tone, charac-ters, and plot.

Oftentimes when the BBC producers gave input on a pitch, they usually revealed a wish for plots that incorporated what they understood to be common African problems. Thus, several themes appeared repeatedly in the *African Theatre* productions. The most common theme was the conflict between older, past ways of life in African society, and new, Western practices and technologies. There was also the regular theme of the morality play, which was common in other parts of postcolonial broadcasting and publishing.[98] Another version of this conflict that appeared quite often on *African Theatre* described religious differences between past and present Africa, with local witch doctors often playing a large role. Family life and urbanization were two other reliable story lines.[99] For example, the South African writer Alfred Hutchinson wrote six plays for *African Theatre* during the 1960s, including one titled *Pirate Taxi*, which told of a man's shock at urban life after moving to Johannesburg from a rural region. British producers enjoyed the play because they believed the difference between rural and urban life was true across Africa.[100] But when Hutchinson submitted a play that they felt was too intrinsically local to South Africa, the BBC producers rejected it, saying it did not consider the diverse broadcast audience enough.[101] Every week if not every day, the team behind *African Theatre* made pronouncements about what and who was included in their efforts to capture the best African writing of the era. Some of the decisions, such as what work was best-suited for the radio play format, stemmed quite logically out of their role as radio play producers. However, BBC producers did not think their authority as broadcasting experts stopped there. Instead, their decisions about African drama also showed them deliberating about who fell into the category of "African writer," what made a work African enough, and what themes African listeners would feel most personally.

As its reputation grew during the 1960s, the BBC African Service received hundreds of submissions from writers all over the world. For producers, this fact alone reinforced their self-image of encouraging African writers and writing. While the BBC highlighted the advantages of having one's works produced in London, African writers were aware of the disadvantages. They saw an inherent problem in the premise of *African Theatre*, which was its disconnect between the writing, production, and listening phases of a play. This disconnect was apparent in several ways. Many African writers whose plays the BBC produced never actually heard them on the radio. Imagine the frustration of one writer in Lagos, who wrote to London describing how he had tried to pick up the BBC signal on the day his play was to be broadcast: "Radio Moscow, Deutshe Welle [*sic*], Voice of America, a good many oriental stations and even the greatest nuisance, Radio RSA [S. Africa] came on the dial but BBC would just not turn up!"[102]

In addition, in any given *African Theatre* production the cast originated from many different places in Africa. While the British broadcasters celebrated the diversity and Pan-Africanism of their productions, it presented a problem for some writers and listeners. One Nigerian writer commented on the production of his play, "The pronunciation of names was annoying to Nigerian ears."[103] His complaint led the BBC to ask writers to submit phonetic descriptions of all African words and names with their scripts. But British producers could not resolve all issues so easily. Other listeners complained, for example, that it was difficult to believe that a Ghanaian woman was the mother of a character from South Africa.[104] Whenever the BBC heard complaints such as these, it defended itself again through the quality and reach that it offered African writers. As one producer stated in 1970, while their presentation of a play might not be 100 percent authentic in accent or feel, "our standard of radio acting and broadcasting technique achieves a result nearer to the author's ideal realization of his material."[105] In the BBC African Service, the discussion raises a situation where African writers identified ways British agencies exhibited control over their artistic output. As the next chapter will demonstrate, this was far from a rare occurrence.

THE RELATIVE FORMS OF BROADCASTING VIRTUES

This discussion began by probing the BBC's self-affirmed reputation for disinterested, high-quality, wide-coverage news. In conclusion, it seems that while there was some evidence the BBC did achieve what it thought it was trying to do in postcolonial Africa, the evidence was neither as absolute nor as extensive as British broadcasters chose to believe. Yes, African audiences continued to listen to parts of the BBC transmission, but they did so selectively, both in choosing which parts of the British content they sought and fully realizing why it was that they sought them. It might seem like only a slight difference, and indeed, British politicians during the period might not have cared. After all, if their main purpose was to measure the outcome—that African audiences listened to the BBC—then they were less concerned with whatever their audience's conflicted feelings were about British content.

After comparing the different protocols that British, Kenyan, and American broadcasters followed in putting together the news, it becomes all the more evident why the history of British colonial broadcasting was important. African audiences associated the BBC with strengths like professional quality and worldwide coverage that were rooted in the structure of British colonial broadcasting in Africa. Even if listeners had suspected the BBC in the past because of its association with colonial rule, British content was a known entity—which made it less suspicious than other international broadcasters, whose new arrival to the field tainted them from the start.

After showing how the BBC's virtues were only ever heard in relative forms, I can underline the real power of this history, which comes not from what the BBC did but from what it *thought* it was doing. Having to compete for audiences for the first time might have appeared daunting at the time, but in the long run it provided a new source of strength in how British broadcasters thought of their work. After finding evidence that a portion of African publics *chose* to listen to the BBC over all their other options, British broadcasters and British proponents more generally were spurred forward. They had permission to rethink their recent history, such as their role in colonial rule, and replace it with a narrative about serving demands and providing a useful service to postcolonial Africa. Within this narrative though, British broadcasters faced difficulty resolving their colonial-era attitudes about their African audiences. The BBC's self-affirmation of itself as broadcasting that upheld principles of journalistic independence thus assumed audiences were discerning enough to recognize what made the BBC news better than the others. This did not pair, however, with Britain's constant concerns that African listeners were easily distracted and persuadable, and thus susceptible to state and foreign propaganda. Yes, it was true that the BBC relied on its African audiences to retain relevancy in the decolonized world, but an essence of colonial paternalism remained nonetheless.

Although the above discussion centered on the news, several of the attributes it examined, like wide coverage and professional quality, extended across the BBC brand, including its cultural programming. The BBC's programming for entertainment thus joined the programs of education and information to continue building what colonial broadcasters had tried to do in Britain's African colonies during the late 1950s: construct a thriving and diverse public sphere that encouraged democratic participation and critical thinking. In addition, in *African Theatre*, we see the BBC make a similar argument that at the heart of its productions was a desire to serve Africans' needs. As mentioned earlier, the BBC producers behind the program sought specific African writers whose names could enhance their program lineup. How did these producers select which authors to solicit? They relied on the British publishing industry, which identified, judged, and launched a group of African writers as part of its new publishing strategy in postcolonial Africa.

Patrons of Postcolonial Culture

British Publishers and African Writers

In 1961 one of the London editors of Oxford University Press traveled to newly independent Nigeria in search of "budding Shakespeares and Byrons."[1] The editor expected to discover the next famous African writer, take his works back to London, and publish his writing worldwide. After a yearlong search, Rex Collings believed he had found what he was looking for: a Nigerian playwright named Wole Soyinka, whose writing was so creative that Collings proclaimed it should be published on its merit alone. But, as Collings well knew, merit was not the reason OUP's educational division typically brought a work to press. Therefore, when Collings sat down to explain why it was urgent that the press publish Soyinka, he made a different argument. "I am convinced that there is still a place for us in African publishing if we can plainly show that we are not in fact only interested in selling enormous quantities of primary school books by expatriate authors. . . . Politically therefore it is also important that we should publish. If we don't, I think we will have missed the bus."[2] What Collings argued for was more than just a single title—it was a different outlook. As he carefully explained, British publishers now operated in an entirely different political context than the one through which they had first expanded into Africa. The political environment called for a different publishing strategy—a strategy that found a way to accommodate their postcolonial critics.

In chapter 2 of this volume, I showed how British colonial rule supported commercial book publishing in regions such as East Africa. That chapter left off right at the moment of independence, when British firms such as OUP had tried to anticipate political change by creating branches that did local publishing. This chapter begins by continuing that story and showing how a branch like OUP

Eastern Africa fared after independence. OUP branch managers realized that their future hinged almost entirely on the national state, which set policies regarding foreign-owned businesses as well as educational curricula. The branch managers therefore set out to demonstrate how useful their operations could be to a developing nation, including their willingness to show flexibility in the authors and works they published. As becomes clear quite quickly, however, branch managers did not have the final say over their publishing strategies; instead, they had to answer to the parent company in London, which had its own priorities.

When thinking through how a firm's organization shaped the literature that it published, I am helped considerably by literary publishing histories, some of which focus on the same examples I examine here.[3] In particular, Caroline Davis's study of the Oxford University Press Three Crowns series draws from Bourdieu's theory of cultural production to show how British multinational firms tried to integrate cultural production and economic production within a single company.[4] Meanwhile, some of the other histories of publishing in Africa, and especially studies of Heinemann's African Writers Series, revel in personal anecdotes meant to show British publishers' faith and support for new African literature.[5] The latter are meant to stand as defenses against cries that European structures, language, and values became entrenched while profits flowed back to Europe, making the publishing industry just one more example of Western neocolonialism. The following discussion historicizes that critique to a degree by showing how it was present at the very start of the postcolonial period. African writers—the very writers whom British firms sought to publish—protested and then organized against the system of exclusion that they encountered.

That gets one to thinking about who exactly Rex Collings had in mind when he proposed British publishers foster goodwill in Africa. In terms of personal politics, Collings was deeply liberal—a political outlook that he shared with many of the British individuals working in publishing in Africa and the Caribbean during the early postcolonial era. Looking around in the early 1960s, he and other British publishers were most concerned about African states either directly or indirectly hurting the publishers' ability to conduct business and thus limiting the possibilities for a flourishing industry. Collings thought the way to pacify African states was by convincing them that British multinationals' aims aligned with the same aims of the African states: mass education, encouraging African creativity, and promoting African creative work outside the nation's borders. British publishers did not yet fully recognize that the most severe condemnation they would face would not come from African states. Instead, it came from the African intellectuals and writers they sought to publish. That relationship— the relationship between British publisher and African writer—thus became the most crucial for explaining how British publishers legitimized their work after African independence.

LOCAL *BRITISH* PUBLISHING

British colonial rule established a somewhat rivalrous, commercial publishing industry in East Africa where almost all the dominant players were British. Kenya's independence in 1963 did not appear to threaten this status quo at first. Now operating out of its new Eastern Africa branch in Nairobi, OUP was pleased to see Kenya's educational system remained organized around the Cambridge School Certificate examinations, and headmasters and teachers still had a degree of autonomy in choosing their texts. That meant that OUP continued to profit from the earlier era, when colonial officials hinted strongly that Oxford's series were the best. OUP's profit-and-loss accounts confirmed the pattern: due almost entirely to textbook sales, the branch's sales rose steadily over its first eight years, so by 1971 OUP Eastern Africa showed branch publication sales over £580,000 and net profits over £41,000.[6]

The very features that OUP celebrated, however, newer publishing outlets scorned. Two years after Kenya's independence, a former district officer named John Nottingham tried to establish his own independent publishing company in Nairobi, the East African Publishing House (EAPH). Nottingham found himself confronting what he called a "deep attachment to the British educational legacy," that was almost impregnable because it was everywhere: teaching methods; personnel; curricula; examination standards; and, of course, books.[7] As much as Nottingham objected to that system, a small publisher like the EAPH and a large multinational like OUP shared a common fear: the prospect of state-controlled publishing. During the 1960s, they had already seen African states such as Zambia, Tanzania, Uganda, and Ghana take control over educational publishing by setting up state publishing houses with the help of another British publishing firm, Macmillan. The typical contract had Macmillan holding 49 percent of the shares while the African government held 51 percent. Individual British firms such as OUP and Allen and Unwin saw clear threats to their profits because state control stifled any efforts to encourage market competition, while Macmillan's capital and management deprived private firms of their comparative advantages.[8] The UK Publishers Association also registered its clear objections to the state publishing houses but framed them in terms of more broad-minded values. "When State participation in publishing combines with monopoly and with the vitiation of copyright, inevitably education progress will be arrested, creative expression in literature and the arts stifled, and the stimulus of ready access to the resources of world literature lost."[9] From Britain, publishers framed the prospect of state control as a danger to intellectual property and freedom of speech.

Although Kenya did not go the route of its neighbors in terms of state-controlled publishing, the Kenyan government did take smaller actions that cut into British firms' sales. Already during the 1960s there were signs Kenyan ministers were going to demand a much more rigid national curriculum that removed headmasters' and teachers' abilities to select books themselves. Instead, textbook decision-making started to take place inside the Ministry of Education and its offshoot, the curriculum development and research center at the Kenya Institute of Education (KIE). In a move that directly cut into foreign publishers' profits, the state also started a pipeline for KIE-authorized books to schools through a new parastatal, the Jomo Kenyatta Foundation. (This was Kenya's second parastatal in publishing; the East African governments also had the East African Literature Bureau, whose staff by now was fully Africanized.) The combination of losing most of its primary and secondary sales in Uganda and Tanzania, plus the KIE's preference for the Jomo Kenyatta Foundation during the early 1970s, meant that during the 1970s the OUP Eastern Africa branch publication sales fluctuated wildly. In some years, the branch registered significant net losses, and in other years it barely held even.[10]

Even against this worrisome political climate, the publishers at OUP Eastern Africa believed there were still paths to profits—they just hinged on the good graces of the Ministry of Education officials. OUP publishers were especially interested in the market that first attracted Oxford to the region: primary school education. The publishers in Nairobi reported primary school enrollments back to London each year, claiming that even if a course required a large initial investment, the payouts for Oxford could be enormous. Such reports also contained what the publishers viewed as political intelligence concerning trends and tensions among policy makers and bureaucrats. For example, the branch's annual report in 1976 spelled out what publishers thought of as their political strategy, given the "complex and chancy" intricacies of primary textbook selection. "The best hope of getting a book on the recommended list [is] to enlist the help and 'sponsorship' of a senior Ministry of Education official or inspector. One has an even better chance if ones author *himself* is a MOE official or inspector, or if ones Course (as with *Progressive Peak*) is the officially endorsed series."[11] OUP was certain, therefore, that there were ways it could play the system correctly and attain the profits that had drawn them to East Africa.

If it needed further evidence, Oxford could look to one instance where it did win a lucrative Kenyan contract for teaching English to schoolchildren. Independence in Kenya had not immediately prompted a major overhaul of the educational curriculum, which meant that most primary students learned in vernacular languages for the first several years and then began receiving English-language lessons gradually. There was also a group of primary schools that used English as the language of instruction across all years and subjects; indeed, the demand for English-stream education was one of the measures that publishers such as OUP closely tracked (see figure 9). The Progressive Peak English Course, the series that effectively replaced the *New Oxford English Course* in OUP's East African catalog, was a KIE initiative.

FIGURE 9. Children in an English-stream class in Kenya learn arithmetic while speaking English. The colonial information office's caption explains that the course is part of a curriculum that encourages English at the primary level, which it describes as "a remarkable achievement since most African children in Kenya hear no English in their home environment." The National Archives, Kew, United Kingdom, INF 10/159/64 (1962).

During the early 1970s, the state agency developed books for standards 4 through 7 and oversaw publication through the Jomo Kenyatta Foundation. By 1974, officials in KIE's English-language division had begun to turn their attention toward the first three grades, when they were jolted by President Kenyatta's announcement that he was abolishing school fees for the first four years of primary school—effective immediately. Without any prior notice, the government expected to quickly get hold of hundreds of thousands of new textbooks—not only English, but also all the other lower primary subjects—of which the parastatals could provide only a fraction. Therefore, KIE needed to find private partners. When the news reached OUP, its officials thought their long wait had paid off. Here was the national government acknowledging the benefits of commercial publishing and extending opportunities to British publishers once again.[12]

Oxford University Press's approach to this series of primary-level English textbooks looked quite different than the top-down, Eurocentric approach it took during the colonial era. Most of the differences stemmed from the fact that the process was almost entirely out of Oxford's hands. For example, Oxford did not independently select the authors. To write the books, KIE turned to two individuals working in KIE's English language section: one a Kenyan teacher named Lorna Wandera, and the other a British man named Clive Brasnett, whom the British Council had seconded to KIE for three years through its Aid to Commonwealth English scheme.[13] Brasnett trained as a linguist before joining the British Council and had done work related to English-language teaching (ELT) in the Middle East, India, and Southeast Asia before his arrival in Nairobi. Despite being so experienced, he recalled later, he was still somewhat taken aback that someone without any African experience would be asked to write a course for millions of African schoolchildren.[14]

Brasnett's misgivings appeared to be fleeting, however, and he described the Progressive Peak series as a perfect collaboration between his ELT know-how and understanding of narrative structure with his Kenyan colleague's "watchful eye."[15] Describing how the process of writing the books unfolded, Brasnett remembered how he would write something that was in his mind sensible, but then Wandera or another Kenyan informed him why it needed to be different for Kenya. For example, for Book Two, Brasnett wrote a lesson in which a group of children prepared a soup next to the river and then became ill. The lesson's aim was to teach negative injunctions, such as "Never drink water from the river." However, when Brasnett presented an early copy to a KIE committee, the committee's head, Mr. Chinmungeni, demanded he change the line because despite what Brasnett knew about health, rivers were a common source of drinking water in Kenya.[16] Another instance along this pattern involved the series' illustrator, an Italian expatriate named Mara Onditi. (The addition of Onditi to the project was one of the main ways OUP supported the project. Brasnett gave a great amount of credit to Onditi's illustrations for helping the books look professional, but he also hinted quite strongly that OUP underpaid her.) As Brasnett described in his memoirs, the first cover Onditi presented for Book One showed the two characters, Mary and Tom, running barefoot across a field. When Wandera objected, the two Europeans—Brasnett and Onditi—both protested that during their journeys up-country they had indeed seen most children without shoes. However, as Brasnett explained decades later, Wandera insisted that Kenya was a country of aspirations, an argument for which Brasnett had no response. Indeed, however inaccurate Brasnett may have regarded it, the final cover showed the children wearing shoes.[17]

The point of retelling all of this is to emphasize that the publisher—OUP—remained far in the background of the writing process. As Brasnett's retelling reveals, OUP's arrangement with KIE occurred separate from his and Wandera's pedagogy and creative input. The two agencies had already agreed that OUP was going to publish whatever books KIE produced, and that as OUP's sole customer, the Kenya Ministry of Education would order hundreds of thousands of copies. The only place where the negotiations might have stalled was over pricing. As the negotiations for Book Three exposed, price was the one part of the publication arrangements where Oxford had somewhat of a say.[18] When the OUP branch manager, Roger Houghton, proposed what he thought was a reduced price, the state officials balked. Despite the increase in primary enrollment, the state had not increased its book-buying budget for primary schools.[19] In the ensuing talks, Oxford agreed to come down in price somewhat, namely by eliminating author royalties because Brasnett and Wandera already received salaries from the British Council and the government of Kenya respectively.

Decades later, another British Council official asked Brasnett whether he thought Oxford University Press made any money at all on the books, and he said he assumed so. In his reasoning, Brasnett explained that all the while he was in Kenya, he kept hearing that it was only textbooks like his that even persuaded OUP to keep a presence in East Africa.[20] Brasnett's supposition was correct in that 1975—the year the first Progressive Peak title came out—Kenya's textbook order led the OUP branch to post its largest profits of the 1960s and 1970s—more than £87,000. The profits were not lasting however, and in later years, once the government obtained the books it needed, the OUP branch in Nairobi had trouble even staying in the black.[21] Regardless, Oxford publishers never questioned their decision to take up the Kenya state's offer.

After independence, private British companies such as Oxford University Press and Longmans set out to prove their willingness to go along with the calls to decolonize educational content, as long as it did not threaten their market position. In his negotiations with Kenyan officials, Houghton did not mention the Oxford brand or the necessity of top-quality production; instead, his focus was on meeting the Kenya government's deadline and finding cost-cutting measures.[22] By this point, British publishers saw that part of the Kenya government's demand was that there be Kenyan authorship and that accommodating this demand gave the publishers a greater chance of success in an otherwise chancy process. Even if it stemmed from political considerations and nothing more, Lorna Wandera and other Kenyans' role in the production of the texts and the fact that their feedback was sometimes listened to was a stark contrast to how Frederick George French wrote the New Oxford English Course two decades earlier. Oxford's experience with the Progressive Peak English Course reveals a reversal in how the company treated teaching and learning. Overall, OUP's attitude during the publication was, "tell us what the demand is, and we will publish to meet it"—a reversal of OUP's supply-led confidence during the colonial era.

Even when they received lucrative education contracts, OUP Eastern Africa staff still had to contend with being viewed as outsiders. The politics between foreign, indigenous, and state-sponsored publishing outfits spilled into and then came to dominate their own trade association, formed in 1970. At its inception, the Kenya Publishers Association (KPA) was supposed to be a venue for all publishing bodies in Kenya to work together for their mutual interest.[23] John Nottingham of the East African Publishing House was one of the proponents behind forming a trade association, believing it would help smaller agencies such as his to ally with wealthier and more politically connected agencies. In organizing the first KPA meeting, Nottingham ensured that all types of agencies—from Oxford University Press to the Jomo Kenyatta Foundation—were in attendance. The Kenyan association decided it would model its constitution on that of the Nigeria Publishers Association, which also had to consider the different multinational and national interests within its membership. In terms of its membership, the Kenya Publishers Association distinguished between companies that "carried on the business of book production" in Kenya and those that merely distributed books published elsewhere. The former group, which included the parastatals, Nottingham's EAPH, OUP, and Longmans, were full members, and each held two votes, while the latter, which included other British firms such as Heinemann Educational Books (HEB), Cambridge, Evans, Nelsons, and Macmillan, were associate members with only one vote.[24]

Although the Kenya Publishers Association worked together effectively on certain matters, its deliberations were increasingly hamstrung by splits within the membership. There were several occasions when KPA members successfully lobbied the government about issues that affected all KPA members' publications. During the early 1970s, for example, the cost of paper rose rapidly in all parts of the world; yet, the Kenya Ministry of Works refused to pay higher prices to publishers. Since there was no paper mill in Kenya, all KPA members were affected; therefore, the members united to lobby the government as one.[25] But this type of unity was harder to find later in the decade. In a meeting in 1975, John Nottingham joined with other indigenous and state-controlled agencies to proclaim that British firms were using the Kenya Publishers Association as a front for pursuing their neocolonial interests.[26] The KPA amended its constitution to give wholly Kenya-owned companies more power, but that only settled the matter for a short period. By 1979, the association's meetings often broke apart into argument, where several of the Kenya-owned companies railed against any publishers that were not completely Kenya-owned. Nottingham decried that besides dominating the market, companies such as OUP, Longmans, and Heinemann Educational Books devasted the KPA's ability to lobby the government because ministers dismissed the whole KPA as a neocolonial body. Another Kenyan publisher, Fred Ojienda of Foundation, stated that publishing was first and foremost a cultural enterprise, meaning only Kenyan publishers could truly speak to Kenya's book needs.[27] These arguments repeatedly arose during the later decades.[28] Although this wasn't the end of the KPA, which still operates today, it demonstrates how the questioning of British publishing interests spread throughout all levels of the industry.

Like the BBC, British publishers faced an unfriendly political environment when they tried to continue their African business after independence. Even if Kenyan ministers and other critics did not attack British business with real teeth, British publishers still felt compelled to show how they were making tangible contributions to society and development around them. Acting as the government's contractor was one route, but a firm such as OUP recognized that it should spread out its risk and pursue other routes toward acceptance at the same time. Whether it was out of defensiveness or cunningness, British firms started looking around them and thinking of other ways they could generate feelings of goodwill. That brings the discussion back to Oxford University Press at the beginning of the postcolonial period and the race to publish African literature.

THE DISCOVERY OF AFRICAN LITERATURE

When Rex Collings traveled to Nigeria in 1961 in search of "budding Shakespeares and Byrons," he was part of a new scramble for postcolonial Africa.[29] Instead of rushing to claim land and resources, British publishers now rushed to claim writers and titles for the new market of Third World literature.[30] Although only a handful of African novels appeared on the metropolitan scene before the 1960s, it was enough to prompt British publishers to eye the continent carefully. For many, the first novel from sub-Saharan Africa they had read was Amos Tutuola's *The Palm-Wine Drinkard*, which Faber and Faber published in London in 1952. Tutuola was a Nigerian writer who based his narrative on Yoruba folktales, which he depicted through a modified Yoruba English. British and American critics received the text with enthusiasm but described it in terms of primitiveness and naivete. For example, Dylan Thomas wrote in the *Observer* how it was a "brief, thronged, grisly and bewitching story" written in "young English," while the *Listener* called it a "very curious" work that had "much in common with other primitive literature."[31] When critics and intellectuals in Nigeria read these reviews, they were alarmed. They feared Tutuola's text reinforced Western ideas of Africa as backward and thus crowded out other styles of writing from international publication in the future.[32] Their fears only subsided six years later, after another Nigerian novel of a very different style reached the metropolitan literary scene. This was when William Heinemann, Ltd. published *Things Fall Apart* by Chinua Achebe, the volume that would become the most widely read African novel in the world. The publishing company received the manuscript through Achebe's supervisor at the BBC in London, where the novelist was training as a broadcaster.[33] Nigerian critics were relieved to see that with Achebe, British critics evaluated an example of African writing outside the confinement of naive art. The *Times Literary Supplement* said,

"His literary method is apparently simple, but a vivid imagination illuminates every page, and his style is a model of clarity."[34] Despite such positive reviews, however, *Things Fall Apart* did not get enough attention for William Heinemann to sell the paperback rights to a mass-market British firm, such as Penguin. As a second option, therefore, the firm subcontracted the rights in 1962 to its educational company, Heinemann Educational Books (HEB). Thus, *Things Fall Apart* was republished in paperback as the first title in the African Writers Series.[35]

As some of the first writers to see their novels published outside Africa, Tutuola and Achebe were forerunners of the true scramble for African literature that started during the 1960s. Their works came out through London presses and were directed at the metropolitan market, meaning the titles were not part of the regional trade described in chapter 2. Yet, just the snapshot of British and African reactions to *Palm-Wine Drinkard* and *Things Fall Apart* gives some insight into the central questions about African literary publishing during the 1960s. Should African literature be judged by the same standards as Western literature? What types of narrative and language did Western publishers and audiences expect to find in an African novel? Which markets were these books meant for? That the *Times Literary Supplement* even reviewed Tutuola's and Achebe's works was only because British firms had published them, and in hardcover editions. These same factors made it much less likely audiences in Nigeria, where the novels were set, would ever read the works.

The prospective markets for a given title depended on the different ways multinational publishers siloed their books. The previous discussion of the publishing industry in East Africa demonstrated how a firm such as OUP established overseas branches in places it believed had a substantial educational market. In each location, the branch manager oversaw local editorial and publishing operations, including assessing titles in terms of local curricular needs and national policies. Branch managers reported to the parent company's overseas division, which was in London in OUP's case.[36] As separate companies within a publishing group, branch rights differed from metropolitan rights. An author's contract specified one or another—that is, the Oxford University Press Eastern Africa branch in Nairobi or Oxford University Press in London. The distinction determined how widely OUP expected to circulate the title; while branch publications were almost entirely contained to a specific region, London titles went to markets in Britain and around the world. Such a model was not unique to OUP. A similar model was apparent at Heinemann Educational Books, another firm that became very active in East and West Africa during the 1960s.

With both Heinemann and Oxford, the organizational and legal details are important because they provide insight into how metropolitan publishers viewed the world in which they worked. The fact that overseas markets were now what was keeping their companies in the black did not affect how London officials provincialized regional markets and branch publications. (The importance of book exports and overseas markets cannot be overstated though: in 1967, these markets represented almost three quarters of OUP's total turnover.)[37] Nevertheless, London-based publishers believed the function of the branches was to publish textbooks and bring in profits, not to become involved with promising authors or new literary genres. They reasoned that if an overseas author had real talent, his or her writing should come out through the London firm, which would elevate the work and allow it to reach readers worldwide.

As will be seen, the institutional structures of publishing in Africa had profound implications for local writers who hoped to see their work in print. Despite the growing number of publishing outfits in countries such as Nigeria and Kenya, the vast majority were offshoots of British companies that had to refer all non-educational submissions to London. If an African writer hoped to see his or her work published, they had to write in a European language, adhere to European conventions, and produce a narrative that would be of interest to European audiences. It was all to have their writing reach *any* audiences, whether in Britain, other parts of the world, or even the region of Africa where they lived. These points are important to consider when examining the specific publishing strategies behind two of the different options an African writer could consider: Oxford University Press's Three Crowns series and Heinemann Educational Book's African Writers Series.

ANOTHER SCRAMBLE FOR AFRICA

Rex Collings, the Oxford publisher who went to Nigeria to discover a budding African Shakespeare, was from OUP's London business. Before moving to London, Collings had worked at Oxford's office in Nairobi under Charles Granston Richards. Although Collings's understanding of African literature was more evolved than Richards's missionary zeal, Collings used some of the same language when describing his role in discovering and guiding African cultural production. Working within OUP's overseas editorial division, Collings thought a big part of his role was to advocate for African literature within the press's profit-oriented structure. Therefore, Collings preemptively framed his reasons for publishing African literature not around merit, but rather through economic and political justifications that even risk-averse editors might respond to. The quote at the start of this chapter, which came from Collings's appeal to publish Wole Soyinka's *The Lion and the Jewel*, shows how Collings presented African literature as a long-term strategic move. He explained that in addition to textbooks, African schools also required literary works to teach language and literature—and after independence, national governments would want that literature to be more African than European. Perhaps even more important, however, were political considerations, where Oxford had to face up to its precarious position as a foreign company. All of this led Collings to conclude, "Politically therefore it is also important that we should publish. If we don't I think we will have missed the bus."[38]

Collings might not have been able to argue with such force if it were not for Wole Soyinka. During his trip to West Africa the OUP editor heard from Joan Littlewood (an acclaimed theater director from London) that there was a Nigerian playwright whose works blew her over. She hoped to produce one of his plays in London very soon.[39] Collings arranged through the OUP Ibadan branch to find the playwright and have his scripts sent to London for review. Although Collings would speak excitedly about his "discovery," Soyinka was already a well-known figure in Nigerian artistic circles by 1962. In the mid-1950s, Soyinka studied at the University of Leeds; while he was in the United Kingdom, he also edited a satirical student magazine, contributed to the BBC program "Calling West Africa," and worked as a script reader at the Royal Court Theatre. Between 1957 and 1960 several of Soyinka's plays were produced in Ibadan (*The Swamp Dwellers, The Lion and the Jewel*, and *The Trials of Brother Jero*), the cultural center of Nigeria, and a few works were produced in London (*The Swamp Dwellers* and an excerpt from *The Invention*). In 1960 Soyinka received a Rockefeller Research Fellowship to return to Ibadan, when he formed his first theatrical company 1960 Masks. They premiered Soyinka's *A Dance of the Forests* as Nigeria's official independence performance in October 1960. When Rex Collings visited Nigeria in 1961, therefore, Soyinka was already a common name across Nigeria with an enormous range of theatrical, poetic, and prose writing to his name.

Even if they had never heard of Soyinka before, the editors at Oxford University Press were quickly aware of the level of talent they had encountered.[40] After detailing how impressed he was by the sophistication of *The Lion and the Jewel*, an OUP manager concluded, "As an authentic African play it certainly deserves publication by somebody, and possibly by us."[41] The reader reports they solicited from British Africanists provided confirmation of the literary merits, but that was not enough to guarantee publication.[42] Where editors had doubts was the question of educational sales, which still loomed over any final decision. Several editors were concerned about the sex and violence in Soyinka's plays because it might dissuade schools from assigning them, thus limiting sales.[43] When the press finally decided to take Soyinka's works, the publishers still saw it as a risky move on principle, one justified only by the quality of the material. In September 1962, Soyinka signed contracts with Oxford University Press for *The Lion and the Jewel* and *A Dance of the Forests* to be published the following year in the Three Crowns series, the press's new venture into African literature.

Between 1963 and 1969, Oxford University Press published seven of Soyinka's plays; however, the Nigerian remained an exception, rather than the rule, to the press's general approach to publishing African literature. A few years later, in an exchange about possibilities for African fiction, one Overseas Editorial editor explained, "We are less likely to promote a single work on its own merits than we are an author, such as Soyinka, who shows signs of ability to develop and mature. This means, as far as new creative literature is concerned, we tend to think in terms of authors in our list rather than of individual titles."[44] A clearer way to explain Oxford's decision-making might have been: "With the exception of Wole Soyinka, we require proof of an educational market." Throughout the 1960s the Three Crowns series suffered from somewhat of an identity crisis over the tension between literary importance and educational sales.

A large problem in establishing a clear identity for Three Crowns lay in the aforementioned relationship between London and the overseas branches. From London, Rex Collings wanted to see the series grow larger and cover all types of creative literature. But he was up against the press's general policy that its London division did not publish literature that was just for an overseas market—those titles should be left to the branches.[45] By the mid-1960s, however, overseas branches such as OUP Eastern Africa were starting to hurt from national policies, such as the creation of parastatals, and branch managers did not want to publish anything that did not have an obvious place in schools. Given how much published material was already available in English, the branches saw novels in English to be a risky venture. With both the London and the African arms of OUP oriented toward educational sales, there was very little space to publish African literature in English. The narrow pathway that existed was for a title to have both international appeal and obvious educational merit.

Unsurprisingly, therefore, the Three Crowns list remained fairly small during the mid-1960s. What Three Crowns did publish was mainly plays, which Collings and other OUP editors viewed as having a better chance of educational sales than the saturated field of novels.[46] (Their reasoning sounded quite similar to the British Council officials who had started to promote drama export as a useful tool for language practice.) An additional advantage in publishing drama was that the London editors had more measures for what qualified as publishable work that would sell. They looked for pieces that were successfully performed and acclaimed in an overseas region such as West Africa. They also saw competitions held by the British Council, the Congress for Cultural Freedom, and the BBC African Service as a way to discover new plays and playwrights to consider.[47]

Whether it was a play or a novel, commercial pressures dominated decisions of whether to publish or not. Here, the school certificate reading lists were everything. All British publishers in Africa, whether they worked for OUP, Longmans, Heinemann Educational Books, or another company, paid close attention to the deliberations going on in the West and East African Examinations Councils as to how the school certificate selections would change after African independence. As they did, the British publishers were acutely aware that they were one another's competition. After learning of a new play or an unfamiliar playwright, the Oxford publishers rushed to see the manuscript, hear advice from African experts, and inquire with their exam council contacts—all in a race against time. As an Oxford representative in West Africa described, "The worst thing would be to decide what we wanted to do to [the African plays] and to find them taken up elsewhere."[48] He sent memos to London with titles such as "Disasters: Or Rumours of Disasters." In that one, he reported hearing Heinemann had gotten Raymond Sarif Easmon's *Of Parents and Ogre*, and—worse—the play might appear on the first-year literature course in West Africa.[49]

As much as publishers in postcolonial Africa thought the exams councils determined their fates, the councils felt they were similarly dependent on the publishers. When choosing their set books, the West and East African Examinations Councils could not rely on a robust bookselling industry. They did not want to set a book for which there were not enough copies, nor did they want to change their lists too drastically from year to year, which schools could not afford.[50] Both of these concerns played into the larger publishing outlets' hands, as they were more able to promise large orders quickly. An exchange from 1963 conveys how the relationship between exams council and publisher played out. In March 1963, the West African Examinations Council informed the Oxford publishers it was prepared to prescribe two of the plays that Oxford was considering (*Sons and Daughters* by Joe de Graft and either *Foriwa* or *Edufa* by Efua Sutherland) for the 1966 examination—*if* OUP could guarantee it would publish the works by early 1964. The Oxford publishers responded within a week to say they had moved ahead on the de Graft publication.[51] (The resulting prescription did great things for de Graft's sales, and he quickly became the second-highest-selling writer in the Three Crowns series, after Wole Soyinka.)[52] The letter from the exam council concluded with a mention that it was also speaking with Heinemann, as if Oxford didn't already know who its prime competitor was in the field of African literature.

LARGER, MORE SUCCESSFUL, BUT STILL COMMERCIAL

At first glance, Heinemann's African Writers Series (AWS) appeared quite similar to what Oxford was doing with Three Crowns.[53] Both series launched in the early 1960s, with their respective editors wanting to model themselves after Penguin paperbacks. Each series focused on African literature in English. Each series featured leading West African writers: for Heinemann Educational Books (HEB) it was Chinua Achebe and for Oxford it was Wole Soyinka. Each series came out of the company's educational arm in London, instead of its branches and offices in East, West, and southern Africa. Yet, as many similarities as there may have been, there were also several ways in which the AWS publishing strategy diverged quite abruptly from that of Three Crowns. Those differences came to have a large impact in how African writers regarded their options.

While OUP imposed strict parameters around its African literature series, Heinemann's AWS editors had more room to experiment.[54] As mentioned, James Currey and other HEB editors imagined the African Writers Series as a Penguin for Africa: in other words, cheap paperback editions of general books by Africans. Rex Collings at Oxford had also tried to follow the Penguin model with the Three Crowns series, but he ran into problems with his press's policies about literary and noneducational works. In comparison with Three Crowns, the African Writers Series came much closer to the Penguin model. The extent to which Heinemann emulated Penguin's success could be seen in the African Writers Series' covers: novels and other fiction were brought out with orange covers, like Penguin books, while nonfiction works, such as Kenneth Kaunda's autobiography *Zambia Shall Be Free*, had blue covers, like Pelican titles.[55] (In Africa, the signature orange cover was associated with Heinemann and not Penguin, and within a few years, African university bookshops were advertising that they carried the "orange series.") The first titles in Heinemann's series were mostly reprints of books that William Heinemann or other publishers had produced in hardcover. These included *Things Fall Apart* and its sequel *No Longer at Ease*, as well as *People of the City* by the Nigerian writer Cyprian Ekwensi, and *Mine Boy* by the South African writer Peter Abrahams.[56]

But Heinemann quickly saw there was not a large enough body of African-authored published works to publish only reprints. This brought the series' editors to express interest in new novels and writers to debut in their series. The first author where this was the case was Ngũgĩ wa Thiong'o (then James Ngugi.) In the span of one year, Ngũgĩ had two novels published in the African Writers Series: *Weep Not, Child* and *The River Between*. As chapter 2 described, an earlier version of *The River Between* won a prize in the East African Literature Bureau competition and prompted Charles Granston Richards to pass the manuscript to Heinemann. At almost the exact same moment, the Heinemann editors learned of Ngũgĩ's *Weep Not, Child* through an entirely separate avenue: a conference of African writers at Makerere University in 1962. The way the story goes, Chinua Achebe was in his guesthouse one evening when Ngũgĩ knocked on the door, introduced himself, and handed Achebe the manuscript. Achebe was so impressed by it that he passed the manuscript to his Heinemann editor, who was also attending the conference. The editor phoned London, where he took Alan Hill out of a meeting to ask if he would take on the book unseen. Hill gave his approval on the spot, and Heinemann signed Ngũgĩ.[57]

With the publication of *Weep Not, Child*, the Heinemann publishing group had to decide how it was going to release new African writing. British publishers in the 1960s saw paperback as a relatively new format, reserved mostly for reprints.

Its cheapness had made it an obvious format for the first African Writers Series books, where they thought the primary market was in Africa. For its previous AWS titles, Heinemann was not concerned the paperback format would prevent reviews or lessen library sales in Britain because the titles were reprints. But with Ngũgĩ's novels the Heinemann educational editors wanted to attract reviews and library sales in Britain too, so they proposed the parent company, William Heinemann, publish a hardback edition at the same time the African Writers Series paperback came out. This made Ngũgĩ's contract somewhat more complicated. One of the editors, Keith Sambrook, explained to the parent company, "Now, the most one can offer a writer through the A. W. S. is a paperback market in Africa and 7½% royalty. We want to be able to offer a hard-covered edition, world sales, full promotion and royalty on the hard-cover of at least 10%. We need to be able to do this to get and keep the best writers."[58] Sambrook was able to persuade the reluctant British publishers they had some interest in producing a few carefully selected African writers in Britain. However, Sambrook had to give in on publishing in Britain and Africa simultaneously. Instead, William Heinemann managers insisted on the conventional eighteen-month delay between editions of *Weep Not, Child*, to ensure the paperback sales did not cut into hardcover profits. They would do the same for *The River Between* and Ngũgĩ's third novel, *A Grain of Wheat*, in 1967.[59] This arrangement allowed Ngũgĩ to be read and reviewed by broader international audiences, but delayed his introduction to African audiences. It also revealed how metropolitan interests trumped African interests, even at Heinemann.

Heinemann's African Writers Series had one great advantage over Oxford University Press and other British publishers in its recruitment of African writers. That was Chinua Achebe. Getting Ngũgĩ demonstrated to the Heinemann editors how Achebe was a magnet for emerging African talent. Later that year they asked the author if he would work as editorial adviser to the African Writers Series, and he accepted the position despite its very low pay.[60] As the Heinemann editors had presumed, Achebe was much closer to literary developments in Africa than his British colleagues in London. For example, four months after he had joined the African Writers Series, Achebe alerted the London editors that Mbari Publications of Nigeria had just got hold of a short novel that had been smuggled out of South Africa. Heinemann pursued the work—*A Walk in the Night and Other Stories* by the activist Alex La Guma—and secured the rights in 1967.[61] Another of Achebe's contributions was to push editors to look beyond the familiar area of West Africa for new authors and works. With his endorsement, for instance, they signed the preeminent Sudanese author Tayeb Salih.[62] (It is notable from these two examples alone, that there was no political litmus test in place in HEB's—or any major British firm's—assessment of potential writers; La Guma was an anti-apartheid activist with strong communist ties, while Salih's novel explored the brutal impact of European colonialism on modern Sudan. Instead, as publishers' editorial files reveal, sales remained the central concern in their decision-making.) Whether indirectly or directly, Achebe's presence helped Heinemann bring one hundred titles from twenty-one countries to press during the first ten years of the series. Also, remember that Achebe's contributions as an editorial adviser came on top of the profits brought by his own writing. William Heinemann was the originating publisher for all five of Achebe's novels and controlled the subsidiary rights; then, the African Writers Series brought paperback editions to the mass market. In the mid-1980s, looking back over the AWS's twenty-year history and more than 250 books, a William Heinemann editor realized almost one-third of total revenue came from Chinua Achebe's titles.[63] While an impressive feat of Achebe's, that statistic starts to point at questions about how widely spread AWS's reach truly was.

With African editorship and a much longer booklist, Heinemann believed it succeeded where Oxford did not, in terms of being more authentic in its patronage of African writing. The African Writers Series published 100 titles in its first decade and 140 more in its second. During the early 1970s, an average of 20 titles a year came out in African Writers Series covers. James Currey, one of the series editors, would later say, "A lot for a single publisher. Not many for a continent."[64] He meant for the comment to be exculpatory, or to show that the African Writers Series did everything it could and especially much more than any other metropolitan effort. It was certainly true that while the Heinemann series published a long list of authors and works, Oxford's Three Crowns editors continued to belabor the question about whether it wanted to support African literary writing. Some of the Three Crown titles met success, namely Soyinka's single plays, such as *The Lion and the Jewel*. However, the OUP editors in London struggled to find African authors of a high enough quality to sit next to Soyinka on a bookshelf.[65] In addition, they found themselves constantly defending the series' place within Oxford's overall business plan. Rex Collings—the editor who argued the hardest for Oxford to publish African literature—became so frustrated with Oxford's reluctance to pursue anything other than sales that in 1965 he left the company and moved to Methuen. Four years later, Collings started Rex Collings, Ltd., a publishing company focused on the African market. His departure really hurt the Three Crowns initiative—in part because it lost its headliner, Soyinka, who decided to move with Collings.[66] Without Collings arguing otherwise, the Oxford managers became more insistent that the only creative writing they publish was that which would be adopted by teachers and examiners.[67] They pursued this despite what they were hearing from their African branch managers, which was that with each passing year Oxford University Press needed all the public goodwill it could get.[68]

In addition to publishing a much longer booklist of African creative writing, Heinemann editors also spoke proudly about the ways they enabled African literature to be published in African languages. One of their many avenues for

doing so was the Swahili-language list called Waandishi wa Kiafrika—a translation of African Writers Series—that the HEB branch in East Africa started during
the late 1960s. The correspondence between London and Nairobi reveals that
the reasons for doing so were more calculating than altruistic, as the Nairobi
editors feared the Kenyan government was serious this time about its intent to
replace English with Swahili in schools.[69] Although the HEB (East Africa) branch
intended to produce original works too, most of the titles that came out of the
series in the early 1970s were translations of AWS bestsellers, such as novels by
Achebe and Ngũgĩ.[70] Its editors proclaimed that translating these works into
African languages would enhance Heinemann's brand because it would serve as
further proof the company was serious in its mission to expand access to African literature. Looking more closely at the contracts and the ensuing correspondence, however, reveals what the British publishers truly felt about locally run
publishing and African languages.

What might have appeared to be rather straightforward for Heinemann—confirm the rights, line up translators, and quickly churn out these titles—turned into
a rather chaotic ordeal. A big part of that was due to confusion over whether HEB
even held the translation rights to its AWS bestsellers. The branch publishers in
Nairobi were disappointed to discover that earlier in the 1960s Alan Hill of the
parent company had promised some of the Swahili translation rights—including
Things Fall Apart—to John Nottingham at the East African Publishing House.
Nottingham was the British expatriate, mentioned earlier, who started an independent firm in the mid-1960s, and he was a leading voice against British publishers for what he deemed a neocolonial monopoly.

Nottingham's firm was very small compared to his competitors, but with the
Swahili-language rights to *Things Fall Apart*, he held something that those British firms—both Heinemann and Oxford University Press—desperately wanted.[71]
When Nottingham was slow to show that he was moving forward on the title,
HEB began to accuse Nottingham and the EAPH of sitting on the rights. During
their increasingly heated exchanges, it became evident how little regard the British
publishers had for Nottingham or his firm. When Nottingham still did not have
anything in press by 1970, HEB negotiated a new joint publishing arrangement
with him; yet Nottingham kept promising them the proofs and failing to deliver.[72]
By the end of 1972, with still nothing in press, HEB's manager in East Africa had
reached his breaking point and wrote to London that it was time to get tough.
"John Nottingham considers that the world should lay at his feet, the oysters in
the publishing ocean and that he may vacillate, delay, annoy, renagle, and generally play hell with contracts and rights just because he is a semi-indigenous publisher in a developing country."[73] In Heinemann editors' minds, this was about
more than just the one title; this was about British firms having to cede to local
endeavors just because of the political context.

During Heinemann's prolonged fight to get the translation rights to Achebe's preeminent work, however, British publishers started to think Swahili literature was not the meal ticket they had once imagined. In 1970, when the HEB branch in East Africa put together the proposals for a handful of the first Swahili titles, their bosses in London underscored the company's view that Swahili was a very risky market. James Currey in London explained that even though they kept hearing Swahili was on the rise, vernacular publications never sold—regardless of the price—unless they were on a school list.[74] Therefore, the London office insisted HEB give much lower royalties for Swahili titles than it did for English, even to their bestselling authors. The royalties to Ngũgĩ for a Swahili version of *Weep Not, Child* and to Achebe for a Swahili version of *Man of the People* were 5 percent for the first ten thousand copies and 7.5 percent after that, although publishers were very skeptical sales would get anywhere near ten thousand.[75] (Moreover, the Swahili translators did not receive a royalty; rather, Heinemann paid a one-off fee for the translation, delivered at completion.)[76] Even with such low royalty rates, Heinemann editors in London said they could not subsidize the sale price of the books or do a large print run—it was far too much of a gamble.

Although James Currey and other London editors admitted they did not know a word of Swahili beyond "*Jambo,*" they controlled these publications just as they controlled the English-language counterparts, from the page proofs to the price.[77] When they were pricing the Luganda-language version of Achebe's *Things Fall Apart*, it came in at 14/50 East African shillings, when the English-language copy was only 5/- shillings.[78] The London editors thought that made sense, saying that from a business standpoint these were two entirely different products. "We sold half a million copies of one and we printed 3,000 of the other," James Currey pointed out.[79] But to their colleagues in East Africa, who were closer to African consumers, this was the wrong attitude to take. They pointed out that in this instance, where they were speaking about an African-language edition of a famous African novel, the man on the street in Kampala would only see them charging more than twice as much for him to read the book in his own language.[80] The history behind Heinemann's African-language African Writers Series thus became more evidence of what Africans saw when they looked at the publishing industry around them.

Although the African Writers Series offered more possibilities for publication than its counterparts, African writers became critical of what they saw as the essentialization of African culture. After publishing two novels with Heinemann, Nigerian writer Kole Omotoso condemned the series for lumping together an enormous number of diverse and unrelated writers. With the same inevitable cover design (often from a clichéd motif of African life) and a string of African-sounding names, the series led overseas audiences to believe all African writing was alike.[81] Wole Soyinka picked up with the same point when he labeled the series an "orange ghetto" of African writing and hoped none of his titles would ever appear there (a hope that was denied).[82] Heinemann produced an enormous number of titles, but on terms that were usually less favorable to the authors than even those offered by its competitors. For example, Oxford gave authors in its Three Crown series royalties of 15 percent, which was double what they would receive under a standard Heinemann agreement.[83] Ayi Kwei Armah, a Ghanaian writer who had five novels published or republished by Heinemann, used even stronger terms than Soyinka or Omotoso when he described the African Writers Series. He called it, "a neo-colonial writers' coffle owned by Europeans but slyly misnamed 'African.'"[84] All of these charges stood as proof that even Heinemann was not exempt from the growing criticism leveled at British publishers working in Africa. The next part of the discussion will describe how, upon realizing the direction in which African literature had been set, African writers sought to circumvent the domination of British publishing.

AFRICANIZING AFRICAN LITERATURE

In June 1962, more than thirty English-speaking African writers met at Makerere University in Uganda for a conference organized by the Mbari Writers' and Artists' Club of Ibadan, Nigeria. The Mbari Club was established the year before by a group of intellectuals who represented a sort of "Who's Who" of Nigerian creative arts, including Wole Soyinka, Chinua Achebe, J. P. Clark, and Christopher Okigbo.[85] Mbari's activities were funded by an international organization called the Congress for Cultural Freedom, which operated out of Paris, and which also funded the 1962 conference.[86] The chairman of the Makerere meeting explained how an Africa-wide conference would extend what had already started in Nigeria to other parts of the continent. "Mbari wanted writers to meet and know one another, talk about common problems and derive a sense of fellowship in a continent where, owing to vast distances and poor communications and educational facilities, Africans tend to write in isolation."[87] The 1962 conference was a landmark event in postcolonial African writing, most notably in the numbers and names it brought together. The thirty authors, playwrights, and poets who convened in Makerere hailed from Ghana, Nigeria, Kenya, Uganda, Tanganyika, Southern Rhodesia, and South Africa. The American writer Langston Hughes and the Jamaican playwright Barry Reckord attended as guests, as did three observers from French-speaking West Africa. Within the group, there was certainly overrepresentation of nationalities that were publishing in greater amounts (nine Nigerian writers and seven South African writers were in attendance) at the expense of the areas perceived as "unproductive" in comparison.[88] The attendees noted the imbalance, but referred to it as another way the conference could foster fellowship, where West Africans could use their experience to help East Africans catch up, so to speak. The same was said for established writers, such as Achebe and Soyinka, and hitherto unpublished writers; indeed, it was at the Makerere conference where the student James Ngugi gave Chinua Achebe his *Weep Not, Child* manuscript.

In the effort to identify the common problems they shared, the ensemble of English-speaking writers quickly focused on the issues of audience and language. They had come together on the basis that they all wrote in English; therefore, the discussions around language and audience were most focused on *how* to use English, not whether African writers should be using English at all. (The latter question would come to dominate discussions in later years.) But many of the writers who spoke still described the difficulties they had in translating their thoughts and feelings into a colonial language that foreign audiences would read. As South African writer Ezekiel Mphahlele explained, this hindered writers' abilities to be creative. "Because [the African writer] has to be published overseas, he has to chop and change his material and adapt his diction for his would-be publisher's audience. His tone automatically changes too. He slips into prosy explanation of his setting and gets bogged down in anthropological information."[89] In Mphahlele's mind, this was why the predominant theme of West African writing had been of the encounter between an indigenous and a European culture; West African writers thought about how they wanted to put themselves across to a foreign audience, and that was the subject they always returned to.

The issues the writers had with audience, language, and style constantly returned to the institutional structures through which African literature was published in the 1960s. It is important to note, however, that the Makerere conference represented an effort to *reform* British publishing, not to *remove* it. This was obvious from the get-go, as a group of European publishers had been invited to attend the meeting. The publishers in attendance included Charles Granston Richards (then at the East African Literature Bureau), Van Milne (Heinemann), Andre Deutsch (representing himself), and representatives of Oxford, Cambridge, and Northwestern University presses. The final day of the conference featured a panel on publishing, when five of the publishers explained how they evaluated African writing. During the question-and-answer portion, the writers in the audience criticized several parts of the publishing process, especially when they heard that the editors did not make it a point to consult African readers in determining what works to deem publishable. The leading publishers instead relied on reports from British Africanists, namely, a small group of literary scholars. Several writers pointed out that Amos Tutuola's *Palm-Wine Drinkard* would never have been published if the British editors had consulted an African critic before taking it up.[90] At the same time, the writers cautioned, what were very good works could easily get overlooked when African readers were not consulted. As more writers chimed in, several of the publishers staunchly defended their good faith and intuitive experience. Their closing words to the writers were simply that the writers needed to trust them.[91] The publishing panel was one of many moments during the Makerere conference when African writers questioned if British publishing best served their needs. They left the conference with the feeling that they must each do more to develop and identify good writing in their local areas, taking advantage of writers' workshops, local publications, and local literary journals whenever possible.[92] Again, all of these proposals aimed to supplement British publishing, not displace it altogether.

The writers assembled in Makerere in 1962 were in agreement that the development of indigenous publishing was important for the future of African writing. Over the rest of the decade, new ventures that aimed to diversify African writers' opportunities appeared around the continent. The ventures did not usually focus on removing British influence altogether; rather, they saw British firms as partners in the larger enterprise to increase African titles overall. One of the better-known ventures was Mbari Publications, run out of the Mbari Club in Ibadan. From its inception, Mbari set out to publish writing that overseas firms were not yet or would never be interested in.[93] Mbari published poetry collections, plays, and novels throughout the first two-thirds of the decade and was the first publisher for many major literary figures, including Wole Soyinka, J. P. Clark, Christopher Okigbo, and Kofi Awoonor. Mbari also welcomed writing by black South Africans whenever they were able to smuggle their works to Nigeria. Whenever Mbari Publications had a new work, the Mbari Club would advertise it through its newsletter, which had a subscription list across Africa, Europe, and the United States. But the Mbari Club also promoted other publishers' titles this way too. The newsletter's reading recommendations listed African writing from all different publishers—most of them British.[94] Mbari Publications had a greater reach than most indigenous publishers in the mid-1960s, but it did not try to compete with British firms.

Like almost all African publishers, Mbari struggled to fund its publications. Mbari was luckier than most African publishing initiatives because it had the support of an international agency, the Congress for Cultural Freedom. Other African projects looked into forming a partnership with a British firm, which could provide capital at the beginning, offer expertise, and reduce some the of the risk involved in publishing. This was the avenue the governments in Ghana and Zambia pursued with firms such as Longmans and Macmillan to publish their school textbooks and reading materials.[95] A British-African partnership was also behind the start of John Nottingham's East African Publishing House that started in Nairobi in 1965.[96] Even with foreign assistance or investment, however, funding remained an enormous barrier for indigenous publishing. In large part that was because profitable titles proved hard to come by.

British firms interested in African writing found local publishers such as Mbari to be very useful for identifying emerging writers and titles. They treated Mbari as a feeder list; the African publisher would test local interest and sales, then the British publisher could decide whether to commit. That was how Wole Soyinka and J. P. Clark came to be published in Oxford's Three Crowns series and Alex La Guma and Christopher Okigbo in Heinemann's African Writers Series—all the authors were first published by Mbari. The more successful the Mbari publication was, the more likely it caught a British firm's attention. The British firms fought for originating rights, and when they got them, took over all future profits. African publishers were thus in a catch-22: either they took on works at a loss, or they started to break even and quickly lost the titles.

By the middle of the decade, several of the more successful African writers sought to use their acclaim to break the cycle. In 1965, Wole Soyinka wrote to his editors at Oxford University Press that he had started a new publishing venture in Ibadan called Orisun Editions. He explained, "We are going in for the Nigerian market principally—short stories, one or two books of Poetry etc etc., but we feel that the greatest market will be in cheap acting editions for schools and the constantly expanding amateur groups." The Nigerian writer made it clear he was not trying to cut ties with the British company, saying instead, "We are entirely in favour of some kind of working arrangement with Oxford University Press especially anything that will take the actual burden of publishing off our backs."[97] Soyinka therefore wanted to inquire about Oxford's position on titles in the Three Crowns series. He was especially interested in learning who held the rights to his works.

Soyinka did not expect there to be a problem with his plans to publish acting editions of his own plays. In a more detailed set of plans he sent a few months later, he showed how he planned to use the original type that was set up for the Mbari editions, from back before he signed with Oxford. Yet, as innocently as he presented these plans, they set off alarms in London. With Orisun he planned to print nine thousand copies initially each of *Swamp Dwellers* and *The Trials of Brother Jero*. Both titles had appeared in *Five Plays*, a collection Oxford had brought out the year before.[98] The Ibadan OUP branch wrote to Rex Collings, "As you can see, a real copyright problem is involved. Whereas the sale of such editions might not militate against the sale of 'Five Plays,' it would certainly not help it."[99] The British editors were even more concerned with Soyinka's plans for the future. In a year or two he wanted Orisun to produce an edition of *The Lion and the Jewel*, which was his most profitable title with Oxford and had been prescribed by the West African Examinations Council. Allowing for local editions of this title was "out of the question," the Oxford editors told one another, because it "would kill our edition for schools."[100] Furthermore, Soyinka's ultimate vision for Orisun extended outside Nigeria's borders. Part of his mission, he had explained, was to take the profits from the acting editions, use them to publish original works, and then expand the company to other markets.

Orisun Editions never became any sort of competition for British publishers, for a few different reasons. First, the initial profits did not appear: Oxford did not relinquish rights to Soyinka's major plays, and the African venture was only able to publish a few of the smaller titles. Second, increasing government censorship and the secession of the Eastern Region overtook Orisun, Mbari, and many other literary initiatives coming out of Ibadan in the 1960s. (Another of those ventures was Citadel Press, the publishing company Chinua Achebe and Christopher Okigbo tried to start in 1966. Like Soyinka, they hoped having titles by authors of their fame would provide the lift-off the company needed.)[101] The Biafran War split parts of the Nigerian literary community, as Chinua Achebe, Gabriel Okara, and Christopher Okigbo went to work for the Republic of Biafra, while Wole Soyinka was arrested. Though Orisun's fate was not entirely due to the domination of British publishing in postcolonial Africa, it demonstrated how large a battle it would be for an African venture to even get off the ground as well as the myriad of other local conditions African publishers had to contend with.

By the early 1970s, there had been an obvious hardening of opinion against British publishing in Africa. A large conference on publishing and book development held in Ife, Nigeria, in 1973 concluded that African-British partnerships had thus far failed. This was primarily because the African partner had been "invariably used as representatives of publishers, not publishers themselves."[102] The African publishers, booksellers, and writers in attendance at the conference decried the continued domination of British publishing as neocolonialism. In its place was a more unified, stronger demand for indigenous African publishing than there had ever been before.

But when it came time to discussing remedies, the conversation shifted toward blaming African writers. (It should be noted that although more than one hundred African, European, and American delegates attended the conference, with the publishing, bookselling, and library professions well represented, almost no African writers attended.) The conference recognized that publishing through a British firm could bring an author critical attention, monetary rewards, and literary prizes, all of which were very tempting. But, the delegates implored, African writers had to resist the urge to write for the overseas market, even when it meant forgoing "the jingle of foreign exchange and the glitter of foreign fame," as one presenter described.[103] As one of the few writers present, Chinua Achebe mostly agreed. In his response, titled "A Writer's View," he said he and his fellow writers had a responsibility to support indigenous publishers and should be prepared to gamble on such publishers' chances at least once or twice in their writing careers.[104] He himself had tried this route earlier in the decade when he arranged to have a new Enugu press, Nwamife Publishers, publish his poetry collection *Beware, Soul Brother*. In that instance, Achebe's experience with lending his name to an African publisher went better than Soyinka's had in 1965. Heinemann Educational Books did later obtain the title for its African Writers Series, but the British firm sub-contracted the rights from the original African publisher. In addition, the agreement was for the Commonwealth market *excluding* Nigeria, which was left all to Nwamife Publishers.[105] In Achebe's mind, the relatively unprecedented agreement was a move in the right direction.

Of course, there was only one Chinua Achebe. The problem remained for how new African writers could ever get to a position like his where they held that sway. Although a chorus of criticism against foreign publishing came out of the University of Ife conference in 1973, the conference did not affect the structure of publishing that was in place. African publishers continued to feel they only saw a manuscript after European and American firms had passed on it. They did not have the capital reserves to take on unknown or risky titles. Meanwhile, British publishers at the top of the hierarchy continued to dictate who and what to publish in African writing, and on what terms.

THE GOOD, THE BAD, AND THE WICKED

The Kenyan publisher Henry Chakava once explained that British publishers could be described in three ways. "[There are] the good, who are sensitive to political change and developing economies; the bad, who attempt to continue a relationship of colonial privilege after history has passed them by; and the wicked, whose motivations are entirely commercial." He went on, "Sometimes one can find all three attitudes in the same company."[106] Having worked at one of Heinemann's branches in Africa, Chakava's words point at the commercial, political, and cultural strategies British publishers deployed both before and after African independence, strategies that sometimes overlapped and other times worked against one another. However, no matter how many relationships they fostered or titles they produced, the fact remained that companies such as Oxford University Press and Heinemann Educational Books were in Africa to make profits.

It is no revelation to say that the entrenchment of British publishing structures in the former empire was a clear form of cultural imperialism. Through systems of capital and international copyright, British publishers had a large say in how, what, and who was published out of Africa. Foreign publishing structures impacted more than just the unprofitability of African publishing, as new African writers made decisions about language, subject, and style based on the overseas publisher and the overseas audience. Many African writers resisted these structures in their writing and in their organizing. However, when writers sought local alternatives, they were also unsatisfied, as political and economic conditions often made it difficult for African initiatives to establish themselves and build readerships. Altogether, this explains how foreign publishing in general, and British publishing in particular, continued to dominate the avenues for publication in

Africa. The writers who were most capable of circumventing the British publishing control were the Soyinkas, the Achebes, and the Ngũgĩs—writers with international reputations. Once there was a demand for their writing, these individuals demanded alternative means of making their voices heard.

That sets up a salient discord between how British and African actors each look back on the same history. British publishers' accounts—of which there are many—portray themselves embracing a new role as patrons of African writing. Whether speaking about Rex Collings at Oxford, or Alan Hill or James Currey at Heinemann, they tell a history of African literature where African writers are peripheral personalities. The British publishers share the language of uplift and patronage to paint themselves as confident and daring, all in the name of bestowing African writing to the world. They could not make these claims if not for the postcolonial writers that they speak of. The writers who enter into British publishing histories and who become the evidence of British accomplishment also look back on this history in their own writing. Beginning in this period and carrying forth to today, African writers continue to contest the aesthetics, forms, and language that British colonialism first imposed and cultural imperialism still imposes on them. In their writing, they continue to resist British cultural imperialism, while British publishing firms continue to publish them.

6

From Culture to Aid to Paid

Cultural Relations after Empire

Colin Perchard remembers Malawi's independence celebration very clearly—it took place just two weeks after he had arrived in central Africa to begin his first British Council posting. Perchard, then twenty-three years old, had joined the council straight out of university. Having studied modern history, he had a choice of careers, but he was attracted to the council's work because it seemed to him, he recalled decades later, "a kind of secular missionary work."[1] His first several months with the council were meant to prepare him for such service: after an introductory course in London, the class of recruits moved to Madrid for three months to gain a background in teaching English. Toward the end of that stay, each man received a letter from the council's headquarters that contained their first posting. Perchard remembers opening the letter and then, in what was a sort of rite of passage for the council's recruits, scrambling over to an atlas to find where Nyasaland was. Then, before he knew it, he was aboard a ship heading south.

Colin Perchard and the other men in the 1963 class of recruits were part of a new generation inside the British Council. After a Treasury-imposed hiring freeze for much of the 1950s, the council had only recently begun recruiting career officers once again. Lifting the freeze was one part of the government's renewed support for the British Council in an attempt to respond to changing global politics. As chapter 1 discussed, the British government's support came with the expectation that the council would orient itself toward new populations, pivoting away from Europe and elites and devoting itself more to Africa, Asia, and the Middle East and mass audiences. While that chapter showed how the council changed the message behind its promotion of British arts, the even larger pattern over the next several decades was that those activities, like the arts, became less and less central to the council's work.

To Perchard and other council officials of his generation, the beginnings of a dramatic transformation of the council's work became apparent from the very start of their service. When Perchard arrived in then-colonial Nyasaland in June 1964, he was the second of two London-appointed council officers. He spent most of his first year doing, in his words, the council's general dogsbody work, overseeing the library service and touring the northern part of the country with film reels of *Richard III*. Even during this year, though, Perchard could see change on the horizon. Directives from the council's London headquarters instructed him to take over more administrative work for Britain's technical cooperation training, until the council officials were essentially the in-country agents for British technical aid to Malawi. From the British Council office, they arranged for British scientists and engineers to visit Malawi and provide consultation services for the University of Malawi's new science department. The council also became the overseas arm of Britain's Voluntary Service Overseas (VSO) program, which meant Perchard's office was responsible for placing and managing more than seventy-five VSO volunteers in Malawi each year. Although Perchard continued to do the Shakespeare film tour and library services (tasks he called "1950s British Council work"), administering technical aid came to occupy more and more of his time each year. By the time he left the position four years later, the council's office in Malawi employed five London-appointed staff, including two English-language teaching specialists. When Perchard returned to central Africa in 1980, the council oversaw more than £1,690,000 in expenditures in Malawi alone.[2]

Beginning their careers in the early 1960s, Perchard and others like him had front-row seats to the ways that decolonization was a shockwave to the British Council's role and activities in most parts of the world. The council remained Britain's official cultural relations body, but the bulk of its activity changed profoundly during the decades after Britain lost its empire. At the start of that period, the council anticipated much greater involvement in English-language teaching, itself a field that underwent a large transformation during this time. As an activity that fit squarely within its original mission from the 1930s, the council viewed teaching English as the most natural way for it to expand its presence in Africa, Asia, and other parts of the decolonizing world. Yet, as Colin Perchard's experience in Malawi reflected and as the rest of the chapter describes, English-language activities were not all the council was doing. The British government now defined its former colonies as developing nations, which brought them into the realm of the British development apparatus. Seeing the government place increasing attention (and money) into the category of overseas aid brought the council to want "in" on the action. It succeeded, and by the middle of the 1970s—a decade that council officials remembered as the watershed years—the British Council oversaw local administration of all overseas educational aid, over £25 million each year. By the 1980s, the council was still described in broad terms as a cultural institution; yet its activities in most parts of the world comprised management and administration.

"How did the Malawians react to you? Did they see you as a postcolonial institution or somebody who could give them genuine help?" The question—which another retired council officer posed to Perchard in the middle of an oral history interview—interrupted what was a free-flowing conversation until that point. Perchard took a deep inhale, followed by a pause before he answered. "That's a very difficult one. Ah. . . I think as our profile grew, they came to appreciate us more." He went on to describe the specialists the British Council started to bring out in science and mathematics education and the increasing numbers of VSO volunteers and finally arrived at the answer that yes, the Malawians appreciated the British Council.[3] The question—and the hesitation it prompted—gets at the tension that hovers over this history, not only of the British Council's work after empire, but also the history of the cultural project of empire more broadly. In this case, the interviewer was asking Perchard to interrupt his telling of his well-meaning hard work to state whether it had forged any relationships or even done any good. Perchard's audible reaction reflected that he was, in many ways, uncomfortable with having to question whether postcolonial populations were convinced that Britain sought an entirely new relationship with them—or whether it was empire in another guise. Whatever his thoughts, what Perchard landed on was quite similar to how BBC broadcasters or British publishers might have responded—namely, to underline Britain's tangible assistance as something that more than compensated for any of Africans' lingering emotions.

Raising the question, and the answers it provoked, points at the significance of questioning how the British Council and other British institutions forged roles for themselves in postcolonial Africa. This period of the council's history reveals a series of struggles over the extent to which the British Council would hold fast to what it offered to nations or change its offerings depending on how it understood a new nation's needs. When Perchard's generation of council officials, whose careers span the decades under study, look back on their role in these decisions, they now describe the decades after empire as a period when Britain lost something valuable. They were attracted to an imperial mission that hinged on the power of British culture; yet, over their careers, they saw that mission fade away, replaced by a set of skills and a management style. As they explained, the British Council went too far in the name of political necessity—it contorted British cultural relations too much, until it lost hold of the power of British culture, and with it the endeavor of liberal empire.

"FROM CULTURE . . ."

When British Council officials learned of a British colony attaining independence, there was one word on their minds: *opportunity*. Political independence (and more importantly, the resulting departure of the British colonial government) would lift the constraints of the definition document, leaving the council free to bring its work to any parts of a population it wanted. At the British Council headquarters in London, officials spoke excitedly about all the new activities their organization could finally take up in more parts of the world, including bringing African civil servants to the United Kingdom for training programs, more extensive library services, and more elaborate English-language teaching schemes.[4] These were activities that they performed regularly in foreign territories and felt should have been part of their work all along because it tied to their mission of propagating knowledge of British behavior and culture to influential populations around the world.

Among all the council's activities, the one at the center of its officials' minds at this time was English. Their rationale was quite straightforward: the council already oversaw the direct teaching of English to foreigners through its British Institutes in Europe, Latin America, and the Middle East, and new national governments would undoubtedly demand the same. In addition, the council was confident that encouraging the use of English overseas was central to its directive to promote an understanding of Britain overseas—in contrast to the questions that arose over the meaning of "British culture," everyone knew what the English language was. Therefore, when council officials planned for English-language teaching to be the spearhead of their expanded involvement in new nations, they did not think there would be any ambiguity over how to approach the teaching of English or over what form of spoken English they should aim for.

Prior to the 1960s, the council saw English as a form of cultural knowledge about Britain that should be learned in conjunction with other components of British culture. One of the main ways the council supported the teaching of English as a foreign language was through *English Language Teaching*, the monthly periodical for overseas language teachers it started in 1947. Under the editorship of the council's linguistic adviser, A. S. Hornby, the journal's first volumes contained articles on sentence patterns, exercises, and corrective treatments that reflected a very practical approach to linguistic pedagogy. However, these early volumes also reflected Hornby and the council's anxieties about being *too* pragmatic in how they described their language. In the inaugural editorial, Hornby dismissed the thought that foreign language study should be described in utilitarian terms, and instead described language as having a much higher value for one's knowledge and contributions to civilization.[5] In the second issue, Hornby felt compelled to explain that although at face value this was a journal that propagated technical aspects of teaching English, there was a profound danger of putting too much attention on techniques. He expressed his fear that language learning would become too "dehumanized and mechanized," as teachers might become so caught up with teaching skills that they failed to teach literature and other humanities.[6] Hornby was not alone in his anxiety; during this same era, the British Council established a new English Studies advisory panel that struggled over whether language or literature should be at the heart of its subject matter. Like Hornby, the panel decided that the English language was not a standalone subject and must instead be treated through its integration with literature and other forms of cultural knowledge.

With *English Language Teaching*, the British Council established itself as an authority in a fledgling field of linguistic study. The journal drew most of its editorial board members from University of London staff, but although several were academic phoneticians, they were not specialists in English-language teaching. Most of that was because during this era—the 1940s and 1950s—there was no such specialized field. The second editor of the journal, Raymond Butlin, commented in 1952 that the field was so small there were only a handful of people he could ask to write contributions. That certainly bore true for the first five years: out of the 144 articles that appeared in the issues, over half came from just nine authors. (Hornby himself wrote 20.)[7] Instead of an academic background, almost all the contributors worked for the British Council, where, like Hornby, their familiarity with the subject came from experience working overseas, not specialized training. For the first half of the 1950s, the council continued to draw its authority in English-language study from its experience working within cultural relations, not from academic research. Nevertheless, its activities—the periodical, the English Studies advisory panel, and direct teaching at British Institutes—were enough to make it stand out as a leading body in what remained an embryonic specialty.

As tempting as it might be to dismiss *English Language Teaching* as an amateur publication, its appearance was significant in a few ways that would be important later. First, as a council publication, its issues were automatically distributed worldwide to the council's representations and libraries in over seventy colonies and nations. Second, the publication reflected how the British Council had begun to connect with several other British institutions that had direct interest in growing the number of English speakers around the world. Their names will sound familiar: British publishing firms, such as Oxford University Press and Longmans, and the BBC. The council hoped to develop reciprocal relationships with each of these bodies; thus, it ensured its journal helped sell their products. Therefore, *English Language Teaching* contained a book reviews section, where one found reviews of student readers, translation dictionaries, books on pedagogy, and the like. It also contained advertisements. In addition, the journal ran articles by the BBC's R. J. Quinault on the usefulness of the "English by Radio" programs.[8]

Although the council's direct teaching of English during the 1940s and early 1950s was hardly worldwide, activities such as the *English Language Teaching* periodical laid groundwork for the reciprocal links between British institutions that the worldwide English-language industry would grow around.

Political circumstances—namely, anticipating the loss of the empire—finally forced the British Council to speak more pragmatically about the English language and how it could be used. Although the council took steps to promote some of the more practical aspects of language teaching during the 1950s, it continued to treat the English language as one part of British cultural knowledge—not a standalone skill. That tendency was especially self-reinforced in the British colonies, where the council only interacted with educated elites. But during the 1950s, the council received more and more signals that it needed to change how it approached cultural relations work. First there was the Drogheda Report that recommended the council pivot toward Asia, the Middle East, and Africa—regions of the world where educational aid took priority over the cultural arts. The council's new director-general, Sir Paul Sinker, embraced the Drogheda committee's recommendations (as well as the additional funding that came with them) and named educational work as the first of what he termed the council's "Main Tasks."[9] As for exactly what this would mean for English-language teaching, the clearest signal from the government—holders of the purse-strings that it was—came in 1956 with an interdepartmental committee report on Teaching English Overseas. The report quickly dismissed the council's view that English study must be treated in conjunction with other forms of cultural knowledge. Instead, it described the commercial advantages for Britain in much more direct terms.

> English is a commodity in great demand all over the world; it is wanted not only for reasons of friendship and trade with the English-speaking countries but also for other reasons not necessarily connected with any desire to imitate British ways or to understand British history and culture. We are, therefore, looking at the language mainly as a valuable and coveted export which many nations are prepared to pay for, if it can be supplied in the right quantities, and which some others would be glad to have on subsidised terms if they cannot pay the full price.[10]

The report's message to the council was clear: let potential customers learn English for whatever reasons they want. It took the same stance that the council had been making in defense of cultural relations for decades—that English was an export that would attract other exports—but instead of treating English as cultural knowledge, the report treated it as a utilitarian commodity. Even if this view refuted the council's traditional approach, it did not dismiss the agency itself. Instead, governmental reports from the second half of the 1950s expected the council to take the lead in what Britain now needed from English-language teaching programs.

The upswell in the development of English-language teaching expertise and specialization did not begin until the 1960s, and then it was because of demand from the former empire. By the early 1960s, the council had taken its cue from the British government and adopted a more pragmatic way of speaking about the usefulness of English. That came through, for example, when the council expounded upon the importance of a common language for maintaining a cohesive Commonwealth; but instead of describing a shared culture and heritage, now the council's message focused on administrative efficiency and economic efficacy.[11] The Commonwealth also forced Britain to confront the degree to which it was unprepared to help other parts of the world learn English. During the First Commonwealth Education Conference, representatives from new Commonwealth nations emphasized that teaching English as a *second* language (ESL) was different from teaching it as a foreign language in the non-Anglo-world, and therefore necessitated special training and attention all its own. New Commonwealth members demanded more and better-trained ESL teachers, to which the United Kingdom delegation eagerly responded, committing to send large numbers of British teachers overseas and to train larger numbers of Commonwealth teachers in Britain. The UK delegates who made these promises assumed that of course Britain would be able to meet them—after all, Britain was the birthplace of the English language. Only after the conference did the delegates learn that, in fact, Britain was by no means capable of meeting its commitments. Over the following year, linguists repeatedly explained to the British Council's executives that teaching English as a second language was different from teaching it to native speakers, and thus was not something any regular British teacher could automatically do. Instead, to do it well required special training—training that was difficult to obtain in Britain, since very few universities had courses in what was still an embryonic field. (At that time, the only university programs in ESL were at the University of London's Institute of Education, which trained eighteen graduates each year, and the University of Edinburgh's School of Applied Linguistics, with three.) When asked what it would take for Britain to catch up and then lead the field, the linguists' advice was straightforward: encourage research in ESL, establish a clearing-house for new information on teaching English, and create a career structure for English-language teaching professionals.[12]

The discussions in 1960 marked the beginning of a flurry of attention toward English-language teaching over the next several years during which Britain attempted to form specific plans and put them into action. At the Second Commonwealth Education Conference in 1962 in Delhi, where discussion again focused on the scattered, often amateurish quality of English-language teaching, Britain announced its Aid to Commonwealth English (ACE) scheme. The ACE scheme, which was to run through the British Council, responded to the specific criticism that there was no training stream and career structure for English-language teaching professionals. The new scheme stipulated that the British Council would recruit ten trainees a year and fund them to receive a year of training at London, Edinburgh, or Leeds. Then, the council would place each specialist, or ACE, in a Commonwealth member country for three or four years, where they would lend their expertise to the national government as it built its own curriculum.[13]

British officials invested heavily in the potential multiplying power of the ACE scheme. In 1964 at the next Commonwealth Education Conference, Britain announced it was going to double the number of ACE trainees by the end of the 1960s.[14] A handful of English-language specialists had become one more item that Britain offered new national governments in its aid packages, and Britain was encouraged to see African and Asian governments request these experts. The host nation got to determine how to best use their form of British aid, and over the 1960s and 1970s ACEs served in a variety of positions. Several acted as lecturers in teacher-training colleges, some oversaw English-language information centers, and others were seconded to the Ministry of Education where they oversaw textbook and curriculum development. (For example, Clive Brasnett, who was attached to the Kenya Institute of Education and wrote the Oxford Progressive Peak course, was an ACE.) On top of these responsibilities, several nations also assigned the specialists to make purchases for and run new language laboratories, which were sound booths with two-channel tape recorders and other equipment that civil servants and teachers could use to practice their speaking skills (figure 10). Overall, the British Council celebrated the ACE scheme because it added sixty experts to the council's permanent service. When the council started to recruit its first ACE cohorts, it noticed most applicants were former colonial education officials.[15] They would serve overseas once again under the ACE scheme, but now, the council told itself, the officials were equipped with specialized training.

During the 1960s, the British Council strengthened its position within Britain as the authoritative body of English-language teaching. During these years, the British government recognized that in lieu of formal empire it needed to devote resources and attention to the spread of the English language. The government then turned to the council to carry out its aims. As the council was drawn into academic research and specialized training, the council's advisory bodies and publications reflected its commitment to treating English as a technical skill. The council's complete move away from treating English as a type of cultivated knowledge about Britain tracked closely with another shift in attitude at the same time, this one regarding British officials' standards for spoken English.

By the early 1960s, most of the officials at the British Council had embraced a more open-minded, less imperial-sounding, approach to spoken language, meaning that they had broadened their standards for what passed as an acceptable form of the language. The handful of officials who continued to disparage nonnative speakers' diction, grammar, and accents were scorned for their elitist, imperial

FIGURE 10. At the British Council Language Laboratory and Education Centre in Accra, an assistant education officer practices his pronunciation while the British Council's English-language officer looks on. The National Archives, Kew, United Kingdom, INF 10/121/49 (1964).

attitudes. Such was the case in 1963, when the British Council reappointed Richard Frost as representative to Kenya—a position he had held years earlier—just a few months before Kenya's independence. Frost's briefing notes tried to emphasize, "The Kenya you will be returning to is a very different place from the Kenya you left in 1955."[16] Frost still expressed surprise, however, when he realized how much focus he was supposed to devote to black Africans' education. He revealed his attitudes starkly when he wrote back to London comments such as, "I do not know what is meant by Kenyan English. You cannot mean the kind of English which, I am told, is spoke by the ill-educated, who, for instance, when bitten by a snake, might say 'That beef done chop me bad.'"[17] (Frost didn't restrict his comments to

English-speaking Kenyans—he also wrote plenty of disparaging remarks about West Africans and South Asians whose English he had overheard when he was in England.) Frost held fast to the belief that political handover should not change anything; the British Council had a duty, in his view, to display the English language in its proper form for Africans to emulate.[18] These were the same attitudes he held when he worked in Kenya during the early 1950s—but back then, his comments were fairly typical among British Council representatives. When Frost expressed them during the 1960s, on the other hand, other council officials took him to task. The controller for education—who had opposed Frost's appointment and made clear he wanted to see a younger person in the position instead—labeled Frost "disturbingly ignorant" about the council's new educational mission.[19] Frost would only stay in Kenya for two years, which were marked by repeated clashes with London headquarters over his resistance to expanding council activities beyond elite Kenyan circles to the masses. After his departure, the council's top officials explained to the incoming representative in no uncertain terms that the council's primary role was educational work and assisting the development of Kenya's national educational system. Frost, and Frost's attitudes, were on their way out, now replaced with a broader set of standards that was in line with the council's new orientation toward educational aid.

As the British Council investigated how to increase English-language teaching efforts to meet rising demand, there was one obvious group for them to turn to: the Americans. British officials—both government and council—viewed cooperation with the Americans as a way to gain access to much greater funding and resources than they could ever expect from their own Treasury. The more the British Council executives heard about the well-funded activities of USAID and the Ford Foundation, the more they professed the need to collaborate.[20] Starting in 1961, British and American officials began meeting semi-regularly to discuss concrete ways they could work together to foster English-language learning all over the world. The meetings reflected how English-language teaching activities spread across state and nonstate agencies, and representatives from the US State Department, USAID, USIA, the Ford Foundation, the Foreign Office, the Commonwealth Relations Office, the British Council, and the BBC were typically in attendance.

Going into these meetings, the British delegates recognized the need to be diplomatic. This was despite what they said among themselves, when they regularly harped that as plentiful as American resources might be, the United States was crippled by short-termism. British officials expressed horror whenever an American project boldly claimed it could fully meet the demand for English in the span of five years, or that non-expert university graduates—a.k.a. United States Peace Corps volunteers—would carry out teacher training. In their criticism of the Americans, the British implicitly defended their own "British way" that prioritized

long-term quality over short-term quantity and allotted resources toward a professional career track, complete with specialized training.[21] But despite their pri-
vately held opinions, during the first meeting the representatives from the United
Kingdom were careful to acknowledge that the English language did not belong
to Britain alone, and that Americans also had a place in the history of English-
language teaching around the world.[22] The 1961 meeting was largely exploratory
but opened channels of communication as each nation built up its ELT infrastructure over the following years. In London, the British Council established the
aforementioned clearinghouse, the English Language Information Centre, while
in Washington, the Ford Foundation funded the Center for Applied Linguistics.
The stated aim of both centers was to act as a repository and collection of all current research being done in the field, and to link academic research with actual
teaching on the ground.

As might have been expected, the prospect of cooperation forced Britain and
the United States to discuss what version of English they wanted to promote
around the world. In what became labeled an issue of "intercomprehensibility,"
some attendees at a 1963 meeting observed that English in one part of the world
could be vastly different from that in another, to the point that not all English
speakers could even understand each other. These American and British officials
did not believe that the main difficulties were between their own Englishes, but
rather between variants of English among nonnative speakers. To address this
issue, British and American officials declared that their outward position—or
what they would tell populations in different parts of the world—was that British
and American English were really quite similar. To help with this, the BBC and the
Voice of America agreed to work together on a joint series of ten programs that
demonstrated how learners of one variant or the other could readily understand
other English speakers.[23] Meanwhile, the British Foreign Office began reminding
its embassies that "our object was not to attempt to standardise English speech,
but rather to ensure that local variants did not exceed the limits of mutual com-
prehensibility."[24] Many of the British Council's officials already held this view,
as the prior condemnation of Richard Frost had revealed, and even the council's
governing board had come to embrace that new tolerance. For instance, in the
mid-1960s, the council's executive committee discussed the signs that an Indian
form of English was developing and concluded that this was probably inevitable
and they would not stop it, provided that Indians could still communicate with
people in other parts of the world.[25]

All of this was meant to demonstrate to potential learners of English that English
was a welcoming language and a language for practical use. (The British meant
to show that English was quite different from, say, French, where they believed
French-language instructors made a mistake in fixating on only one academic-
level language.)[26] Anglo-American cooperation around English-language teaching

as well as Britain's embrace of variants of English reflected how Britain sought to promote English after empire. Looking forward, Britain downplayed a nationalist version of the English language and replaced it with an inclusive and malleable language that anyone in the world could take up and use.

The council's new attitude toward the inclusiveness and usefulness of English tracked with changes that were happening in the profession, as English-language teaching was increasingly recognized as its own specialization. The first half of the 1960s were pivotal for the field of English as a second language, when state officials, private entities, and academics in both Britain and the United States began to respond to overseas demand and address deficiencies in how they approached the subject. Applied linguists who entered the profession during these years remember feeling that they were a part of something on the cusp of taking off. Individuals such as David Crystal, whose imposing career dates back to this era, credit the British Council with providing the administrative support and connective fascia that his field desperately needed. In particular, Crystal pointed to the council's new corps of English-language specialists as the pivotal element that professionalized British ELT overseas.[27]

Crystal's praise was somewhat self-congratulatory, as he and other academics like him enjoyed a symbiotic relationship with the British Council throughout their careers. The council helped develop the market for ELT research and publications, for which Crystal directly benefitted. In exchange, Crystal's lengthy CV made him a valuable expert for the council; in addition to a long tenure on the English Studies Advisory Committee, Crystal later sat on the council's board of governors—his presence a signal of how central ELT was to the council's operations. The British Council also pushed for the establishment of an international professional association, and the International Association of Teachers of English as a Foreign Language (IATEFL) started in Britain in 1967. There was no doubt about it—in comparison to where it was just one decade earlier, by the late 1960s English-language teaching was a recognized profession bolstered by academic research, specialized training, a market for its materials, and professional associations. The British Council saw that it had a hand or a connection in each of these, allowing the council to maintain its position as Britain's authoritative body on English-language teaching.

After spending several decades preserving the national character of the English language, the British Council adopted a new attitude in a fairly short period of time. Between the late 1950s and early 1960s, Britain's official cultural propagation agency stopped promoting the English language as something attached to British culture and civilization, and instead began speaking of spoken English in inclusive and pragmatic terms. During these same years, accelerating demand from new Commonwealth nations exposed how amateur Britain's approach to English-language teaching had been previously, and so the council also oriented itself around a more research-driven and technical approach to the English-language teaching profession. Academic research, increasing professionalization, and the prospect of collaboration with the Americans only accelerated the speed at which the English language lost its specifically national character as something explicitly British. The British Council remained an active participant in the process, which showed that it viewed it as a politically necessary direction for British cultural relations. The council's transformation reflected what it anticipated as the new direction of its work after the end of European imperialism—work that would focus less on culture and more on the delivery of educational aid.

"... TO AID ..."

As much attention as it gave to language teaching, the British Council expected English to be merely the spearhead of a whole slew of new activity in Africa. But before the council could deploy all its plans, it first had to make sure that host governments would allow it to work in their nations. Many of the top officials at the council recognized they needed to appear as conciliatory and unobtrusive as possible. After visiting Nigeria, for example, the director-general, Sir Paul Sinker, commented that "In spite of their anxiety for continued British educational aid, and in spite of the very easy personal relations that exist between British and Nigerians, there is still a strong latent suspicion of anything that might appear to Nigerian susceptibilities to savour of the Colonial period." He went on to explain how the council had to adopt its approach around these attitudes. "[Therefore] it is important that the Council should not give any impression to trying to push. We must be content, where necessary, to wait—a policy that paid off well in India and Pakistan—and to get the Nigerians to push us in the direction we want to go."[28] On the ground in new nations like Nigeria, British Council representatives leaned on their personal relationships with members of the new administrations. In conversation, they stressed the council's neutrality—that it had not really been a part of the colonial administration, that it was not really Britain's official diplomatic body—to make their intentions appear benign. The goal, the director-general stressed, was to present the council as the "unobtrusive link" between national authorities and the British High Commission—all the while, of course, acting as the "eyes and ears" for British development agencies.[29]

English-language teaching was the inroad to greater and greater involvement in a nation's educational system. During that same Nigeria trip, Sinker met with the federal prime minister Abubakar Tafawa Balewa, whom he said spoke with "special warmth" about British assistance for English learning. When Sinker relayed the conversation back in London, he explained that through the subject of English the groundwork was laid for the council to be drawn into Nigeria's entire educational system. Then, when other African nations gained independence later, the council could point to Nigeria as a model of what it could do.[30] The council's high hopes for Nigeria came in part from the relatively good relationship Britain had with the nation during the years right after independence, but even in less friendly nations Britain could still rely on at least some demand for English. Take Ghana, for instance, where Kwame Nkrumah and his ministers frequently railed against Western neocolonialism, yet still declared English as their national language and pursued English-language teaching assistance.[31] The council's representatives in Ghana realized they needed to be sensitive (among other things, they trained themselves to call English a *Ghanaian* language, not a foreign one, so that it might appear more savory to the government) but believed that most of the Ghanaian ministers' rhetoric was just bluster.[32] In their contact with new national governments in Africa, most council officials relied on an argument that their agency's intentions were benign. While making this point, council officials also sought to persuade African ministers of how useful the British Council could be for them, especially while national governments designed their educational systems. Meanwhile, back in London the council engaged in a very different sort of politics as it carved out a role for itself in Britain's development aid apparatus.

During the early 1960s, the council found itself in a whole different position than it had been in a decade earlier. In stark contrast to the austerity measures and constant fear of elimination, the council saw that now when it requested additional funds, it received them. For example, for the 1963–64 budget year, the council received over £1 million more from the Treasury than it had the year before, bringing its annual budget above £8.5 million. Besides covering its rising costs, the council had also requested funds to expand in certain activities and regions— which it received. Half of those expansion funds were meant for English-language teaching and education specifically, and another quarter were to increase representation and services in the continent of Africa.[33] The next year, the council again received a budget increase of almost £1 million for new activities. Even when the organization did have to contemplate cuts later in the decade, it did not even consider cutting any English-language teaching activities, proposing instead to reduce services in Jamaica and Barbados (where there was no scope for ELT) as well as places such as the Congo and Aden, where it was having a lot of difficulties doing work anyway, due to the violent conflicts taking place there.[34] By the end of the 1960s, the council's budget reflected the degree to which English-language teaching in the developing world, and especially Africa, had become strategic priorities for the British government.

The council's relative comfort during these years reflected a larger shift within the British government, which started to see overseas development as one of its central functions. The British Council ensured it was part of that conversation. Over the 1960s and 1970s, successive British governments reorganized the administrative structures that oversaw British aid, whether it was the Department of

Technical Co-operation (DTC), the Ministry of Overseas Development (ODM), or the Overseas Development Administration (ODA).[35] Whatever the name and place of the department or ministry, British Council officials saw a constant during these decades—namely, that overseas aid could provide them with a new imperative and new funding. During the mid-1960s, the director-general used the creation of the new ministry for overseas development as a chance to secure another arm of funding. He underlined that most of what the council was now doing to promote Britain in the "developing world" incidentally contributed to development; therefore, a portion of the council's funds should come out of the ODM vote. He recognized the ODM vote was structured differently from the funds from the overseas departments, which distributed budgets by representation (colony or nation) and to council departments in London (such as arts, books and periodicals, or the English language.) In contrast, the ODM's budget was broken down into specific projects to which ODM awarded funds. During the mid-1960s, the council successfully bid to act as an agent of ODM for educational work in Sudan, Ethiopia, and Brazil. In its bids, the council emphasized what it felt was its strongest argument: economy to Her Majesty's Government.[36] The council already had an operation on the ground in each nation, it explained, as well as a relationship with each national government. Getting these bids marked the beginning of a pattern that would hold for the next decade and a half, where the ODM or ODA provided the funds and the council's offices and officials administered the work. The activities included teacher training and English-language services (what the council had been doing for years) as well as investment in new facilities and supplies—a new type of work for the council.

Over the next fifteen years, agency work along these lines came to represent almost all the council's funds in the developing world. Starting in 1966, when the ODM contributed 36 percent of the council's grant-in-aid from the government, direct funds from the ODM plus agency work through the ODM became a larger and larger portion of the council's budget (see figure 11). This signified not just that the council had continued to move away from Europe and other developed parts of the world, but also the degree to which the council's activities were now in the name of overseas development. Meanwhile, the council's relationship with the ODM was gradually becoming more formalized; after a series of inquiries over the second half of the 1960s, the Mark/Philips Report in 1969 determined that the council would automatically act as the agents for all British educational aid. The government expected the council to recognize the different sources of its funds as "information" and "aid" strands (depending on whether the funds came from the FCO or ODM votes) and the government would set the ratio between those activities that the council needed to adhere to.[37]

The council was no longer an organization that feared its elimination; instead, it was the organization that swallowed other smaller bodies. The British Council

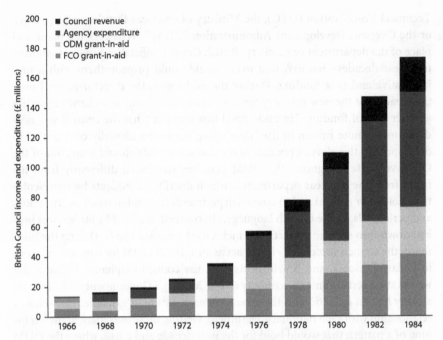

FIGURE 11. British Council annual expenditure in £ millions, broken down by income source. (Sources: *British Council Annual Reports*; Frances Donaldson, *The British Council: The First Fifty Years*, appendix A)

was already the overseas arm for VSO and two other British volunteer programs, meaning that council officials overseas helped select volunteers, initiated and vetted in-country placements, and then acted as the volunteers' contact should problems arise. The council also administered the Aid to Commonwealth English (ACE) scheme and the Technical Cooperation Training Program (TCTP). Then, in the early 1970s, the council became the overseas arm of the ODA's Centre for Educational Development Overseas (CEDO), which provided training courses and support for education development in other countries. When the council formally took over CEDO in 1974, it acquired large science education and visual aids departments. Brian Vale, a council official who had pushed for the council to merge fully with CEDO, reasoned later that it was only logical, as the council needed these resources so it could deliver even more aid.[38] The government's efforts to reduce the number of overseas development quangos did not end there. It expanded the council's official remit yet again in 1981, when the council absorbed both the Inter-University Council for Higher Education Overseas (IUC) and the Technical Education and Training Organisation for Overseas Countries (TETOC).[39] By gaining the latter, the council was now in an even stronger position to undertake training projects outside the field of education: technical, industrial, agricultural, vocational, management training, etcetera. Altogether, the pattern of the 1970s was of the council's role growing larger in every direction: the ODM gave it ever increasing funds for it to administer an increasing number of projects that were also growing larger in scope. The council's executives pursued every avenue; in their minds, each opportunity for expansion was further protection against any talk that their organization was redundant. Another way to phrase it, from the perspective of someone lower down in the council's ranks, was that the 1970s were the decade of the ODM "milk cow."[40]

As the council's funding and activities changed, so did its staffing. Over the 1960s and 1970s, the council's staff reflected the degree to which it had become increasingly oriented toward overseas development. As mentioned at the start of this chapter, the council started its general career service entry scheme in 1956 after a seven-year hiring freeze. Until this point, the typical council official had come to the organization after already gaining experience in another field—perhaps as a university lecturer in the humanities, perhaps a distinguished writer or poet. That was when the council still described an important part of its overseas work as forming personal relationships; however, this group also contributed to the council's reputation as nothing but a group of elitist, long-haired aesthetes. In the mid-1950s, the council received word that it could resume hiring at the same time that the government instructed it to build much more of a presence in the so-called developing world, especially by extending its educational services. Top officials at the council designed the new career service entry scheme accordingly, planning to recruit about a dozen entrants a year and gradually build a cadre of general-ists who could carry that new work forward. Starting in the late 1950s the council sought men such as Colin Perchard: fresh-faced graduates with no experience whom the organization could mold into able senior officials through a variety of postings abroad and in London.[41]

Viewing the diplomatic service as the council's main competition for gradu-ates, the council's recruiting materials depicted British Council work as more idealistic, more creative, and more varied than diplomatic work.[42] A 1965 recruit-ment pamphlet went into more detail about the personal attributes the council sought:

We therefore need men and women of intelligence and warmth who enjoy work with people. They must have good university qualifications to enable them to hold their own in local academic circles, but a wide range of interests outside their own field is almost as essential. They need more vitality than most people since they are always at the centre of a wide circle of acquaintances to whom they give time, sym-pathy and help, while they themselves are having to get to grips with a new environ-ment, a strange society and often another language. They must be clear-headed and commonsensical, able to talk reasonably well and to organize their time so that they can carry a fairly heavy administrative load without letting it get them down or get in the way of more creative activities.[43]

How did the council measure such attributes? Recruits who entered the council's career stream during these years do not remember the interview process being all that hard. One Cambridge graduate remembers hearing that it was vital to smile a lot during the interview.[44] Another Cambridge graduate, who applied in 1968, remembers being asked about Prime Minister Harold Wilson during his interview, and that he answered with a personal anecdote the interviewers seemed to enjoy.[45] While both of them were among the high percentage of general service entrants who came from Oxbridge and public schools, by the end of the decade the council expressed slightly more interest in diversifying. That was why the council considered Peter Elborn, who grew up in a Gospel Oak council flat and failed his 11-plus, but ultimately went to Swansea University. (After joining the council, Elborn was still somewhat of an anomaly; his first boss used to introduce him to others by saying, "You know, this boy failed his 11-plus. Honestly, he did! Quite extraordinary!")[46]

But by the later part of the 1960s, the council was expanding quickly, and the career generalists were only one small part of its growth. Julian Andrews, who worked in the council's Personnel Division, said this growth was because suddenly there was much greater demand for the council's work than before, and that required it to bring in a great number of staff all at once. The British Council was another government body (alongside the FCO and the ODM) that absorbed large numbers of former colonial officials. But Andrews was careful to stipulate that with only a few exceptions, the ex-colonial officers were not naturally suited for council work, mostly because they were not dynamic enough. He and others in the Personnel Division thought of most former colonial officials as time servers (i.e., in it to get their pensions) who were not actually interested in the cultural outreach mission.[47] The Personnel Division therefore parachuted the ex-colonial officers into the type of work they were suited for—what they deemed "ODA work," or the new positions responsible for overseeing aid and development projects.

The pressure to add staff did not let up over most of the 1970s, and even the injection of former colonial officers could not make up the gap in the council's staffing needs. By this point, the council's new staff were primarily specialists— whether in science education, finance, English-language teaching, etcetera—and in technical administration. Colin Perchard directed the Technical Cooperation Training Department, which was responsible for funding, placing, and overseeing six thousand to seven thousand overseas students' technical training in the United Kingdom every year. The department had a budget in the millions because training represented a large chunk of many foreign countries' overall allocation of British aid. Over the 1970s, the department grew to over one hundred development staff in size, plus ancillary staff—an "empire unto itself," as Perchard described it.[48] Many of the staff coming into the department were in their early twenties and new to the British Council, but in contrast to Perchard—who worked in Malawi, India, and Korea during his first fifteen years with the council—these men and women were unlikely to ever be posted overseas. Rather than the catch-all of tasks Perchard performed, the new staff who came to the British Council in the middle or late 1970s worked in much more focused departments, performing administrative or specialist work. By the early 1970s, the type of varied and creative work that overseas posts once entailed was now becoming increasingly rare, although the Personnel Division preserved what was left of it for their most generalist generalists.

The 1970s were a transformative decade for the council, during which Britain's premier cultural relations body came to look and act like a development agency. After the end of British rule in most of its African colonies, Britain had determined its primary way of interacting with the region would be through development and aid. The British Council followed that cue and, led by its increasing involvement in English-language teaching, more and more of the council's organizational structure grew around the delivery of technical assistance. This was especially true with regard to its funding source, its activities, and who worked for the council. During the peak of these years, such as, say, the mid-1970s, when ODM agency work surpassed £25 million per year, there was a sense in the British Council hallways that any insecurity about the agency's relevance or future was no longer pertinent. Council officials thought that now, as an essential part of Britain's delivery of aid, their future was secure. For the British Council officials who professed such confidence, the end of the 1970s would prove quite a shock.

". . . TO PAID"

Once the British Council started to become a development agency, it could not stray from the path. The more overseas development work the council did, the more the ODA controlled the council's fate; this was a point many in the council were aware of, but could not see what they could do to change it. That point comes through, for example, in a memory of David Waterhouse, who was another of the career generalists who joined the council in the early 1960s and served in Nigeria, Zambia, Nepal, and Thailand during his career. In an interview years later, Waterhouse recalled being in Thailand and preparing for a tour by the ODA chief education officer. He remembered thinking at the time that this was the most important visit the representation could possibly have, and—given how much the ODA controlled their funds—it was far more important than a visit from the council's top management. "I suppose that's a slightly dangerous position?" the interviewer pressed him. Waterhouse answered that it was what it was, and then reasoned that if not for the ODA work, many of the council's representations around the world would have been closed.[49]

Outside of its agency work for the ODM, the British Council also pursued other streams of revenue. Starting in the mid-1970s, the council got into what was essentially a business of development, where it turned what it had once offered for free into products that were available for purchase. The first such product was the British Council's consultation and administration services. After the oil crisis in the early 1970s, a handful of British Council officials saw pound signs in the requests their organization received from nations such as Saudi Arabia, Venezuela, and Nigeria. Starting in 1975 through a new section called Paid Educational Services, the council offered oil-rich developing nations a range of options for British-assisted educational services. Britain could still do the basic job, council officials explained, or if the nation wanted, Britain could provide more—for a price. In the first Paid Educational Services contract, which was a £13 million contract to build an English Language Centre at King Abdul Aziz University in Saudi Arabia, the council earned £1.6 million in eight years. (The council's official historian pointed out one of the perks of working with the Saudi Arabian government was that it paid in advance—over half the net income came from interest on advance payments.)[50] In these instances, the British Council acted as the overseas clientele's entry into the entire British specialist market. The council put together the proposal, but the various elements came from British firms and services. The thinking behind paid services commodified the council's contacts with British agencies and companies and the management expertise it had accumulated doing agency work for the ODM.

Although its consultation services were valuable, they were nothing compared to the council's real product: English. At this same time during the mid-1970s, the British Council renewed its interest in the direct teaching of English, something it had not given priority to for almost two decades. Since the British Council started giving focus to the developing world during the late 1950s, its involvement in teaching English occurred at a level removed; the council focused on training teachers and consulting on curricula instead of directly teaching students. However, the second half of the 1970s saw the council set up commercial teaching centers in many of the nations it worked in. By the mid-1980s, the council's direct teaching facilities around the world had an annual turnover of £16 million.[51] The direct teaching of English operation reflected something that a government paper from the late 1950s had observed: English was so valuable that nations would be willing to pay for it. Foreign students showed willingness to pay for the product of English as well—a demand that fueled the number of English-language schools, centers, and programs opening back in Britain, in addition to the council's direct teaching of English overseas. During the 1970s, the council had an abundance of ODA work but also sought revenue streams outside Treasury funds. Each of the avenues it pursued—Paid Educational Services and the direct teaching of English—commodified expertise and activities the council previously propagated for free under the guise of cultural diplomacy. The contractor-client principle at the heart of both pursuits exposed the governing rationality that by this point had crept close to the center of the council's administration. At the same time, this was also a revealing moment to several inside the council, when they started to realize how far the council's mission had strayed.

Even with its new profit streams, during the late 1970s the British Council came under the British government's scrutiny. In August 1977, the think tank named the Central Policy Review Staff published what became known as the Berrill report on overseas representation.[52] In stark contrast to previous inquiries, which sometimes described overseas information as an antidote to economic decline, the Berrill report said that Britain could no longer afford to act like a great power. As its introduction stated, "In today's world a country's power and influence are basically determined by its economic performance. Inevitably, therefore, the UK's ability to influence events in the world has declined and there is very little that diplomatic activity and international public relations can do to disguise the fact."[53] After identifying redundancies in the information services and inefficiencies in the delivery of overseas aid, the report proposed severe cuts to the BBC external services and abolishing the British Council all together.[54] British Council officials working in the London headquarters later described how the arrival of this report essentially traumatized the organization, especially after the false sense of security they had acquired over the past several years. With their budgets rising each year and with their relevance going unquestioned for almost two decades, council officials had lost some of the sharpness with which they defended their loftier mission. Then the Berrill report came out and MPs started debating the organization's future, meaning the British Council found itself catapulted into a defense it did not have time to prepare. One of the council's officials, Trevor Rutter, remembered feeling put on the spot and struggling to explain what cultural relations were to people who had no understanding of the concept: "We were having to defend and expound what seemed to us self-evident and obvious that what we were doing was totally worthwhile, entirely in the British interest. . . . We were arguing to skeptical think tank people and skeptical politicians."[55] This crisis, which Rutter termed the first in a series of traumas, subsided in 1978, when the British government decided to keep the council in place. (The British Council actually expanded shortly thereafter, when the government decided to merge the IUC and TETOC into the council.) But it was only a short period before British Council officials experienced the next trauma, this one with more lasting effects.

While the council responded to the Berrill report crisis by defaulting to a cultural relations defense, the council's response to the next crisis looked far more businesslike. One of the main things that Trevor Rutter took away from his interactions with the Central Policy Review Staff was how difficult it had been to establish any sort of dialogue. As he explained, "We were coming from different points of the compass," where the council could not find the right language or evidence that would map onto the think tank's terms of reference or impetus to think boldly.[56] That experience revealed to Rutter, who would soon become an assistant director-general, that the council needed to externalize that it governed itself as a firm and construed its activities in market terms.[57] Almost immediately after taking office, Prime Minister Margaret Thatcher announced the council's budget was to be reduced by 18.5 percent over the next three years. This time, the council reacted the way that a firm would. For the first time, it hired a director of public relations, who was responsible for directing a proactive public relations campaign. They rallied British industries to lobby the government on the council's behalf. Therefore, in place of the council making nebulous claims about goodwill and friendship, there were British trade associations and businesses speaking in concrete terms. The British publishers spoke forcefully about their industry's reliance on overseas sales, for which the council's book exhibitions and contacts were crucial, while British universities demonstrated how international student fees helped offset their expenses, again due to the council's overseas presence. Finally, Britain's English-language industry—meaning the more than one hundred English-language schools and centers offering language classes to foreigners—chimed in that the council's endless promotion of the value of English and of the British "brand" was what attracted thousands of foreign visitors to Britain each year.

As much as the council and its constituencies detailed the ways cultural diplomacy enhanced British exports, a large part of the council's fate came down to personality. In 1977, the council got a new chairman—Dick Troughton, a businessman who had previously served as the chairman of W. H. Smith. Rutter and the director-general, Sir John Burgh, cited Troughton as the factor that ultimately convinced the Thatcher administration to lessen the first round of cuts. Recalling a crucial 1980 meeting between Troughton and the prime minister, Rutter explained that Troughton knew instinctively how to speak to the Thatcher administration. "He accepted lots of briefing, but he didn't talk in our terms, he talked in *his* terms."[58] For his part, Burgh recalled also being meant to attend that meeting, but then he and Troughton decided against it because they knew how much the prime minister disliked civil servants.[59] Troughton's approach worked; three weeks after the meeting, the council received word its budget cut was not as severe as originally announced.[60] And yet, when speaking about the entire ordeal decades later, Trevor Rutter adopted a regretful tone nevertheless. "Value for money, show us the bottom line, and all of that. . . . [We were] put to the test by the standards of business operations, which weren't terribly relevant for an organization that was quite rightly dealing with less tangible things. But again, we had to contort ourselves to defend and respond."[61]

This moment in the early 1980s was only the beginning of what council officials would later describe as the Thatcher onslaught. Over the following decade, the British Council continued to adjust its working methods and govern itself more like a firm. For the first time, the council began accepting business sponsorship of its arts events and conferences. After public relations, the next new department was industrial relations—important, it turned out, since the government forced the council to reduce its staff and commitments. Like other agencies in this same time, the British Council's executives examined the different aspects of the organization's work with an eye to deciding which services could be contracted out or eliminated altogether. The assistant director-general, Trevor Rutter, recalled how heretical their discussions seemed at first, but then, as he and the other managers kept looking at it, the more it made sense to, for instance, cannibalize the council's expensive book supply department and tender for private contractors instead.[62] He found other decisions much more regrettable, however. Over the 1980s and early 1990s, the government continued to demand the council find parts of its budget to cut. For several years in a row they relied on what Rutter termed "salami cuts," slicing bits of the budgets in each area of the world. Finally, during a year when he was forced to find £2 million in the budget somewhere, he made the dire suggestion they close two representations in Scandinavia. Looking back, Rutter said that in his heart he wanted the cuts to appear in Africa instead, but he knew they could not propose such a thing because it would only be further proof to the ODA that the council was unworthy of its trust.[63]

Among the council's contortions during this period, it was its commitment to a project-based approach to work that ultimately determined its future. Project-based work had been part of the council's activities since the 1960s, when the organization began its relationship with the ODM, and then the council's growth during the 1970s was primarily among the specialized staff and departments that did this project-based agency work. None of this went completely unnoticed; beginning in the early 1970s certain council staff started murmuring that the organization had gone a little too far in its pursuit of ODA work and should correct course by, say, hiring more generalists instead of specialists. Most of the talk stayed as just murmurs, although there were some louder calls as well. For instance, in a 1974 memo titled "What the Council Is About," an assistant director-general described how the council's success at chasing aid funds and roles could reach the extent whereby it proved its own redundancy. He warned that if the pattern continued, there might be a moment in later years when someone asked, "If there is no distinction between the ODA and the British Council in function and motivation . . . why should the council exist?"[64] His warning certainly prompted some discussion among his colleagues in the London headquarters, but it did not lead to any action. Instead, council executives who enjoyed the feeling of security reassured themselves the line between educational aid and information work was

very often quite blurred, and the council could use that to its advantage. Whatever was happening right then, they told themselves, down the road the council
could quietly ease some of its aid-funded resources over to the informational and
cultural side, like they had once done when they used educational funds to promote Shakespeare performances.[65] Looking back decades later, one council official
scoffed at how ridiculous he and his colleagues had been in thinking they could
push back against the ODA. "We were bound to lose," he realized; "the ODA had
control over *its* budget."[66] As quick as the council had been to pursue the ODA's
funds, it was much slower to recognize the degree to which it committed itself to
parameters that the development agency decided.

Despite what they had told themselves earlier, during the 1980s the council's
management dedicated an increasing amount of its organization to a project
approach as a way of trying to stay in the government's favor. In the overseas
representations—what had been seen as the remaining space for so-termed traditional cultural outreach—representatives found themselves subject to management plans, strategic objectives, and achievement metrics.[67] The group of career
generalists who had once been recruited for their varied interests and interper-
sonal skills were now forced into the roles of managers and administrators, spending their time on bureaucratic procedures instead of individual relationships.
Meanwhile, Paid Educational Services and the direct teaching of English, which
were both continuing to grow, were premised on contractor-client relationships,
an arrangement that only further accelerated the trend. In Trevor Rutter's words,
he and his colleagues contorted themselves to the extent that they were more than
just businesslike, they were full-on businessmen. It was all part of the Thatcher
revolution, he explained, but it was also a "false holy grail."[68] The problem with
project work, as the council would soon discover, was that it did not necessarily
have to be the council that carried it out.

Over the second half of the 1980s, the ODA stopped seeing the British Council
as its agent and more as its competition. This happened for two reasons. First,
the ODA believed the council's revenue-earning departments, such as its paid
contracts and English courses, directly hurt the ODA's own efforts in those fields.
Second, the arrangement that was once heralded as efficient was now framed as
government waste. One council official remembered a famous occasion during
the late 1980s when a Commons select committee asked the ODA permanent
secretary whether he could say the British Council gave value for money—and
the permanent secretary said he could not.[69] From that point forward, the relationship between British development bodies and council officials deteriorated
quickly, both in London and on the ground in nations like India, Pakistan, and
Nigeria, where they were committed toward working together on projects worth
thousands or sometimes millions of pounds. Finally, in 1991 the ODA announced
that it was no longer going to rely on the British Council as its sole agency. Instead,

the administration would put contracts out to competitive tender and the council would have to compete, just like any other agency.

NOSTALGIA FOR LIBERAL EMPIRE

In its contortions of the 1960s, 1970s, and 1980s, the British Council reframed how it understood and described the "British culture" of British cultural relations. In contrast to earlier decades, when the council was preoccupied with the *content* of cultural promotion, beginning in the 1960s the British Council became increasingly oriented around the *managerial* component of its work. Because of the aid business, by the 1980s very little of the British Council's attention went toward the promotion of the British arts, particularly in the developing world. Instead, when the council pursued contracts from the British ODA, foreign governments, or the World Bank, its emphasis was on the value its administrative apparatus offered, regardless of the project or content. Even the council's own conception of its mission came to reflect this change. In 1981, facing government cuts, the director-general John Burgh held a senior staff conference at Ditchley Park, where the organization would have an opportunity to reformulate what the British Council's objectives had become. This would replace the council's old mission statement from the first decade of its establishment when it heralded the essentialness of British culture. The outcome of the 1981 meeting was a single sentence that described the British Council's objectives: "To promote an enduring understanding and appreciation of Britain through educational, cultural, and technical cooperation with other countries."[70] The council finally acknowledged in official terms that the ubiquitous, hard-to-articulate, harder-to-pin-down term *culture* was not its singular objective any longer. Instead, culture followed education, and both appeared in the same phrase as technical cooperation.

Of course, there were some at the British Council who praised the overall transformation, believing that it signaled how Britain could adapt to changing global circumstances. For example, Brian Vale was one of the individuals behind creating the Paid Educational Services division in 1975, and he viewed that as well as other organizational changes to be some much-needed flexibility. The 1970s were a battle, as Vale described it, between some of his colleagues, who held on to an old idea of a secular cultural mission, and he and other forward-thinking officials who crucially recognized that Britain needed to be pragmatic in how it approached other nations. For Vale, the British Council promoted Britain's interests overseas by doing whatever the situation most called for. He explained, "If you're in France you do cultural work, if you're in Zambia you do aid work. . . . If the Saudis wanted to solve their scientific and educational problems by throwing money at them, then we were on hand to provide the resources that they were willing to pay for."[71] Overall, therefore, this was the time when Britain's cultural relations agency truly came to reflect all aspects of overseas life: "the cultural was now 'Cultural, Aid, and Paid.'"[72] To hear Vale describe it, the transformation to British cultural relations after the end of the British Empire was pivotal because otherwise Britain would have lost its relevance in the world.

But Brian Vale was an exception. Many of his contemporaries at the British Council now speak regretfully about the changes they experienced in terms of what it meant to do cultural relations work. Coming into the council during the early 1960s, they were excited to be part of an organization that would carry Britain into the era after empire. While other British agencies might have been concerned with what decolonization would mean for Britain's global role, men like Colin Perchard and his peers felt emboldened that British cultural relations could ensure there was continuity, and Britain could continue to have prestige and influence in the world.

When these former British Council officials think back on the beginning of their careers, it is with profound nostalgia for a different way of forging relationships with people in other parts of the world. They describe the 1960s as a period when British cultural relations still included some creativity and serendipity, all the way down to the people it sought to employ. For instance, Audrey Lambert (who stands out as one of the very few women of this generation) reminisced that when she first joined, the council still had a number of "eccentrics" who worked for it, including distinguished writers and poets. "By the time I left, there was just no time for that. There was so much administration, so much bureaucracy, so much worry about finances all the time, about making money as opposed to just managing, bidding for contracts with the World Bank, etcetera, etcetera. There was no time to sit down and write poetry, which I think is sad because I think the council lost some of that."[73] When accounting for their own experiences, she and others framed the changes to their day-to-day workload—which they clearly resented—as something more meaningful by saying British cultural relations lost an important way of connecting with individuals. Across their recollections, this is an idea that former council officials keep returning to—that Britain once distinguished itself in the cultural relations field because it focused on meaningful, individual relationships. However, over their careers they saw that slip away. During an oral history interview in 2007, Peter Elborn said he cringed whenever he read or heard that the British Council now reached millions of people in the world, because he believed it spoiled the council's true mission.[74] Trevor Rutter said his decision to take early retirement during the 1990s occurred when he realized the British Council had replaced individual bonds with client relationships.[75] Their tones reflect not so much anger at their organization as a general regret about how the world changed in a way that the sorts of relationships they remembered had become much rarer.

When this group of British officials explains how the British Council's remit changed, they describe an organization that abandoned its liberal mission in the face of temptation. One official wrote that the moment the council began ODM work was the moment it "lost the purity of its ethos."[76] Using less formal terms, another explained that the British Council effectively prostituted itself for money and put on display its willingness to give up the careful thought that once drove British cultural relations.[77] He wished his organization had protected its original mission, "We were not in the aid business. Full stop finish—that's what we should have been saying, very clearly. Our business was a different one."[78] Thus, these British individuals portray themselves as the last bearers of a view that was in danger, the view that no, Britain should not adjust its cultural relations approach according to what another nation most needed. Instead, they are saying that what the whole world really needed, whether it realized it or not, was British culture: British arts, British literature, British traditions, and British political values.

If what they envisioned sounds familiar, it is because it was. Their notions of a purity of ethos, careful thought, and an original mission expressed the same commitment to progress, optimism for the impart of knowledge, and faith in British relationships that had propelled iterations of British liberal imperialism for more than a century and a half. At its inception, the cultural project of the late British Empire was rooted in a fundamental set of values: the unrestricted circulation of knowledge, encouragement of creativity, and critical debate. Although British authorities did not feel African publics were ready for such values during the 1930s, over the resulting decades the British Council, the BBC, and British publishers had encouraged these values with increasing frequency and intensity. They did so against the backdrop of a changing political order—decolonization—where the formal loss of territory and the anxieties it produced about Britain's place in the world led Britain to question how hard it should work to convince others of the universalism of its culture. Be it through plays, books, broadcasts, or other forms of expression, the work that British cultural agencies carried out during this era was an imperial encore. Like all encores though, it remained to be seen whether the performers were about to end and exit gracefully or would turn to another sheet of music and find a way to play on.

Epilogue

In 2013, one of Britain's top cultural awards sought to break with its imperial roots. Since 1969, the Booker Prize had been awarded each year to what its judges deemed the best English-language novel by an author from the United Kingdom, Ireland, or the Commonwealth. Throughout the decades, the Booker Prize stood as another way that metropolitan publishing authorities asserted that they helped postcolonial writers attain legitimacy. The prize's proponents boasted that being shortlisted alone brought significant international renown to an author and his or her national tradition, citing names such as Salman Rushdie as their proof. Indeed, when scanning the list of novels that have won the prize, the degree to which the empire lingers in the British literary scene is striking, both in the authors' nations of origin and in the pervasive themes of the winning fiction.[1]

But in 2013, the prize announced it was doing away with its "empire-only" rules and that writers from anywhere in the world could enter—so long as they wrote in English. The chairman of the Booker trustees proclaimed the move reinforced the global prestige of the award—and would thus subsequently boost the global prestige of British publishing all the more.[2] But however he tried to sell it, there was an outcry from some of Britain's most esteemed authors, agents, and critics. They predicted that American novels would flood the competition and prevent a lesser-known talent—the next Salman Rushdie—from getting discovered. As one author wrote in the *Guardian*, "From next year, the floodgates open, and we can expect never to hear again from an Indian novelist."[3] Across the outcry there was a sense that changes to the Booker award diluted an identity that cultural authorities should have seen reason to preserve. The BBC quoted John Mullan, a literary critic and a former Booker judge, who said the Booker's uniqueness had been that you got books "from all over the world that are bound together by common identity."[4] Of course, the identity that he spoke of—what an Irish writer and an Indian writer might share—was being part of the British imperial world, most often unwillingly.

Hearing this debate unfold—the chairman's confidence in the global prestige of British publishing, respondents' nostalgic evocation of imperial patronage—one cannot help but think back to the history told in the preceding pages. The contention over the Booker captures a much lengthier and more tangled set of deliberations that lie at the center of this book. Was British culture a dynamic and expansive category that was no longer constrained by national boundaries? Or was it just a fleeting version of an earlier self, diluting itself to obsolescence? Moreover, how did we get here, and what does it say about the endurance of British imperialism?

The British officials who feature in this history provided us with an unending debate around what British culture entailed. Their deliberations centered around two sets of questions—what was culture, and what could make it British. First, throughout the late colonial period there were debates about whether the "culture" of British culture was confined to traditions, language, and the arts, or whether it should be more broadly thought of as a wide-ranging group of values and practices. This question materialized when the British Council decided how to disperse its resources among its departments, and again when the BBC put together its program schedule. However, by the 1960s, the prospect of political and economic change forced those who proclaimed a narrow understanding of culture to rethink their view. From that point forward, one saw British cultural agencies reaching for a very broad set of objects—including the BBC's disinterested news, OUP's editorial standards, and the British Council's managerial style—and grouping them together in the British culture that they sold.

The larger and more complicated question about British culture was what made it recognizably *British*. As the second half of this book shows, formal decolonization compelled British cultural agents to turn away from a fixed view of who and what was British. Thereafter, the British agencies examined here set out to show that theirs was an inclusive culture that could be embraced, molded, and used by diverse groups of people. The shift in their mindsets could first be seen in the subject matter of their broadcasts, books, and plays. The BBC switched out its home news for the world news, British publishers pointed to the new sections of their catalogs titled World Literature, and the British Council celebrated adaptations of *Julius Caesar* set in 1960s Africa. In order to carry out these changes, British officials found they needed to recruit new partners from overseas, such as the African broadcasters who read and edited the Swahili news, the African writers who wrote world literature, and the African university students who took Shakespeare plays on tour. All of these different changes took place within a very short period—namely, the late 1950s and early 1960s, or the moment when these British agencies recognized that decolonization was imminent. In response, they tried to anticipate and provide what overseas listeners and markets would demand once the colonial apparatus fell away. But as much as the BBC and OUP hoped to deflect indictments of neocolonialism, their activities became new fuel for their critics.

The critique of British cultural imperialism enters this history at several different points, sometimes quietly and other times more emphatically. Looking at British broadcasting, for example, saw BBC officials confront rejection of their principles immediately after African independence, when they watched political elites take over colonial broadcasting infrastructures and put them in service of their own power. Often this meant abruptly moving away from the journalistic practices that British broadcasters took pride in—practices that were rooted in freedoms of the press and speech for the very reason that they encouraged critical debate. Meanwhile, in publishing, British firms also faced a chorus of criticism, only this time it came from their own authors, individuals whose creativity the publishers had heralded. In both their writing and in organized venues, African writers became among the loudest critics of the colonial structures that endured in postcolonial Africa. The writers resoundingly proved that as much as British cultural agencies had broadened their understanding of culture and tried to incorporate outside elements into their work, certain aspects of the British cultural project went unchanged. British actors continued to cast themselves in the center of a global network as gatekeepers who then handed a specific culture down to Africans. Whether or not that made their output British, it certainly made it imperial, and suggested that the sun still had not set on the British Empire.

But as powerful and pervasive as the postcolonial critique became over the following decades, it did not disarm what British cultural agencies set out to do after formal decolonization. Instead, by the late 1970s, the BBC was still a news source for Africans, while OUP and other British firms still dominated book publishing. What's more, the presence of the postcolonial critique actually strengthened British cultural imperialism and gave its agencies new claims to legitimacy. The BBC found that the loss of the colonial monopoly strengthened the corporation's brand far more than it could have imagined, as it could now full-heartedly claim that even when they had other options, African listeners sought out the British world news. It reinforced British broadcasters' view of their product as a universally valued commodity. Meanwhile, British publishers absorbed and commodified their loudest critics by continuing to publish them. Like British broadcasters, they were thus able to demonstrate that their aims and activities could exist alongside those of their loudest critics.

It became clear, then, that British culture was reinvented after empire. The proponents of British cultural imperialism set out to subsume postcolonial culture and claim it as part of the British world. The endurance of the BBC World Service and the Booker Prize winners proved that they succeeded to an enormous degree. But within these efforts, another older anxiety started to make itself evident once again. Was there also a risk of Britain distancing itself too much from *British* English, *British* values, and *British* culture and replacing them with a more generic global form? After all, if the Britishness became unrecognizable, Britain would lose its distinguished position as the link between parts of the global audience. The outcry over the new Booker Prize, where authors and publishers described the dilution of a British identity, illustrated this fear. "Without a cohesive identity, what would Britain have left?" they seemed to ask. Nor were they alone. Their point that Britain was on the verge of diluting its cultural heritage to obsolescence reflected the same alarm seen elsewhere in this volume—namely, in the reflections of British Council officials who commented on the fading-out of Britain's mission of liberal empire.

They would always have English. When tracing when and how the English language appears in this history, it becomes apparent that in many ways it *is* the historical transformation described above. During the late colonial period, the British Council, the BBC, and publishers embraced an exclusive idea of the English language that mapped closely with the categories of race and class as another tool for differentiation within African society. However, in the course of decolonization, those same agencies reframed how they spoke about and taught their language, replacing a rigid set of rules with a fluid language that had endless accents and variants. Moreover, the British were buoyed by all the signs they received that their language was in demand. Whether it was the BBC's round-the-clock service, Heinemann's African Writers Series, or the British Council's overseas courses, the consumption of English reinforced Britain's faith that it helped connect global audiences to one another. English was at the center of British cultural imperialism after empire, but it was also at the core of the postcolonial critique. Even when looking back on the Booker Prize for English writing, one sees some of the past African and Indian recipients speak about how complicated their relationship with the colonial language has been.[5]

Through English, the British actors in this history hoped they could have it both ways: a language that was dynamically global as well as one that was perpetually theirs. After decolonization, British agencies knew what they had with English and recognized that the language could make it possible for them to retain relevance around the world. It was the "golden egg," according to the British Council's official historian, and "Britain's real black gold" according to its director-general, John Burgh.[6] They both spoke during the middle of the 1980s, when the British Council and other organizations were looking for new ways to brand British English and capitalize on overseas populations' eagerness to learn it. Such business models rested around the assumption that foreigners would always want to learn English in the original, or "purest," form of the language; or, in other words, that as many spoken varieties as there may be, the world would still know that the standard lay in Britain.[7] Several decades later, the critics of the new Booker Prize did not believe this to be true. When faced with a suggestion that the prize could be both global and British at the same time, they assumed that the former—the universalizing global English language—would immediately swallow the national particularities of the latter.

Threaded throughout this history, then, is the question of whether and how something can be both global and British. It is a question that can be asked about the Booker Prize or the English language, or it can be asked just as easily about the cultural agencies at the center of this history. The BBC World Service, Oxford University Press, and the British Council are all still in operation around the world today, a fact that stands as further proof of their abilities to evolve so they can endure. More important than where they work is how they each make their expansive reach a main feature of their self-portrayal as global organizations. The most recent *BBC Annual Report* announced that after a boost of government funding, the broadcaster's international audience was soaring, with 394 million people around the world consuming the BBC News each week, a rise of 14 percent since the prior year. (Notably, the new audiences came largely from three particular countries—India, Kenya, and the United States—all of them once part of the empire.) "Reflecting the United Kingdom, its culture and values to the world," the glossy report proclaimed, "We continued to bring the BBC's impartial, independent journalism to a world where the media is often becoming less, not more, free."[8] Using this one British institution as an example shows how there remains to this day a powerful influence of an imperial internationalism first conceived a century earlier.

Yet even as these institutions seek to prove their global reach and their global audience, they take faith that at the end of the day, what they deal in will be recognized for its Britishness. Therefore, when the World Service boasts that it does more to improve perception of Britain overseas than any other brand or institution, it is saying that, as global as it may be, listeners know that they are listening to something from Britain.[9] The same is true when the British Council speaks about the trust that Britain gains because it operates overseas centers for learning English.[10] What they want to convey in these and all the other studies and discussions about the role of cultural outreach today, is that there is a way to preserve national identity even while acting globally.

After empire, British cultural imperialism reinvented itself as a new version of global Britishness. Its elements overlapped with Western values more generally, such as freedoms of speech and the press that ethical journalism and a competitive publishing industry both celebrate. It also overlapped with international patterns, such as the diversity of spoken English. Nevertheless, the British cultural institutions studied here are certain that at the heart of their work is a revered and unquestioned Britishness that should be spread to the world. It shows that the imperial endeavor is still very much present, fueled by a cultural self-confidence that guides—some would say blindly—the role Britain still seeks for itself in the world today.

NOTES

INTRODUCTION

1. For a fuller discussion of the British world-system, including the extraordinary range of relationships it contained, see John Darwin, *The Empire Project: The Rise and Fall of the British World-System, 1880–1970* (Cambridge: Cambridge University Press, 2009), 1–17.

2. Alfred Zimmern, *The Third British Empire: Being a Course of Lectures Delivered at Columbia University, New York* (London: Oxford University Press, 1927); John Darwin, "A Third British Empire? The Dominion Idea in British Politics," in *The Oxford History of the British Empire, Volume 4: The Twentieth Century*, ed. Judith Brown and Wm. Roger Louis (Oxford: Oxford University Press, 1999), 64–87; Mrinalini Sinha, "Whatever Happened to the Third British Empire? Empire, Nation Redux," in *Writing Imperial Histories*, ed. Andrew S. Thompson (Manchester: Manchester University Press, 2014), 168–87.

3. P. J. Cain and A. G. Hopkins, *British Imperialism: 1688–2000* (New York: Longman, 2002); R. F. Holland, *Britain and the Commonwealth Alliance, 1918–1939* (Basingstoke, UK: Macmillan, 1981).

4. Simon J. Potter, *News and the British World: The Emergence of an Imperial Press System, 1876–1922* (Oxford: Clarendon Press, 2003); Potter, *Broadcasting Empire: The BBC and the British World, 1922–1970* (Oxford: Oxford University Press, 2012). To explain how one of Britain's international rivals viewed British information networks, see Heidi J. S. Tworek, *News from Germany: The Competition to Control World Communications, 1900–1945* (Cambridge, MA: Harvard University Press, 2019), 17–69.

5. Darwin, "A Third British Empire?"

6. Some recent volumes that explore this point are Carl Bridge and Kent Fedorowich, eds., *The British World: Diaspora, Culture and Identity* (London: Frank Cass, 2003); Phillip Buckner and R. Douglas Francis, eds., *Rediscovering the British World* (Calgary, AB: University of Calgary Press, 2005); Kate Darian-Smith, Patricia Grinshaw, and Stuart

Macintyre, eds., *Britishness Abroad: Transnational Movements and Imperial Cultures* (Melbourne: Melbourne University Publishing, 2007).

7. Michael Havinden and David Meredith, *Colonialism and Development: Britain and Its Tropical Colonies, 1850–1960* (New York: Routledge, 1993); Stephen Constantine, *The Making of British Colonial Development Policy, 1914–1940* (London: Frank Cass, 1984).

8. Frederick Cooper, *Decolonization and African Society: The Labor Question in French and British Africa* (Cambridge: Cambridge University Press, 1996).

9. Havinden and Meredith, *Colonialism and Development*; Frederick Cooper and Randall M. Packard, "Introduction," and Frederick Cooper, "Modernizing Bureaucrats, Backward Africans, and the Development Concept," in *International Development and the Social Sciences: Essays on the History and the Politics of Knowledge*, ed. Frederick Cooper and Randall M. Packard (Berkeley: University of California Press, 1997); Joseph Morgan Hodge, *Triumph of the Expert: Agrarian Doctrines of Development and the Legacies of British Colonialism* (Athens: Ohio University Press, 2007).

10. D. A. Low and John Lonsdale, "Introduction," in *History of East Africa, Volume 3*, ed. D. A. Low and Alison Smith (Oxford: Clarendon Press, 1976).

11. To cite some of these, Ronald Hyam, *Britain's Declining Empire: The Road to Decolonisation, 1918–1968* (Cambridge: Cambridge University Press, 2006); Darwin, *The Empire Project*.

12. Frederick Cooper, "Possibility and Constraint: African Independence in Historical Perspective," *Journal of African History* 49, no 2 (2008): 167–96; Martin Lynn, ed., *The British Empire in the 1950s: Retreat or Revival?* (New York: Palgrave Macmillan, 2006).

13. Wm. Roger Louis, *Ends of British Imperialism: The Scramble for Empire, Suez, and Decolonization* (Oxford: Oxford University Press, 2006).

14. Caroline Elkins, *Imperial Reckoning: The Untold Story of Britain's Gulag in Kenya* (New York: Henry Holt, 2005); David Anderson, *Histories of the Hanged: The Dirty War in Kenya and the End of Empire* (New York: W.W. Norton, 2005).

15. For the left, see Stephen Howe, *Anticolonialism in British Politics: The Left and the End of Empire 1918–1964* (Oxford: Oxford University Press, 1993). For the Conservative-led government, see Harold Macmillan, *Pointing the Way, 1959–1961* (London: Macmillan, 1972); Philip Murphy, *Party Politics and Decolonization: The Conservative Party and British Colonial Policy in Tropical Africa, 1951–1964* (Oxford: Oxford University Press, 1995); as well as many of the chapters in Larry Butler and Sarah Stockwell, eds., *The Wind of Change: Harold Macmillan and British Decolonization* (Basingstoke, UK: Palgrave Macmillan, 2013).

16. The work of Frederick Cooper is important here, especially Cooper, *Colonialism in Question: Theory, Knowledge, History* (Berkeley: University of California Press, 2005); Cooper, *Africa in the World: Capitalism, Empire, Nation-State* (Cambridge, MA: Harvard University Press, 2014).

17. Wm. Roger Louis and Ronald Robinson, "The Imperialism of Decolonization," *Journal of Imperial and Commonwealth History* 22, no. 3 (1994): 462–511.

18. Frances Donaldson, *The British Council: The First Fifty Years* (London: Jonathan Cape, 1984); Wm. Roger Louis, ed., *The History of Oxford University Press, Volume 3: 1896–1970* (Oxford: Oxford University Press, 2013); Asa Briggs, *The History of Broadcasting in the United Kingdom*, 5 vols. (Oxford: Oxford University Press, 1961–1995); Gerard Mansell, *Let*

Truth Be Told: 50 Years of BBC External Broadcasting (London: Weidenfeld and Nicolson, 1982); Andrew Walker, *A Skyful of Freedom: 60 years of the BBC World Service* (London: Broadside Books, 1992).

19. There are numerous studies that examine public diplomacy, cultural diplomacy, and how they demonstrate the use of soft power, stemming from Joseph S. Nye, *Soft Power: The Means to Success in World Politics* (New York: Public Affairs, 2004). For studies that debate the role of the state and how to categorize institutions such as the BBC World Service or the British Council, see Nicholas J. Cull, "Public Diplomacy: Taxonomies and Histories," in "Public Diplomacy in a Changing World," ed. Geoffrey Cowan and Nicholas J. Cull, special issue, *Annals of the American Academy of Political and Social Science* 616, no. 1 (March 2008): 31–54; Tim Rivera, *Distinguishing Cultural Relations from Cultural Diplomacy: The British Council's Relationship with Her Majesty's Government*, USC Center on Public Diplomacy Perspectives series (Los Angeles: Figueroa Press, 2015).

20. Edward W. Said, *Culture and Imperialism* (New York: Vintage Books, 1994). Other examinations that inform this history include Ngũgĩ wa Thiong'o, *Decolonising the Mind: The Politics of Language in African Literature* (Portsmouth, NH: Heinemann, 1986); and Gayatri Chakravorty Spivak, "Can the Subaltern Speak?," in *Marxism and the Interpretation of Culture*, ed. Cary Nelson and Lawrence Grossberg (Urbana: University of Illinois Press, 1989), 271–13.

21. Said, *Culture and Imperialism*, 9.

22. Ibid., 212.

23. Ngũgĩ wa Thiong'o, *Decolonising the Mind*.

24. For a sampling of the different ways that new scholarship is making this point, see Hodge, *Triumph of the Expert*; Sarah Stockwell, *The British End of the British Empire* (Cambridge: Cambridge University Press, 2018); Emily Baughan, *Saving the Children: Humanitarianism, Internationalism and the British Empire, 1914–1970* (forthcoming, 2021); and Charlotte Lydia Riley, "'The Winds of Change Are Blowing Economically': The Labour Party and British Overseas Development, 1940s–1960s," in *Britain, France and the Decolonization of Africa: Future Imperfect?*, ed. Andrew W. M. Smith and Chris Jeppesen (London: University College London Press, 2017), 43–61.

25. Christopher Lee, "Between a Moment and an Era: The Origins and Afterlives of Bandung," in *Making a World after Empire: The Bandung Moment and Its Political Afterlives*, ed. Christopher J. Lee (Athens: Ohio University Press, 2010), 5.

26. Jordanna Bailkin, *The Afterlife of Empire* (Berkeley: University of California Press, 2012); Rob Waters, *Thinking Black: Britain, 1964–1985* (Oakland: University of California Press, 2019); Bill Schwarz, *The White Man's World* (Oxford: Oxford University Press, 2011); Elizabeth Buettner, *Europe after Empire: Decolonization, Society, and Culture* (Cambridge: Cambridge University Press, 2016).

27. Bailkin, *The Afterlife of Empire*, 11–15; Jean Allman, "Phantoms of the Archive: Kwame Nkrumah, a Nazi Pilot Named Hanna, and the Contingencies of Postcolonial History-Writing," *American Historical Review* 118, no. 1 (February 2013), 104–29; Jeffrey Ahlman, *Living with Nkrumahism: Nation, State, and Pan-Africanism in Ghana* (Athens: Ohio University Press, 2017). See also, Antoinette Burton, ed., *Archive Stories: Facts, Fictions, and the Writing of History* (Durham, NC: Duke University Press, 2006).

28. Spivak, "Can the Subaltern Speak?"

29. Antoinette Burton and Isabel Hofmeyr, "The Spine of Empire? Books and the Making of an Imperial Commons," in *Ten Books That Shaped the British Empire: Creating an Imperial Commons* (Durham, NC: Duke University Press, 2014), 13.

30. Ibid., 3–4.

CHAPTER 1. SHAKESPEARE IN AFRICA

1. "Shakespeare and Shaw in the Sun," *Stage and Television Today*, 4 April 1963, 16; Simon Carter, interview, *Africa Abroad*, no. 66, Transcription Centre, 16 December 1963, transcript, Transcription Centre Records, Harry Ransom Center, University of Texas at Austin, container 5.2 (hereafter cited as Transcription Centre Records); Judi Dench, *And Furthermore* (New York: St. Martin's Press, 2011), 31.

2. Correspondingly, the scholarship on British overseas publicity during the 1940s and 1950s also focuses very heavily on Western and Eastern Europe ("Britain and the Cultural Cold War," ed. Tony Shaw, special issue, *Contemporary British History* 19, no. 2 [2005]: 109–262) and the Middle East (James R. Vaughan, *The Failure of American and British Propaganda in the Arab Middle East, 1945–57: Unconquerable Minds* [Basingstoke, UK: Palgrave Macmillan, 2005]). A few exceptions are Susan L. Carruthers, *Winning Hearts and Minds: British Governments, the Media, and Colonial Counterinsurgency, 1944–1960* (Leicester, UK: Leicester University Press, 1995); Maria Hadjiathanasiou, "Colonial Rule, Cultural Relations and the British Council in Cyprus, 1935–55," *Journal of Imperial and Commonwealth History* 46, no. 6 (2018): 1096–124; Mark Hampton, "Projecting Britishness to Hong Kong: The British Council and Hong Kong House, Nineteen-Fifties to Nineteen-Seventies," *Historical Research* 85 (2012): 691–709, but besides Carruthers, Africa gets little mention.

3. For an official history of the British Council, see Frances Donaldson, *The British Council: The First Fifty Years* (London: Jonathan Cape, 1984).

4. Colin Perchard and David Waterhouse in Perchard, interview by David Waterhouse, 5–6 November 2006, C1083/37, audio file, British Council Oral History Collection.

5. "British Culture Abroad," *Times* [London], 20 March 1935, 13, Times Digital Archive.

6. Janet Horne, "'To Spread the French Language Is to Extend the *Patrie*': The Colonial Mission of the Alliance Française," *French Historical Studies* 40, no. 1 (2017): 95–127, https://doi.org/10.1215/00161071-3686068.

7. Stephen G. Tallents, *The Projection of England* (London: Faber and Faber, 1932). For a more complete account of the debates over Britain's use of overseas publicity, see Philip M. Taylor's scholarship, including Taylor, *The Projection of Britain: British Overseas Publicity and Propaganda, 1919–1939* (Cambridge: Cambridge University Press, 1981).

8. Donaldson, 29–67.

9. Ibid., 1–2.

10. Ibid., 29–67.

11. This discussion comes from the official historian's description of the council's involvement in the Middle East, although she openly shares the same attitudes as the council officials about whom she wrote. Ibid., 91–93.

12. Ibid., 46–50.

13. Alan Burns to Arthur Creech Jones, 12 April 1947, UKNA, BW 93/6.

14. A. P. Williams to controller of the Empire Division, 21 April 1947, UKNA, BW 93/6.

15. The policy that became known as the "definition document" was circulated in a dispatch from Arthur Creech Jones regarding aims and work of the British Council in the colonies, 9 August 1948, UKNA, CO 875/73/4.

16. Richard Frost to Creech Jones, 25 June 1947, UKNA, BW 95/1.

17. Frost to Empire Division, 2 July 1947, UKNA, BW 95/1.

18. Thomas, British Council policy in Ghana, February 1958, UKNA, BW 93/7.

19. The following discussion relies on the minutes and memoranda of the council's Drama and Dance Advisory Committee (hereafter cited as DDAC).

20. F. R. Leavis, *Mass Civilization and Minority Culture* (Cambridge: Minority Press, 1930); John Reith, *Broadcast over Britain* (London: Hodder and Stoughton, 1924); see also D. L. LeMahieu, *A Culture for Democracy: Mass Communication and the Cultivated Mind in Britain between the Wars* (Oxford: Oxford University Press, 1988), 103–77.

21. Dennis Kennedy, "British Theatre, 1895–1946: Art, Entertainment, Audiences–An Introduction," in *Cambridge History of British Theatre, Volume 3: Since 1895*, ed. Baz Kershaw (Cambridge: Cambridge University Press, 2008).

22. Ibid., 23–24; LeMahieu, *Culture for Democracy.*

23. DDAC, 22 January 1947, UKNA, BW 120/1.

24. See DDAC correspondence in UKNA, BW 120/1.

25. DDAC, December 1957, UKNA, BW 120/1.

26. DDAC, 30 January 1959, UKNA, BW 120/1.

27. J. Hume-Sprey to Foreign Office, 30 October 1947, UKNA, BW 1/24.

28. J. M. Lee, "British Cultural Diplomacy and the Cold War: 1946–61," *Diplomacy and Statecraft* 9, no. 1 (1998): 119, https://doi.org/10.1080/09592299808406072.

29. R. Davies to Lord Lloyd, 2 October 1951, UKNA, BW 1/101.

30. Esher to Butler, 17 December 1951, UKNA, BW 1/101.

31. Ibid.

32. DDAC, 11 September 1945, UKNA, BW 120/1.

33. DDAC, 21 June 1951, UKNA, BW 120/1.

34. Ibid.

35. DDAC, 24 October 1961, UKNA, BW 120/1.

36. Executive committee, 5 December 1961, UKNA, BW 120/3.

37. *Summary of the Report of the Independent Commission of Enquiry into the Overseas Information Services* (Drogheda Report), April 1954, Cmd. 9138, 10–11.

38. Ibid., 32.

39. *Overseas Information Services: Report of the Drogheda Committee*, 13 November 1953, 3, UNKA, CAB 129/64/15.

40. *Independent Commission of Enquiry into the Overseas Information Services* (Drogheda Report), 33–36.

41. DDAC, 8 October 1958, UKNA, BW 120/2. The council's budget for music and drama increased tenfold over the second half of the 1950s, from £6,000 in 1956 to £60,000 in 1961. W. R. Owain-Jones, meeting with Lord Drogheda, 13 October 1960, UKNA, BW 2/660.

42. DDAC, 11 December 1959, UKNA, BW 120/2.

43. For Ghana, see Deputy Controller to Hollyer, 20 March 1957, UKNA, BW 93/7.

44. Philips to regional representative in Sekondi/Takoradi, 19 December 1957, UKNA, BW 93/7.

45. For an account of the US State Department's incorporation of jazz into the ideological battles of the Cold War, see Penny M. Von Eschen, *Satchmo Blows Up the World: Jazz Ambassadors Play the Cold War* (Cambridge, MA: Harvard University Press, 2006). For another examination of the role of race in US cultural diplomacy in West Africa, see Naima Prevots, *Dance for Export: Cultural Diplomacy and the Cold War* (Middletown, CT: Wesleyan University Press, 1998), 105–7. See also David Caute, *The Dancer Defects: The Struggle for Cultural Supremacy during the Cold War* (Oxford: Oxford University Press, 2003) for a broader study of cultural export and the Cold War.

46. Executive committee, draft minutes, 4 July 1961, UKNA, BW 55/12.

47. Sanderson to Commonwealth I, 30 June 1961, UKNA, BW 55/12.

48. DDAC, 9 March 1961, UKNA, BW 120/3.

49. John Bailey, *A Theatre for All Seasons: Nottingham Playhouse, The First Thirty Years 1948–1978* (Gloucestershire, UK: Alan Sutton Publishing, 1994); Anthony Jackson, "1958–1983: Six Reps in Focus," in *The Repertory Movement: A History of Regional Theatre in Britain*, ed. George Rowell and Anthony Jackson (Cambridge: Cambridge University Press, 1984), 132–33.

50. DDAC, 11 July 1962; DDAC, 14 December 1962, UKNA, BW 120/3.

51. Carter, interview, *Africa Abroad*, no. 66, 16 December 1963.

52. Ibid.

53. Dench, *And Furthermore*, 31.

54. J. P. Stevens, general report on Nottingham Playhouse Company tour, April 1963, UKNA, BW 120/3.

55. Carter, interview, *Africa Abroad*, no. 66, 16 December 1963. For more about the power of translating Shakespeare into Krio, see Thomas Decker's introduction to his translation of *Julius Caesar* (Thomas Decker, *Juliohs Siza*, eds. Neville Shrimpton and Njie Sulayman [Umea, Sweden: Umea University, 1988], xv, qtd. in Lemuel A. Johnson, *Shakespeare in Africa (and Other Venues): Import and the Appropriation of Culture* [Trenton, NJ: Africa World Press, 1998], 137–38).

56. Report from Kano regional director, 29 January 1963, UKNA, BW 120/3.

57. Report from UK high commissioner to Ghana, 13 March 1963, UKNA, BW 120/3.

58. Report from Port Harcourt regional representative, 18 March 1963, UKNA, BW 120/3.

59. Report from UK deputy high commissioner to Nigeria, 5 February 1963, UKNA, BW 120/3.

60. Drama and music overseas: The role of the British Council, 20 May 1963, UKNA, BW 120/3.

61. Mauritius representative to drama advisory committee (formerly DDAC; hereafter cited as DAC), 2 December 1963, UKNA, BW 120/3.

62. Shakespeare Quatercentenary tours—progress report, DAC 64(2), 30 June 1964, UKNA, BW 120/3; Richard Pankhurst, "Shakespeare in Ethiopia," *Research in African Literatures* 17, no 2 (Summer 1986): 172–74.

63. H. F. Oxbury to W. R. Owain-Jones, 8 September 1960, UKNA, BW 2/660; DDAC, 11 July 1962; Shakespeare Quatercentenary tours—progress report, DAC 64(2), 30 June 1964, UKNA, BW 120/3.

64. Co-ordinating committee for drama and music tours overseas, 13 November 1962, UKNA, BW 2/660.

65. DDAC, 14 December 1962, UKNA, BW 120/3.

66. DDAC and DAC minutes between 1956 and 1966, UKNA, BW 120/1–3.

67. DAC minutes between 1970 and 1979, UKNA, BW 2/784.

68. John Fraser, *The Bard in the Bush* (London: Granada Publishing, 1978), 10.

69. Director of Enugu quoted in reports on tours, DAC (76)2, 1976, UKNA, BW 2/782.

70. Reports on tours, DAC 77(4), 1977, UKNA, BW 2/782.

71. Reports on tours, DAC 78(5), 1978, UKNA, BW 2/782.

72. Report on forthcoming tours, DAC (64)3, 1964, UKNA, BW 120/3.

73. Western Region representative in 1963–64 annual report for Nigeria, 30 April 1964, UKNA, BW 128/16.

74. Tom Hebert (United States Peace Corps), interview, 9 June 2017.

75. Reports on tours, DAC (64)1, 1964, UKNA, BW 120/3.

76. DAC, 11 May 1965, UKNA, BW 120/3.

77. M. R. Snodin in April 1963–64 annual report for Nigeria, 30 April 1964, UKNA, BW 128/16.

78. James Gibbs, "The Travelling Theatre," University of Malawi Chancellor College—Department of English newsletter, October 1974, Transcription Centre Records, container 3.4.

79. For Makerere, see Cook, "Theatre Goes to the People!" *Transition* no. 25 (1966): 32; for Malawi, see Adrian Roscoe, "Travelling Theatre Broadsheet 1974, No. 1; 1st Chancellor College Drama Festival," November 1974, Transcription Centre Records, container 3.4.

80. Billy Chibber, "Varsity Variety," *Daily Nation*, 12 May 1965, Transcription Centre Records, container 3.1; see also Cook, "Theatre Goes to the People!," 26–27; Lydia Kayanja, "The Makerere Travelling Theatre in East Africa," *Journal of Modern African Studies* 5, no. 1 (1967): 142.

81. Cook, "Theatre Goes to the People!," 23.

82. Ngũgĩ wa Thiong'o, *Decolonising the Mind: The Politics of Language in African Literature* (Portsmouth, NH: Heinemann, 1986), 39–41.

83. Dapo Ajaui, "Danda—Excellent," *Daily Times*, 6 April 1965.

84. David Kerr, "Participatory Popular Theatre: The Highest State of Cultural Under-Development?" *Research in African Literatures* 22, no. 3 (Autumn 1991): 58–59, https://www.jstor.org/stable/3819710; Reinhard Sander, Bernth Lindfors, and Lynette Cintrón, eds., *Ngũgĩ wa Thiong'o Speaks: Interviews with the Kenyan Writer* (Trenton, NJ: Africa World Press, 2006), 145.

85. Wole Soyinka, "Towards a True Theatre," *Transition* no. 8 (March 1963), 22. https://www.jstor.org/stable/2934730.

86. Ngũgĩ wa Thiong'o, "Kenyan Culture: The National Struggle for Survival," 1979, reprinted in *Writers in Politics* (London: Heinemann, 1981), 46–48. See also Ngũgĩ, *Decolonising the Mind*.

CHAPTER 2. "BRINGING BOOKS TO AFRICANS"

1. See Stanley Unwin quoted in [Author unknown] minute to Willis, 28 Oct 1941, UKNA, CO 1045/268; Charles Granston Richards, "No Carpet on the Floor: Recollections and Reflections on the Work of 40 years, 1935–1975, in The Development of Literature and Publishing Chiefly in the Third World" (unpublished manuscript, ca. 1980), 21–22, Charles Granston Richards Papers, PP MS 12, box 1, folder 0, School of Oriental and African Studies Library, University of London (hereafter cited as Richards Papers).

2. I found Burton and Hofmeyr's introduction to their edited volume especially valuable for this discussion. Antoinette Burton and Isabel Hofmeyr, "The Spine of Empire? Books and the Making of an Imperial Commons," in *Ten Books That Shaped the British Empire: Creating an Imperial Commons*, ed. Burton and Hofemyr (Durham, NC: Duke University Press, 2014), 1–6.

3. Recent studies of book history and print culture in Africa underline the extent to which views like Richards's prevailed in African history. See Elizabeth le Roux, "Book History in the African World: The State of the Discipline," *Book History* 15 (2012): 248–300; Isabel Hofmeyr, "From Book Development to Book History: Some Observations on the History of the Book in Africa," *SHARP News* 13, no. 3 (2004): 3–4; Caroline Davis and David Johnson, eds., *The Book in Africa: Critical Debates* (London: Palgrave Macmillan, 2015). Other key titles that explore writing and reading practices in Africa include Karin Barber, ed., *Africa's Hidden Histories: Everyday Literacy and the Making of the Self* (Bloomington: Indiana University Press, 2006); Archie L. Dick, *The Hidden History of South Africa's Book and Reading Cultures* (Toronto: University of Toronto Press, 2013).

4. A detailed assessment of the colonial state's encouragement and support for the private sector during the late colonial period in Kenya can be found in Robert Tignor, *Capitalism and Nationalism at the End of Empire: State and Business in Decolonizing Egypt, Nigeria, and Kenya, 1945–1963* (Princeton, NJ: Princeton University Press, 1997), 293–386.

5. Pierre Bourdieu "The Field of Cultural Production; or, The Economic World Reversed," *Poetics* 12, nos. 4–5 (November 1983): 311–56, https://doi.org/10.1016/0304-422X(83)90012-8.

6. This discussion of newspapers in colonial Africa relies upon Derek R. Peterson and Emma Hunter, "Print Culture in Colonial Africa," in *African Print Cultures: Newspapers and Their Publics in the Twentieth Century*, ed. Derek R. Peterson, Emma Hunter, and Stephanie Newell (Ann Arbor: University of Michigan Press, 2016), 6–11. Book publishing would emerge from the same missionary and colonial government interests as newspapers, but where the newspaper and book industries would diverge was that with the latter European missionary and government entities retained control over editorial decisions and production.

7. For more about the transnational circulation of such texts and the meanings ascribed to them, see Leslie Howsam, *Cheap Bibles: Nineteenth-Century Publishing and the British and Foreign Bible Society* (Cambridge: Cambridge University Press, 1991); Isabel Hofmeyr, *The Portable Bunyan: A Transnational History of* The Pilgrim's Progress (Princeton, NJ: Princeton University Press, 2004).

8. Richards, "No Carpet on the Floor," 10.

9. Margaret Wrong, *Africa and the Making of Books: Being a Survey of Africa's Need of Literature* (London: International Committee on Christian Literature for Africa, 1934), 9.

10. Richards, draft of forward to the work and aims of the CMS Bookshop, Nairobi, 1944, Richards Papers, box 1, folder 7.

11. Ruth Allcock, organization of CMS Bookshop, Nairobi, March 1953, Church Missionary Society Papers, MSS 61/656, Kenya National Archives (hereafter cited as CMS Kenya Papers).

12. Richards, "No Carpet on the Floor," 12.

13. Richards, *Sala Zangu* (Nairobi: CMS Bookshop, 1941).

14. Richards, "Books in the Service of the Church," address to the Cathedral Committee of the Christian Council of Kenya, 16 April 1945, Richards Papers, box 1, folder 9; James A. Lyall, "'Our Part in the Great Priority': The First Annual Report of the Highway Press, the Publishing Department of the CMS Bookshop" 25 October 1950, CMS Kenya Papers, MSS 61/652.

15. Richards, "No Carpet on the Floor," 12.

16. Ibid.

17. Richards, Draft of forward to the work and aims of the CMS Bookshop, Richards Papers, box 1, folder 7.

18. Publishing advisory committee (PAC), 1951–1952, CMS Kenya Papers, MSS 61/652.

19. Lyall, "Our Part in the Great Priority." These figures are from the period January 1950 to March 1951.

20. PAC, 17 Jan 1950, CMS Kenya Papers, MS 61/652.

21. PAC, 17 Jan 1950 and 15 Feb 1950, CMS Kenya Papers, MSS 61/652.

22. Analysis of market—December 1949–June 1950, CMS Kenya Papers, MSS 61/652. At that point the bookshop was selling 16 Kikuyu titles, out of a total active list of 141 titles in nine languages. The next largest share was in Swahili (42 active titles, which accounted for 18% of CMS's sales), followed by English (30 titles, 15% of sales).

23. PAC, 6 December 1951, CMS Kenya Papers, MSS 61/652. For a much fuller discussion of how the Gikuyu used different Kikuyu-language texts, see Derek R. Peterson, *Creative Writing: Translation, Bookkeeping, and the Work of Imagination in Colonial Kenya* (Portsmouth, NH: Heinemann, 2004).

24. CMS Bookshop Nairobi to CMS London, 11 December 1952, CMS Kenya Papers, MSS 61/656.

25. Lyall, Highway Press quarterly report January–March 1951, 5 April 1951, CMS Kenya Papers, MSS 61/652.

26. S. G. Bishop, third annual report, July 1952, CMS Kenya Papers, MSS 61/656.

27. Summary of opinions of CMS Bookshop's European staff, 1952, CMS Kenya Papers, MSS 61/656.

28. Conference of East African governors, July 1947, Richards Papers, box 2, folder 17a.

29. Huxley's political views would come to occupy the center of debates over her life and legacy, with sympathetic accounts like that of her biographer arguing that Huxley's outlook quickly changed with the times during the 1940s and beyond: C. S. Nicholls, *Elspeth Huxley: A Biography* (New York: Thomas Dunne, 2003). African critics, however,

levied brutal indictments. Ngũgĩ wa Thiong'o called her a "racist apologist for European settlerism" in *Writers in Politics* (London: Heinemann, 1981), 17.

30. Conference of East African governors, July 1947, Richards Papers, box 2, folder 17a.

31. Quoted in ibid.

32. This was only one of several literature bureaus the British Colonial Office set up or contemplated setting up in Africa during the late 1940s and early 1950s (G. H. Wilson, "The Northern Rhodesia-Nyasaland Joint Publications Bureau," *Africa: Journal of the International African Institute* 20 [1950]: 60–69; L. J. Lewis, Report on literature production and distribution in British West Africa, 1950, National Archives of Ghana, Accra [hereafter cited as NAG], RG 3/5/1182). See also Evelyn Ellerman, "The Literature Bureau: African Influence in Papua New Guinea," *Research in African Literatures* 26, no. 4 (Winter 1995): 206–15.

33. Ward to Carrington, 24 October 1946, UKNA, CO 1045/267.

34. Executive committee, 9 May 1956, CMS Kenya Papers, MSS 61/967.

35. Richards to CMS regional secretary, Nairobi, 9 August 1955, CMS Kenya Papers, MSS 61/967.

36. Richards sat on CMS committees for the rest of his working life and into retirement (Richards, "No Carpet on the Floor," 17).

37. East African Common Services Organization, *East African Literature Bureau Annual Report 1961–62* (Nairobi, 1962), v. From 1960 to 1964 the Colonial Development and Welfare Fund contributed £40,744 and the East African governments £103,677.

38. East African Literature Bureau, *Annual Report 1959–60* (Nairobi: East Africa High Commission, 1960), 10.

39. Richards, "A Proposed Literature Organization for East Africa," 1947, Richards Papers, box 2, folder 17b, 2–4.

40. Conference of East African governors, July 1947, Richards Papers, box 2, folder 17a.

41. Proceedings of a conference to consider a report by Mrs. Huxley on the establishment of an East African bureau to provide literature for Africans, 15 August 1946, UKNA, CO 1045/267.

42. Richards, "Bringing Literature to the Africans," *East African Standard*, 15 August 1950; Richards, "No Carpet on the Floor," 22.

43. Colonial Office, "East African Literature Bureau," 17 March 1949, UKNA, CO 822/129/2.

44. East African Literature Bureau, *Annual Report 1948–49* (Nairobi: East Africa High Commission, 1949).

45. F. M. Inoti, *Mwari uri muuno uti nda* (Nairobi: Eagle Press, 1949); Emmie Mary Holding, *Ũtheru thĩinĩ wa mũciĩ* (Nairobi: Eagle Press, 1949). For accounts how discourse on morals, sex, and cleanliness fit into British colonial development and welfare, see Lynn M. Thomas, *Politics of the Womb: Women, Reproduction, and the State in Kenya* (Berkeley: University of California Press, 2003); Timothy Burke, *Lifebuoy Men, Lux Women: Commodification, Consumption, and Cleanliness in Modern Zimbabwe* (Durham, NC: Duke University Press, 1996), ch. 2.

46. Richards, "No Carpet on the Floor," 15.

47. East African Literature Bureau, *Annual Report 1958–59* (Nairobi: East Africa High Commission, 1959), 9.

48. Richards, "No Carpet on the Floor," 22.

49. Richards, "Bringing Literature to the Africans."

50. East African Literature Bureau, *Annual Report 1958–59* (Nairobi: East Africa High Commission, 1959).

51. Henry Chakava, interview, 5 July 2013, Nairobi.

52. Duncan Whitefield, photograph, c. 1958, UKNA, INF 10/159/91; East African Literature Bureau, *Annual Report 1959–60* (Nairobi: East Africa High Commission, 1960).

53. For more on photography as a tool of empire, see Paul S. Landau, "Empires of the Visual: Photography and Colonial Administration in Africa," in *Images and Empires: Visuality in Colonial and Postcolonial Africa*, eds. Paul S. Landau and Deborah D. Kaspin (Berkeley: University of California Press, 2002), 141–71.

54. Richards, "Bringing Literature to the Africans."

55. East African Literature Bureau, *Annual Report 1958–59* (Nairobi: East Africa High Commission, 1959).

56. Richards, handwritten note, Richards Papers, box 3, folder 51; Richards, "No Carpet on the Floor," 37.

57. For a separate account of this history, see Nourdin Bejjit, "Heinemann's African Writers Series and the Rise of James Ngugi," in *The Book in Africa: Critical Debates*, eds. Caroline Davis and David Johnson (London: Palgrave Macmillan, 2015), 223–44.

58. E. C. Parnwell to K. Sisam, 19 October 1928, AOUP, 165(1), quoted in Caroline Davis, *Creating Postcolonial Literature: African Writers and British Publishers* (New York: Palgrave Macmillan, 2013), 17.

59. Davis, *Creating Postcolonial Literature*, 48.

60. See John C. Hardy (Educational Director, Thomas Nelson & Sons) to Keith, February 1940, UKNA CO 1045/267; E. Jones (Educational Manager, John Crowther Ltd.) to Christopher Cox, 28 July 1944, UKNA CO 1045/267.

61. For Evans, see P. Sykes to Christopher Cox, December 9 1940, UKNA, CO 1045/265; for OUP, see Parnwell to Humphrey Milford, 16 April 1940, in UKNA, CO 1045/268.

62. C. S. S. Higham to Ward, 6 February 1947, UKNA, CO 1045/266.

63. Ward to Higham, 11 February 1947, UKNA, CO 1045/266.

64. Quoted in Peter Sutcliffe, *The Oxford University Press: An Informal History* (Oxford: Oxford University Press, 1978), 214.

65. Lawrence Faucett, *The Oxford English Course* (London: Oxford University Press, 1933); Faucett, *A Picture-Dictionary: Direct Method* (London: Oxford University Press, 1933); Faucett, *One Hundred Reading Cards* (London: Oxford University Press, 1933).

66. Richard C. Smith, ed., *Teaching English as a Foreign Language, 1936–1961: Foundations of ELT* (New York: Routledge, 2005), xvii.

67. Isabelle Frémont, F. G. French, and Laurence Faucett, *The Oxford Readers for Africa*, Books 1–6 (London: Oxford University Press, 1938–1943).

68. Ibid. The third editions, which appeared in 1949, appeared until the logo "Oxford Progressive English."

69. Ngũgĩ wa Thiong'o, *Writers in Politics: A Re-engagement with Issues of Literature and Society* (Oxford: James Currey, 1997), quoted in John Willinsky, *Empire of Words: The Reign of the OED* (Princeton, NJ: Princeton University Press, 1994), 203.

70. C. W. Jackman, the teaching of English in secondary schools, 30 May 1956, Kenya National Archives, XJ/1/168 (hereafter cited as KNA).

71. G. E. Perren, books on the teaching of English, 12 July 1956, KNA, XJ/1/168.

72. Book One of the Gold Coast series, which came out in 1955, contained English names, but by the release of Book Two in 1956 the characters had West African names. *New Oxford English Course (Gold Coast), Book Two* (London: Oxford University Press, 1956); *New Oxford English Course for India, Book One* (Calcutta: Oxford University Press, 1963).

73. G. E. Perren, vocabulary taught in the first four books of the Oxford Readers for Africa, 17 July 1956, KNA, XJ/1/168.

74. W. A. D. Riach to C. W. Jackman, 14 September 1956, KNA, XJ/1/168.

75. Ibid.

76. Jackman to Riach, 21 September 1956, KNA, XJ/1/168.

77. Sutcliffe, *The Oxford University Press*, 266. For a more detailed examination of the organization of Oxford University Press in this period, see Wm. Roger Louis, ed., *The History of Oxford University Press, Volume 3: 1896–1970* (Oxford: Oxford University Press, 2013).

78. Noah L. Sempira to Oxford University Press, Nairobi, 22 April 1963, Oxford University Press Eastern Africa, MS 19 (hereafter cited as OUP EA).

79. Simon A. de G. Abbott to M. B. Nsimbi, 16 September 1963, OUP EA, MS 19.

80. Abbott to Collings, 21 February 1962, OUP EA, MS 106; Clyde Sanger, "Shakespeare in Swahili Blank Verse," *Guardian*, 27 August 1963.

81. Abbott to Joan Wicken, 7 April 1962; RAC Norrington to Wicken, 22 May 1962, OUP EA, MS 106.

82. Wicken to Abbott, 2 May 1962, OUP EA, MS 106.

83. Julius K. Nyerere, "Utangulizi," introduction to *Julius Caezar*, by William Shakespeare, trans. Julius K. Nyerere (Nairobi: Oxford University Press, 1963), 5.

84. Ibid., 3.

85. John Mbiti, review of *Julius Caezar* by Julius Nyerere, *Africa Abroad*, no. 66, Transcription Centre, 16 December 1963, transcript, Transcription Centre Records, container 5.2.

86. Nyerere, "Utangulizi," 6.

87. Houghton to Howell, 8 April 1963, OUP EA, MS 106.

88. The OUP Eastern Africa editorial files referred to the translated edition as *Juliasi Kaizari*, but the edition that was ultimately published was titled *Julius Caezar* by William Shakespeare, Julius K. Nyerere, trans. (Nairobi: Oxford University Press, 1963).

89. See the communication and estimates in BBC WAC, E1/1446/1.

90. David Cook, "Theatre Goes to the People!," *Transition* no. 25 (1966): 32.

91. OUP EA, MS 119.

92. Wicken to Lewis, 29 April 1969, OUP EA, MS 107.

93. Jonathan Kariara to Lewis, 7 May 1969, OUP EA, MS 107.

94. Quoted in Wicken to Lewis, 2 May 1969, OUP EA, MS 107.

95. Henry Chakava, "Kenyan Publishing: Independence and Dependence," in *Publishing and Development in the Third World*, ed. Philip Altbach (London: Hans Zell, 1992), 120–21.

CHAPTER 3. "THIS IS LONDON . . ."

1. An exception is Gordon Johnston and Emma Robertson, *BBC World Service: Overseas Broadcasting, 1932–2018* (London: Palgrave Macmillan, 2019), 223–79. Otherwise, the most detailed history of the British Broadcasting Corporation is Asa Briggs's five-volume series *The History of Broadcasting in the United Kingdom*, but when it mentions external broadcasting it does not highlight Africa. The past decade has seen a greater amount of scholarship on the BBC external services in other parts of the world; see for example, Marie Gillespie, Alban Webb, and Gerhard Baumann, eds., "BBC World Service, 1932–2007: Cultural Exchange and Public Diplomacy," special issue, *Historical Journal of Film, Radio and Television* 28, no. 4 (2008): 441–623; Simon J. Potter, *Broadcasting Empire: The BBC and the British World* (Oxford: Oxford University Press, 2012); and Alban Webb, *London Calling: Britain, the BBC World Service, and the Cold War* (London: Bloomsbury, 2014). In addition, several former employees of the BBC World Service have authored histories of British external broadcasting, including Gerald Mansell, *Let Truth Be Told: 50 Years of BBC External Broadcasting* (London: Weidenfeld and Nicolson, 1982); Andrew Walker, *A Skyful of Freedom: 60 Years of the BBC World Service* (London: Broadside Books, 1992); and John Tusa, *A Word in Your Ear: Reflections on Changes* (London: Broadside Books, 1992).

2. John Reith, *Into the Wind* (London: Hodder and Stoughton, 1949), 113.

3. Mansell, *Let Truth Be Told*, 3–6.

4. Colonial Office Conference, 1927, Cmd. 2883, 58–60.

5. Trade propaganda committee, minutes, 4 April 1930, UKNA, CO 323/1103/1.

6. Report on Empire Broadcasting, Appendices to Imperial Conference, 1930, Cmd. 3718, 134–36.

7. Minutes from meeting to discuss empire broadcasting service, 11 March 1930, UKNA, CO 323/1103/1. Arnold Hodson was the only colonial governor willing to contribute to the cost of the Empire Service, but he made the offer twice—first as governor of Sierra Leone, then as governor of the Gold Coast. BBC officials wryly suggested the Colonial Office assign Hodson a different posting every six months so that then they would have their funding (Mansell, *Let Truth Be Told*, 32).

8. Mansell, *Let Truth Be Told*, 18–19.

9. The first director-general, John Reith, coined this term in the late 1920s and by the next decade BBC officials regularly used it to refer to their isolated listeners.

10. British Broadcasting Corporation, *The Empire Broadcasting Service* (London: BBC, 1935), 11.

11. Potter, *Broadcasting Empire*, 26–33.

12. BBC, *Empire Broadcasting Service*, 11; Emma Robertson, "'I Get a Real Kick out of Big Ben': BBC versions of Britishness on the Empire and General Overseas Service, 1932–1948," *Historical Journal of Film, Radio and Television* 28, no. 4 (October 2008): 459–73.

13. BBC, *Empire Broadcasting Service*, 6.

14. Ibid., 15.

15. Ibid., 8–13.

16. Ibid., 8.

17. Henry Moore to colonial secretary, 28 June 1943, UKNA, CO 875/4/27.

18. Charles Armour, "The BBC and the Development of Broadcasting in British Colonial Africa, 1946–1956," *African Affairs* (July 1984), 369–71.

19. Manager, Cable and Wireless, to F. A. W. Byron, 14 November 1938, NAG, CSO 7/5/20.

20. Byron, "Memorandum on Wireless and Wire Broadcasting in the African Colonies," 16 October 1943, UKNA, CO 875/1/14. Although less extensive than the Gold Coast, rediffusion systems were already in place in the Falkland Islands and Sierra Leone when the Gold Coast inaugurated its system in 1935. The prior systems were also the initiative of the colonial governor, Arnold Hodson, and his chief engineer, F. A. W. Byron, during their earlier postings. See Sydney W. Head, "British Colonial Broadcasting Policies: The Case of the Gold Coast," *African Studies Review* 22, no. 2 (September 1979): 40–42.

21. Byron, "Memorandum on Wireless and Wire Broadcasting."

22. Colonial Office, *Interim Report of a Committee on Broadcasting Services in the Colonies* (Plymouth Report), Colonial No. 139 (London: HMSO, 1937), 3–4.

23. Ibid., 5.

24. Stephen Constantine, *The Making of British Colonial Development Policy, 1914–1940* (London: Frank Cass, 1984).

25. For some of the scholarship that examines imperial communications links and technology in the late nineteenth and early twentieth centuries, see Dwayne R. Winseck and Robert M. Pike, *Communication and Empire: Media, Markets, and Globalization, 1860–1930* (Durham, NC: Duke University Press, 2007); Daniel R. Headrick, *The Invisible Weapon: Telecommunications and International Politics* (New York: Oxford University Press, 1991); Potter, *Broadcasting Empire*.

26. Model license agreement, enclosed in despatch from Lord Plymouth to the colonies, 16 March 1934, NAG, CSO 7/5/16.

27. Arnold Hodson to William Ormsby-Gore, 25 June 1937, UKNA, CO 323/1495/31.

28. BBC, *Empire Broadcasting Service*, 9.

29. BBC, "The Empire Broadcasting Service," February 1935, enclosed in colonial secretary's despatch of 8 May 1935, NAG, CSO 7/5/13.

30. Ormsby-Gore to Hodson, 26 July 1937, UKNA, CO 323/1495/31.

31. [Author unknown], 17 July 1937, UKNA, CO 323/1495/31.

32. Ormsby-Gore to Hodson, 26 July 1937, UKNA, CO 323/1495/31.

33. BBC, "With the greetings of the BBC," promotional Christmas card, December 1936, National Library of Australia digital collections, MS 1924, series 26, item 1281, http://nla.gov.au/nla.ms-ms1924-26-1281.

34. For detailed staff figures from the period, see Asa Briggs, *The History of Broadcasting in the United Kingdom, Volume 3: The War of Words 1939–1945* (Oxford: Oxford University Press, 1970), appendix A, 663–65.

35. *Report of the Broadcasting Committee 1935*, February 1936, Cmd. 5091 (Ullswater Report), at paragraph 122.

36. Reith to Herbert Morrison, 19 June 1936, BBC WAC, E2/249/1.

37. Minutes, ca. October 1937, BBC WAC, E2/249/5.

38. Suggested use of languages other than English in the Empire Service, June 1937, BBC WAC, E2/249/3.

39. Use of languages other than English in the empire broadcasting service, June 1936, 4, BBC WAC, E2/249/1.

40. Briggs, *History of Broadcasting in the United Kingdom*, 3:18. By the early 1940s the empire was represented through the weekly programs in South Asian and East Asian languages, as well as the Arabic Service, which retained its importance from the late 1930s (Mansell, *Let Truth Be Told*, 119–20).

41. The Caribbean was served primarily by the North American Service, but BBC officials thought the African Service was the more suitable department to put out specialized programs for West Indian audiences (Extract from monthly report: empire countries and USA, 30 October 1941, BBC WAC, E2/3).

42. See Marie Gillespie and Alban Webb, "Corporate Cosmopolitanism: Diasporas and Diplomacy at the BBC World Service, 1932–2012," in *Diasporas and Diplomacy: Cosmopolitan contact zones at the BBC World Service (1932–2012)*, ed. Marie Gillespie and Alban Webb (New York: Routledge, 2012), 6–9.

43. Cecil Graves to Frederick Ogilvie, 5 October 1939, BBC WAC, R49/339.

44. In addition to its three thousand wireless sets, Nigeria also counted twelve thousand wired receiving sets, for a total of fifteen thousand sets, or 1.2 per two thousand people (UNESCO, *Statistics on Radio and Television, 1950–1960* Statistical reports and studies ST/S/8 [Paris: UNESCO, 1963], 56, 60).

45. John Grenfell Williams to E. E. Sabben-Clare, 13 June 1941, BBC WAC, E2/583.

46. Reported in G. C. Latham to Grenfell Williams, 1 August 1941, BBC WAC, E2/583.

47. Bernard Bourdillon to colonial secretary, 14 August 1941, UKNA, CO 875/3/6. For discussion of a similar approach in Kenya, see Fay Gadsden, "Wartime Propaganda in Kenya: The Kenya Information Office, 1939–1945," *International Journal of African Historical Studies* 19, no. 3, 412–13.

48. Grenfell Williams to Noel Sabine, 10 February 1943, BBC WAC, E2/583.

49. Governor of Sierra Leone to colonial secretary, 20 April 1942, BBC WAC, E2/583.

50. Bourdillon to colonial secretary, 16 April 1942, BBC WAC, E2/583.

51. The program was soon renamed *Caribbean Voices*. For more about the BBC's programs for the Caribbean in the 1940s and 1950s, see Glyne Griffith, *The BBC and the Development of Anglophone Caribbean Literature, 1943–1958* (Basingstoke, UK: Palgrave Macmillan, 2016); Anne Spry Rush, *Bonds of Empire: West Indians and Britishness from Victoria to Decolonization* (Oxford: Oxford University Press, 2011), chaps. 7 and 8; and Darrell Newton, "Calling the West Indies: The BBC World Service and *Caribbean Voices*," *Historical Journal of Film, Radio and Television* 28, no. 4 (October 2008): 489–97.

52. Grenfell Williams to Latham, 5 August 1941, BBC WAC, E2/583. For detailed accounts of West Africans in London during this period, see Hakim Adi, *West Africans in Britain, 1900–1960: Nationalism, Pan-Africanism, and Communism* (London: Lawrence and Wishart, 1998); Marc Matera, *Black London: The Imperial Metropolis and Decolonization in the Twentieth Century* (Oakland: University of California Press, 2015).

53. BBC, African Service schedule for week 24, 30 April 1943, BBC WAC, E2/3.

54. Norman Collins to F. Lamping, 15 March 1944, BBC WAC, E2/583.

55. Etienne Amyot to Edmett, 20 June 1944, BBC WAC, E2/583.

56. R. J. Montgomery, Autumn schedule African Service, 10 August 1944, BBC WAC, E2/3.

57. Mary Treadgold to Overseas Presentation, 26 October 1944, BBC WAC, E2/583.

58. Bourdillon to colonial secretary, 19 September 1941, UKNA, CO 875/3/6.

59. The General Forces Programme, a shortwave station, first came into being in November 1942 as the General Overseas Programme and was re-named the Forces Overseas Programme in January 1943. In February 1944 the service was extended to listeners in Britain and became the General Forces Programme (BBC, "The General Overseas Service," 8 November 1946, BBC WAC, E2/336/2).

60. C. F. G. Max-Müller, report on GFP/GOS, 1946, BBC WAC, E2/336/2.

61. Grenfell Williams to Byron, 10 October 1945, BBC WAC, E1/29/1.

62. Grenfell Williams to Goatman, 19 February 1943, BBC WAC, E2/3.

63. Byron to Grenfell Williams, 4 September 1945, BBC WAC, E1/29/1.

64. Based upon a comparison of London Calling with the Gold Coast rediffusion schedule for the week of April 7–14, 1946.

65. Byron to Grenfell Williams, 4 September 1945, BBC WAC, E1/29/1.

66. Grenfell Williams to Byron, 18 October 1945, BBC WAC, E1/29/1.

67. Gold Coast Broadcasting Department, "Your Programme for the Week April 7–April 13," pamphlet, BBC WAC, E1/29/1.

68. The returns came from 4,013 Africans (the majority of whom were either Fante or Ga), 1,539 non-Africans, and 496 schools, offices, and clubs. Gold Coast officials estimated that the result represented a listening audience of over fifty thousand people in the colony and that the largest groups of listeners assembled around African-owned rediffusion boxes (Huxtable to Grenfell Williams, 6 April 1946, BBC WAC, E1/29/1).

69. Ibid.

70. Ibid.; Amyot to Treadgold, 2 June 1944, BBC WAC, E2/583.

71. Huxtable to Grenfell Williams, 6 April 1946, BBC WAC, E1/29/1.

72. Grenfell Williams to Huxtable, 29 April 1946, BBC WAC, E1/29/1.

73. Ibid.

74. Overseas Audience Research, "The Audience of the BBC's General Overseas Service," 1 January 1955, enclosed in Bernard Moore to R. H. Young, 7 April 1955, UKNA, CO 1027/82. Also see Potter, Broadcasting Empire, 147; Gavin Schaffer, "The Limits of the 'Liberal Imagination': Britain, Broadcasting and Apartheid South Africa, 1948–1994," Past & Present 240, no. 1 (2018): 246.

75. In 1955 the BBC estimated that 1 percent of the white adult population in South Africa, or about twenty thousand listeners, picked up its signal every day (Overseas Audience Research, "The Audience of the BBC's General Overseas Service").

76. Ibid.

77. Ibid.

78. Blackburne, verbatim report of evidence to the broadcasting committee, 9 November 1949, UKNA, CO 875/71/1.

79. BBC Board of Governors paper G68/46, 14 November 1946, quoted in Mansell, Let Truth Be Told, 216.

80. BBC, Overseas Presentation Handbook, 3rd ed. (London: BBC, June 1955).

81. Ibid., 28.

82. Ibid., 36.

83. Ibid., 16.

84. Ibid., 22–25.

85. VQ7LO Nairobi (Kenya) Broadcasting Station, 18 February 1947, BBC WAC, E1/10/3. Although the regional stations in the colony often carried the same schedule as Nairobi for certain parts of the day, they also developed their own programming styles, such as the Muslim radio culture and emphasis on local dialect that became more prominent at the Mombasa station over the 1950s. See James R. Brennan, "A History of Sauti ya Mvita [Voice of Mombasa]: Radio, Public Culture, and Islam in Coastal Kenya, 1947–1966," in *New Media and Religious Transformations in Africa*, ed. Rosalind I. J. Hackett and Benjamin F. Soares (Bloomington: Indiana University Press, 2015), 19–38.

86. Gold Coast Broadcasting Department, "Your Programme for the Week April 7–April 13," pamphlet, BBC WAC, E1/29/1; John Wilson, "Gold Coast Information," *African Affairs* (1944): 111–15.

87. BBC General Advisory Council, broadcasts on colonial topics from September 1948 to August 1949, UKNA, CO 875/70/8.

88. BBC General Advisory Council, 28 October 1949, UKNA, CO 875/70/8.

89. Huxtable to Grenfell Williams, 10 May 1946; Grenfell Williams to Huxtable, 18 July 1946, BBC WAC, E1/29/1.

90. See correspondence from March 1950 in BBC WAC, E1/32.

91. M. J. Esslin, 3 July 1950, BBC WAC, E1/32.

92. Two significant reports from this era were *Mass Education in African Societies* (London: HMSO, 1944) and *Education for Citizenship* (London: HMSO, 1948). The topic of mass education in colonial Africa is the subject of numerous studies; see, for instance, D. A. Low and John Lonsdale, "Introduction," in *History of East Africa, Volume 3*, ed. D. A. Low and Alison Smith (Oxford: Clarendon Press, 1976); Charlotte Lydia Riley, "Monstrous Predatory Vampires and Beneficent Fairy-Godmothers: British Post-War Colonial Development in Africa," PhD diss., University College London, 2013; Joanna Lewis, *Empire State-Building: War and Welfare in Kenya, 1925–52* (Athens: Ohio University Press, 2000).

93. Armour, "The BBC and the Development of Broadcasting," 359–60, 376–78.

94. For accounts of these events, see Frederick Cooper, *On the African Waterfront: Urban Disorder and the Transformation of Work in Colonial Mombasa* (New Haven, CT: Yale University Press, 1987); Cooper, *Decolonization and African Society: The Labor Question in French and British Africa* (Cambridge: Cambridge University Press, 1996); Dennis Austin, *Politics in Ghana, 1946–1960* (London: Oxford University Press, 1964), 49–102; and Richard Rathbone, "The Government of the Gold Coast after the Second World War," *African Affairs* 67, no. 268 (July 1968), 210–15.

95. Gadsden, "Wartime Propaganda in Kenya"; Stephanie Newell, "Paradoxes of Press Freedom in Colonial West Africa," *Media History* 22, no. 1 (2016): 107–13.

96. Armour, "The BBC and the Development of Broadcasting," 374.

97. Ibid., 378–80.

98. Colonial Secretary, Special courses for colonial broadcasters, circular 1044/54, 2 November 1954, KNA, AHC 18/77.

99. Ibid.

100. See correspondence in BBC WAC, E31/34/1.

101. Ghana Broadcasting Corporation, *50 Years of Broadcasting in Ghana*, Golden Jubilee pamphlet (Accra: GBC, July 1985), 12–13.

102. See correspondence in BBC WAC, E1/9.

103. For studies that explain some of the ways this occurred, see Daniel Branch and Nicholas Cheeseman, "The Politics of Control in Kenya: Understanding the Bureaucratic-Executive State, 1952–1978," *Review of African Political Economy* 33, no. 107 (2006), 11–31; Justin Willis, Gabrielle Lynch, and Nic Cheeseman, "Voting, Nationhood, and Citizenship in Late-Colonial Africa," *Historical Journal* 61, no. 4 (2018): 1113–35; Cooper, *Decolonization and African Society*, 392–401.

104. J. B. Clark to James B. Millar about Ghana on 1 April 1957, BBC WAC, E1/1431/1.

105. Until 1939 the BBC provided the Empire Service from its license revenues; then, at the outbreak of the war, the Ministry of Information took over responsibility for funding British external broadcasting.

106. *Broadcasting Policy*, 1946, Cmd. 6852, at paragraph 60.

107. *Summary of the Report of the Independent Commission of Enquiry into the Overseas Information Services* (Drogheda Report), April 1954, Cmd. 9138.

108. Ibid., 46–51.

109. James R. Brennan, "Radio Cairo and the Decolonization of East Africa, 1953–64," in *Making a World after Empire: The Bandung Moment and Its Political Afterlives*, ed. Christopher J. Lee (Athens: Ohio University Press, 2010), esp. 174–82.

110. Mansell, *Let Truth Be Told*, 239.

111. For evidence the government already hoped to make sizable cuts to the external services, see draft proposals to the BBC, 1 November 1956, UKNA, CO 1027/78. For discussion about the reaction of different members of the government to the BBC's Suez coverage, see Asa Briggs, *The History of Broadcasting in the United Kingdom, Volume 5: Competition* (Oxford: Oxford University Press, 1995), 73–137. The accounts of the Suez Crisis in Mansell, *Let Truth Be Told*, and Walker, *Skyful of Freedom*, are examples of how the Suez Crisis became portrayed in the corporation's account of its own history.

112. *Overseas Information Services*, July 1957, Cmnd. 225, 5.

113. Clark to controller of overseas services, 6 September 1956, BBC WAC, E2/690/1.

114. BBC WAC, E1/1439/1.

115. Millar to Clark, 17 March 1957, UKNA, DO 35/9648.

116. B. Cockram, note, 21 March 1957, UKNA, DO 35/9648; Clark to Millar, 1 April 1957, BBC WAC, E1/1431/1.

117. [Author unknown] to Clark, 22 March 1957, BBC WAC, E1/1431/1.

118. A. H. Joyce, 2 April 1957, UKNA, DO 35/9648.

119. Sunday Folawiyo, "Why 'Home' News from Britain," *Daily Times*, October 10, 1958.

120. C. F. MacLaren to Winther, 23 October 1958, UKNA, CO 1027/329.

121. Unlike most African states in the 1960s, broadcasting in Nigeria after independence comprised federal, regional, and commercial stations that existed side by side (BBC WAC E1/1430/2).

122. UNESCO, *Statistics on Radio and Television, 1950–1960*, 56, 60. Data about radio ownership was self-reported from each of the colonies and countries. For most parts of Africa in this period the figures are based on extremely rough estimates.

123. GBC, *50 Years of Broadcasting in Ghana*. This wired broadcasting system remained for at least twenty more years; a 1977 article described that the rediffusion system still "survives and flourishes today in Ghana," (Head, "British Colonial Broadcasting Policies," 41).

124. C. A. Hayes to S. O. V. Hodge, 17 June 1953, KNA, DC/TAMB/3/18/4. For more of the history of saucepan radios in Africa, see Rosaleen Smyth, "A Note on the 'Saucepan Special': The People's Radio of Central Africa," *Historical Journal of Film, Radio and Television* 4, no. 2 (1984): 195–201.

125. Myles Osborne, "'The Rooting Out of Mau Mau from the Minds of the Kikuyu Is a Formidable Task': Propaganda and the Mau Mau War," *Journal of African History* 56, no. 1 (March 2015): 77–97.

126. Hodge to district commissioners, 21 May 1953, KNA, DC/TAMB/3/18/4.

127. UNESCO, *Statistics on Radio and Television, 1950–1960*, 60.

128. Low and Lonsdale, "Introduction"; Joseph Morgan Hodge, *Triumph of the Expert: Agrarian Doctrines of Development and the Legacies of British Colonialism* (Athens: Ohio University Press, 2007); Sabine Clarke, "A Technocratic Imperial State? The Colonial Office and Scientific Research, 1940–1960," *Twentieth Century British History* 18, no. 4 (2007), 453–80.

129. See for example, Rosaleen Smyth, "The Development of British Colonial Film Policy, 1927–1939, with Reference to East and Central Africa," *Journal of African History* 20, no. 3 (July 1979): 437–50; James Burns, *Cinema and Society in the British Empire, 1895–1940* (Basingstoke, UK: Palgrave Macmillan, 2013).

CHAPTER 4. ". . . CALLING AFRICA"

1. Gerard Mansell, *Let Truth Be Told: 50 Years of BBC External Broadcasting* (London: Weidenfeld and Nicolson, 1982); Andrew Walker, *A Skyful of Freedom: 60 Years of the BBC World Service* (London: Broadside Books, 1992); John Tusa, *A Word in Your Ear: Reflections on Changes* (London: Broadside Books, 1992).

2. Asa Briggs, *The History of Broadcasting in the United Kingdom, Volume 5: Competition* (Oxford: Oxford University Press, 1995); Alban Webb, *London Calling: Britain, the BBC World Service and the Cold War* (London: Bloomsbury, 2014).

3. For more on the Cold War in Africa, see Odd Arne Westad, *The Global Cold War: Third World Interventions and the Making of Our Times* (Cambridge: Cambridge University Press, 2005); Leslie James and Elisabeth Leake, eds., *Decolonization and the Cold War: Negotiating Independence* (London: Bloomsbury, 2015). On broadcasting in Africa, see James R. Brennan, "Radio Cairo and the Decolonization of East Africa, 1953–64," in *Making a World after Empire: The Bandung Moment and Its Political Afterlives*, ed. Christopher J. Lee (Athens: Ohio University Press, 2010), 173–95; Stephen R. Davis, "The African National Congress, Its Radio, Its Allies, and Exile," *Journal of Southern African Studies* 35, no. 2 (June 2009): 349–73; Gavin Schaffer, "The Limits of the 'Liberal Imagination': Britain, Broadcasting and Apartheid South Africa, 1948–1994," *Past & Present* 240, no. 1 (August 2018): 235–66.

4. Herbert J. Gans, *Deciding What's News: A Study of CBS Evening News, NBC Nightly News, Newsweek, and Time* (New York: Pantheon, 1979); Heidi J. S. Tworek, *News from*

Germany: The Competition to Control World Communications, 1900–1945 (Cambridge, MA: Harvard University Press, 2019).

5. British Broadcasting Corporation, *BBC Handbook 1963* (London: BBC, 1963), 80.

6. "News Ban Defended by Kenya," *Daily Telegraph*, 30 November 1964, in KNA, AHC/1/34. See also, C. F. MacLaren to John B. Ure, 28 November 1964, UKNA, FO 1110/1855.

7. United States Information Agency, 22d Report to Congress, 1 January–30 June 1964, 9–10.

8. BBC African Audience Research, Swahili Service questionnaires—March 1971, 21 May 1971, 7–8, BBC WAC, E1/186/1.

9. For a full accounting of this history, see Briggs, *History of Broadcasting in the United Kingdom, Volume 5: Competition.*

10. Webb, *London Calling*; Michael Nelson, *War of the Black Heavens: The Battles of Western Broadcasting in the Cold War* (Syracuse, NY: Syracuse University Press, 1997).

11. Briggs, *History of Broadcasting in the United Kingdom, Volume 5: Competition*, 708–10.

12. Donald S. Cape to Oliver J. Whitley, 1 December 1969, UKNA, FCO 26/435.

13. Whitley to Cape, 21 August 1969, UKNA, FCO 26/435.

14. Whitley to Cape, 5 January 1970, UKNA, FCO 26/435.

15. Report on Hausa Service, 20 August 1969, UKNA, FCO 26/435.

16. "BBC Maarifa Club," *London Calling* 3, no. 26 (May 1965), 2.

17. The evidence for this is ink stamps that say "African Audience Research" with a date at the top of letters from African listeners in the BBC African Service files. (See, for example, correspondence in *African Theatre* files in BBC WAC, E40/212/1.) Each of the Swahili Service audience reports explains how the audience research department identified its sample, with the vast majority coming from the Maarifa Club mailing list and a smaller percentage from recent listener letters (see 1968, 1971, 1972, and 1973 reports in BBC WAC, E3/186/1.) For more context about the BBC's overseas audience research, see Graham Mytton, "Audience Research at the BBC World Service 1932–2010," *Participations: Journal of Audience and Reception Studies* 8, no. 1 (May 2011): 75–103.

18. Swahili Audience Research, African Service: Swahili Panel Questionnaire—May 1972, September 1972, 2–4, BBC WAC, E3/186/1.

19. Ibid., 4–5.

20. See Daniel Branch and Nicholas Cheeseman, "The Politics of Control in Kenya: Understanding the Bureaucratic-Executive State, 1952–78," *Review of African Political Economy* 33, no. 107 (2006), 11–31. In addition, for thorough accounts of postcolonial Kenya and of Britain and Kenya's relationship during the Kenyatta government, see Daniel Branch, *Kenya: Between Hope and Despair, 1963–2011* (New Haven, CT: Yale University Press, 2011); Poppy Cullen, *Kenya and Britain after Independence: Beyond Neo-Colonialism* (Cham: Palgrave Macmillan, 2017).

21. KANU, press release no. 20, 12 April 1963, KNA, AHC/3/24.

22. P. J. Gachathi to Richard Koske, 11 April 1967, KNA, AHC/1/34.

23. Gachathi to Koske, 7 June 1967, KNA, AHC/1/34.

24. For example, in Tanganyika the annual report for 1961 referred to the broadcaster "preparing itself materially, psychologically, and physically for 9 Dec [independence]

and afterwards" (Annual Report of Sauti ya Tanganyika for the period 1 January 1961 to 31 December 1961, Graham Mytton papers, ICS 115/2/3, Institute of Commonwealth Studies Library [hereafter cited as Mytton papers]).

25. For references from VOK, see Gachathi to Director of Broadcasting VOK and Chief News Editor VOK, 24 March 1966, KNA, AHC 18/16; H. W. Thompson, monthly reports, 1967, KNA, AHC/10/52 and AHC/10/53. For references from Tanganyika, see Annual Reports of the Tanganyika Broadcasting Corporation for 1960 to 1962, Mytton papers, ICS 115/2/3.

26. Timothy Bungey, English Language Services monthly report, July 1964; Koske, Director's report—January–April 1967, KNA, AHC/10/52.

27. J. R. E. Carr-Gregg to B. Cockram, 3 August 1960, UKNA, DO 35/9648.

28. Jomo Kenyatta, 1 July 1964, "Prime Minister Speech on Voice of Kenya" (recording), digitized copy at Kenya Broadcasting Corporation, accessed 15 July 2013.

29. Gachathi to director of broadcasting, 31 March 1966, KNA, AHC/1/34.

30. Ibid.; Gachathi to senior press office and chief editors KNA and VOK, 4 May 1966, KNA, AHC 18/16.

31. Gachathi to director of broadcasting, 31 March 1966, KNA, AHC/1/34.

32. "Outside observer" to Oneko, opinions on KBC news coverage for the week of 11–17 February, n.d., KNA, AHC 18/16.

33. For more about the business of supplying news to a region such as East Africa during the Cold War, see James R. Brennan, "The Cold War Battle over Global News in East Africa: Decolonization, the Free Flow of Information, and the Media Business, 1960–1980," *Journal of Global History* 10 (2015): 333–56.

34. Terry Heron, KBC news division monthly report—March 1964, 1 April 1964, KNA, AHC 18/16.

35. Graham Mytton, notes of interviews with Stephen Mlatie (8 November 1967), Martin Kiama (28 November 1967), and A. Cheche (18 April 1968), Mytton papers, ICS 115/2/5.

36. A. Cheche qtd. in Ibid.

37. For Kenya, Frank Barton to John Ithau, 25 April 1966, KNA, AHC/1/34. MPs in Tanganyika also complained about the reliance on Reuters (Parliamentary Debates (Hansard) National Assembly, 18 February 1964, col. 9, no. 10, in Mytton papers, ICS 115/2/1).

38. For coups, Gachathi to Koske, 21 March 1966; Koske to chief editor, 31 March 1967, KNA, AHC 1/34. For secessionism, Ithau to director of broadcasting, 5 August 1967, KNA, AHC 1/34.

39. Ithau to B. R. Omori (chief editor, VOK), 3 September 1964, KNA, AHC 1/34.

40. Barton to Ithau, 25 April 1966, KNA, AHC 1/34.

41. Mwakio to director of broadcasting, 10 July 1967, KNA, AHC 1/34.

42. Barton to Ithau, 25 April 1966, KNA, AHC 1/34.

43. For Kenya, L. J. Kibui to Gachathi, 21 November 1967; Ithau to Gachathi, 27 November 1967, KNA, AHC 1/34. For Tanganyika, Brian Eccles to S. E. Watrous, 22 February 1962, BBC WAC, E40/202/2.

44. Martin Kiama, interview by Graham Mytton, 7 November 1967, Mytton papers, ICS 115/2/5, no. 6, interview 1.

45. Kenyatta, "Prime Minister Speech on Voice of Kenya."

46. Kibui to Gachathi, 21 November 1967, KNA, AHC 1/34.

47. Ithau to Gachathi, 14 November 1967, KNA, AHC 1/34.

48. Gachathi to senior press office and chief editors KNA and VOK, 4 May 1966, KNA, AHC 18/16.

49. Gachathi to Acting Chief Editor VOK, 8 March 1966; J. Cooper (for Permanent Secretary, Ministry of Housing and Social Services) to Gachathi, 25 March 1966, Jesse Kimani (PIO Embu) to Permanent Secretary MIB, 6 November 1967, KNA, AHC 18/16.

50. Walter Mbotela to director of broadcasting, 13 October 1967, KNA, AHC 18/16.

51. Gachathi to director of broadcasting, 15 July 1965, KNA, AHC 1/34.

52. Gerald G. Marans, Voice of Kenya monthly report, August 1965, KNA, AHC/10/52.

53. Gachathi to Koske, Programmes—Continuity announcers and news readers, 14 March 1968, KNA, AHC/18/16.

54. Governor-general of Nigeria to secretary of state for the colonies, 14 January 1959, UKNA, FCO 141/13703.

55. BBC, *BBC Handbook 1964*, 80; *BBC Handbook 1970*, 99.

56. See BBC WAC, E3/186/1.

57. African Audience Research, Swahili Service Questionnaire—April 1966, 29 September 1966, p. 3, BBC WAC, E3/186/1.

58. Ghana Ministry of Information, Radio Ghana's external broadcasting service, 22 June 1961, BBC WAC, E1/1431/2.

59. BBC, *BBC Handbook 1970*, 111–12.

60. BBC, *BBC Handbook 1963*, 68–69.

61. BBC, *BBC Handbook 1970*, 98.

62. Like its British counterpart, many of the histories of the Voice of America come from VOA broadcasters who offer a principled account of the broadcaster's history rooted in its stated mission. For VOA, the primary example of this is Alan L. Heil Jr., *VOA: A History* (New York: Columbia University Press, 2003), 32, 36–37.

63. Gregory M. Tomlin, *Murrow's Cold War: Public Diplomacy for the Kennedy Administration* (Lincoln, NE: Potomac Books, 2016); see also, Nicholas J. Cull, *The Cold War and the United States Information Agency: American Propaganda and Public Diplomacy* (Cambridge: Cambridge University Press, 2008).

64. Donald M. Wilson to Robert F. Kennedy, preliminary report on USIA, December 1960, US Department of State, *Foreign Relations of the United States, 1917–1972, Volume 6: Public Diplomacy, 1961–1963*, document 3. https://history.state.gov/historicaldocuments/frus1917-72PubDipvo6/d3.

65. *Hearing before the Subcommittee on Africa of the Committee on Foreign Affairs*, 87th Cong. 2 (1962) (statement of Edward R. Murrow, director of the United States Information Agency).

66. Ibid.

67. Mary L. Dudziak, *Cold War Civil Rights: Race and the Image of American Democracy* (Princeton, NJ: Princeton University Press, 2002). Also see Penny M. Von Eschen, *Race against Time: Black Americans and Anticolonialism, 1937–1957* (Ithaca, NY: Cornell University Press, 1997); Kevin K. Gaines, *American Africans in Ghana: Black Expatriates and the Civil Rights Era* (Chapel Hill: University of North Carolina Press, 2006).

68. *Hearing before the Subcommittee on Africa* (statement of Edward R. Murrow), 2–3.

69. United States Information Agency, 22d Report to Congress, January 1–June 30, 1964, 25–26.

70. Konrad Syrop (Head of BBC External Services Productions), "Touting for Custom" in BBC, *BBC Handbook 1963*, 24–25.

71. For more about British broadcasting to West Africa in Hausa and French during this period, see Andrew W. M. Smith, "'Information after Imperialism': British Overseas Representation and Francophone Africa (1957–1967)," in *Imagining Britain's Economic Future, c. 1800–1975: Trade, Consumerism, and Global Markets*, ed. David Thackeray, Andrew Thompson, and Richard Toye (Cham: Palgrave Macmillan, 2018), 205–29.

72. Tony Dean to D. P. Wolferstan, 20 August 1958; G. M. Gaymer to Reiss, 2 September 1958, KNA, AHC 18/77; Gaymer to Chalmers, 25 March 1960, BBC WAC, E30/1/1.

73. Jubb to Wolferstan, 7 September 1959, BBC WAC, E30/1/1.

74. Asher Lee to Watrous, 24 January 1961, BBC WAC, E2/688/2.

75. W. F. Coleman to J. B. Millar, 10 March 1961, BBC WAC, E1/1431/2.

76. Wolferstan to Jubb, 12 August 1959, BBC WAC, E30/1/1.

77. Dean to establishments division, 21 March 1958, KNA, AHC 18/77.

78. Wolferstan to Reiss, 2 September 1958, KNA, AHC 18/77.

79. Quoted in BBC African Audience Research, Hausa Service questionnaire—September 1969, 11 February 1970, 11, BBC WAC, E3/174/1.

80. For examples of complaints about standards of VOK's Swahili news, see Oluoch to Permanent Secretary, 30 April 1963, KNA, AHC 3/24; Koske to A. Senuasi, 28 September 1970, KNA, AHC 1/34. For its part, the Voice of Kenya considered different ways to combat the poor level of spoken Swahili. At one point, it considered sending VOK newsreaders to Tanzania for practice, but the idea was nixed because it was too expensive.

81. "Sauti ya Tanganyika" Annual Report for 1961, Mytton papers, ICS 115/2/3.

82. Angus McDermid, interviewed by Ray Davies, 4 July 1988, C408/004, tapes 5 and 6, British Library Sound Archive, NLSC: Leaders of National Life Oral History Collection.

83. African Audience Research, Hausa Service questionnaire—September 1969, 11 February 1970, BBC WAC, E3/174/1.

84. E. Matu to Gachathi, 4 April 1966, KNA, AHC/1/34.

85. J. F. Wilkinson to G. T. M. de M. Morgan, 17 November 1961, BBC WAC, E40/202/2.

86. See for example Morgan, 3 April 1962, BBC WAC, E1/1439/1.

87. Barton to Ithau, 25 April 1966, KNA, AHC/1/34.

88. For Kenya, see correspondence between Patrick Jubb and Bush House in BBC WAC E1/1450/2; Acting Governor of Kenya to Secretary of State for the Colonies, 22 January 1959, UKNA, CO 1027/330.

89. Graham Mytton, "40 Years of Broadcasting from London in African Languages," in *Africa Bibliography 1996*, ed. Chris H. Allen (Edinburgh: Edinburgh University Press, 1997), xvi.

90. Dawid S. Engela to Copps, programme publicity—week 12, March 1962, BBC WAC, E40/212/2.

91. Shirley Cordeaux, "The BBC African Service's Involvement in African Theatre" *Research in African Literature* 1, no. 2 (1970): 148, http://www.jstor.org/stable/3818573.

92. Cordeaux to Ngũgĩ, 15 January 1965, BBC WAC, E40/212/2.

93. John Gordon to Berridge, 13 October 1969, BBC WAC, E40/212/1; Veronica Manoukin to M. F. C. Roebuck, 27 March 1968, BBC WAC, E40/212/2; Cordeaux to Robin Minney, 27 September 1966, BBC WAC, E40/210/1.

94. See, for example, Gordon to Nkem Nwankwo, 16 October 1967, BBC WAC, E40/212/2.

95. BBC African Service press releases, 1969, BBC WAC, E40/211/1. The discussion about the plays' content is based on the correspondence in the BBC archive, not the plays themselves because those were not preserved.

96. Ngũgĩ to Cordeaux, 3 October 1966, BBC WAC, E40/212/2.

97. Engela, "The producer talks about 'African Theatre,'" broadcast script, 16 April 1963, BBC WAC, E40/212/2.

98. Dina Lingaga, "Radio Theatre: The Moral Play in the Historical Context of State Control and Censorship of Broadcasting in Kenya," in *Radio in Africa: Publics, Cultures, Communities*, ed. Liz Gunnar, Dina Lingaga, and Dumisani Moyo (Suffolk, UK: James Currey, 2011).

99. Cordeaux, "The BBC African Service's involvement in African Theatre," 151.

100. Gordon to Hutchinson, 21 March 1969, BBC WAC, E40/212/1.

101. Ibid.

102. Fela Davies to Gwyneth Henderson, 8 July 1970, BBC WAC, E40/212/1.

103. Ibid.

104. For a sample of complaints, see correspondence in BBC WAC, E40/212/2.

105. Cordeaux, "The BBC African Service's Involvement in African Theatre," 149.

CHAPTER 5. PATRONS OF POSTCOLONIAL CULTURE

1. Rex Collings to J. Rogers, 25 February 1963, AOUP, LG 229/221(1).

2. Collings to David Neale, 4 July 1962, AOUP, OP1619/12161 regarding *The Lion and the Jewel* by Wole Soyinka.

3. For example, Camille Lizarríbar, *Something Else Will Stand Beside It: The African Writers Series and the Development of African Literature* (Ann Arbor: University of Michigan Press, 1998); Gail Low, *Publishing the Postcolonial: Anglophone West African and Caribbean Writing in the UK 1948–1968* (New York: Routledge, 2011).

4. Caroline Davis, *Creating Postcolonial Literature: African Writers and British Publishers* (New York: Palgrave Macmillan, 2013). See also Graham Huggan, *The Postcolonial Exotic: Marketing the Margins* (New York: Routledge, 2001), 50–57.

5. James Currey, *Africa Writes Back: The African Writers Series and the Launch of African Literature* (Athens: Ohio University Press, 2008); Phaswane Mpe, "The Role of the Heinemann African Writers Series in the Development and Promotion of African Literature," *African Studies* 58 (1999): 105–22, doi: 10.1080 /00020189908707907.

6. Davis, *Creating Postcolonial Literature*, 53.

7. John Nottingham, "Establishing an African Publishing Industry: A Study in Decolonization," *African Affairs* 68, no. 271 (April 1969), 140.

8. For OUP see [Author unknown], "Macmillans in Africa," n.d. [1967], AOUP, LOGE 000289; for George Allen and Unwin see John Budds to Charles Furth, 20 January 1966, University of Reading Special Collections (hereafter cited as URSC), AUC 1102/9.

9. Statement by the Publishers Association on State Monopoly Publishing and Distribution and the Erosion of Copyright, 27 April 1967, AOUP, LOGE 000289.

10. Davis, *Creating Postcolonial Literature,* 53–56.

11. East African branch annual editorial report: year ending 31 March 1977, AOUP, CPGE 00047. (Emphasis in original)

12. East African branch annual editorial report: year ending 31 March 1977, AOUP, CPGE 00047.

13. See chapter 6 for more on Britain's Aid to Commonwealth English (ACE) scheme.

14. Clive Brasnett, *Mr. Nirmal's Guru and Other True Tales* (London: Peris Press, 2009), 125.

15. Ibid.

16. Ibid.

17. Ibid., 124.

18. L. Wandera to head of Kenya School Equipment Scheme, 10 February 1977, KNA, XJ/3/141.

19. Davis, *Creating Postcolonial Literature,* 56.

20. Clive Brasnett, interviewed by Brian Hedger, April 26, 2006, C1083/25, tape, British Council Oral History Collection.

21. Davis, *Creating Postcolonial Literature,* 56.

22. Brasnett, interview.

23. Minutes of first meeting of Kenya Publishers Association, 18 September 1970, KNA, RW/2/2.

24. Objects and regulations of the Kenya Publishers Association, January 1971; Minutes of meeting of Kenya Publishers Association, 3 June 1971, KNA, RW/2/2.

25. K. W. Martin, Ministry of Works primary school orders—Kenya, 22 November 1971; Houghton to Sempira, draft letter to MOW, 7 December 1971, KNA, RW/2/2.

26. Nottingham to Houghton, 17 February 1975, KNA, RW/2/3. By this point, John Nottingham represented a new firm called TransAfrica Publishers, after he was dismissed as publishing manager of the EAPH in 1973 (Minutes of KPA meetings, 1973–1974, KNA, RW/2/3).

27. Minutes of annual general meeting of KPA, 19 September 1979, KNA, RW/2/3.

28. Henry Chakava, interview, 5 July 2013, Nairobi.

29. Collings to Rogers, 25 February 1963, AOUP, LG 229/221(1).

30. Ever since Western publishers began thinking of literature from the Global South as occupying a new international market, scholars and writers have fiercely debated the label "Third World literature" and its position in postcolonial studies. As a sample of some of the contributions to this debate, see Fredric Jameson, "Third-World Literature in an Era of Multinational Capitalism," *Social Text* 15 (Autumn 1986): 65–88 and the exchange it prompted with Aijaz Ahmad, "Jameson's Rhetoric of Otherness and the 'National Allegory,'" *Social Text* 17 (Autumn 1987): 3–25; and Emily Apter, *Against World Literature: On the Politics of Untranslatability* (London: Verso, 2013).

31. These reviews and a series of others are quoted in Low, *Publishing the Postcolonial*, 1.

32. Bernth Lindfors, *Critical Perspectives on Amos Tutuola* (Washington, DC: Three Continents Press, 1975).

33. This story is retold in many places, including, "Working with Chinua Achebe: The African Writers Series. James Currey, Alan Hill, and Keith Sambrook in conversation with Kirsten Holst Petersen," in *Chinua Achebe: A Celebration*, edited by Kirsten Holst Petersen and Anna Rutherford (Oxford: Heinemann International Literature and Textbooks, 1991), 49.

34. Philip Stanley Rawson, "The Centre Cannot Hold," *Times Literary Supplement*, June 20, 1958, 341.

35. Currey, *Africa Writes Back*, 28.

36. In Britain, Oxford University Press divided its different imprints between Oxford, where the prestigious Clarendon imprint for academic books was located, and London, where the general and educational divisions were located. The overseas division was in London because it was almost completely concerned with general and educational books.

37. Peter Sutcliffe, *The Oxford University Press: An Informal History* (Oxford: Clarendon Press, 1978), 266–68.

38. Collings to Neale, 4 July 1962, AOUP, OP1619/12161.

39. Collings to T. Tani Solaru, 22 February 1962, AOUP, OP1619/12161.

40. Neal Burton to Solaru, 5 July 1962, AOUP, OP1619/12161.

41. John Bell to Collings, 19 July 1962, AOUP, OP1619/12161.

42. Gerald Moore to Collings, 2 August 1962, AOUP, OP1619/12161.

43. Solaru to Burton, 28 June 1962; Bell to Collings, 19 July 1962, AOUP, OP1619/12161.

44. Anthony Toyne to Solaru, 27 September 1966, AOUP, LG229/221(1).

45. Toyne to Charles Lewis, 22 September 1966, AOUP, LG229/221(1).

46. Burton to Collings, 4 June 1962, AOUP, LG229/221(1).

47. Collings to Neale, 26 June 1962; C. O. Botchway to the Publisher, 20 December 1962, AOUP, LG229/221(1).

48. Burton to Collings, 8 February 1963, AOUP, LG229/221(1).

49. Burton to the Publisher, 8 February 1963, AOUP, LG229/221(1). The rumor was not true, and Oxford came out with Easmon's play the next year.

50. The latter was an enormous concern after Kenya set new literature syllabi in 1980 (see correspondence in KNA, XJ/1/131.)

51. Caroline Davis, "The Politics of Postcolonial Publishing: Oxford University Press's Three Crowns Series 1962-1976," *Book History* 8 (2005): 235, http://www.jstor.org/stable /30227377.

52. S. W. Smith to Lewis, 1967, AOUP, LG229/221(1).

53. In this discussion, I sometimes use Heinemann as shorthand for Heinemann Educational Books (HEB), which was the educational offshoot of the British publishing house William Heinemann, Ltd.

54. The history of Heinemann and the African Writers Series appears in publishers' accounts (Alan Hill, *In Pursuit of Publishing* [London: J. Murray in association with Heinemann Educational Books, 1988]; Currey, *Africa Writes Back;* Becky Clarke, "The African Writers Series—Celebrating Forty Years of Publishing Distinction," *Research in African Literatures* 34, no. 2 [2003]: 163–74, doi: 10.1353/ral.2003.0027), as well as

scholarly works (Low, *Publishing the Postcolonial;* Mpe, "The Role of the Heinemann African Writers Series").

55. Currey, *Africa Writes Back,* 20.

56. William Heinemann published Achebe's *No Longer at Ease* in 1960; it was reprinted in the African Writers Series in 1963 as AWS #3. Cyprian Ekwensi was first published in Nigeria by Onitsha in the late 1940s and had children's works published by Oxford and Cambridge University presses in the 1950s. *People of the City* was his first full-length novel and was published in Britain by Andrew Dakers in 1954. It became AWS #5 (1963). Peter Abrahams's *Mine Boy* was published in 1946 by Dorothy Crisp; it was his third novel to be published in Britain. *Mine Boy* became AWS #6 (1963).

57. "Working with Chinua Achebe," 153; Hill, *In Pursuit of Publishing,* 126.

58. Keith Sambrook in 1963, quoted in Currey, *Africa Writes Back,* 12.

59. Currey, *Africa Writes Back,* 115.

60. In 1963, Heinemann paid Achebe £150 for acting as editorial adviser to the AWS series for the year (URSC, HEB/06/08).

61. La Guma became well known among antiapartheid activists and communist organizations in South Africa during the 1940s and 1950s, leading to his being accused at the Treason Trials of 1956. During the mid-1960s, he and his family went into exile to the UK, which was where he was living when HEB signed him. For more on La Guma's politics and writings during this era, see Christopher J. Lee, ed., *A Soviet Journey: A Critical Annotated Edition,* by Alex La Guma (New York: Lexington Books, 2017).

62. Currey, *Africa Writes Back,* 143, 201–2.

63. Hill, 144.

64. Currey, *Africa Writes Back,* 22.

65. Neale, 8 February 1963, AOUP, LG229/221(1).

66. Davis, *Creating Postcolonial Literature,* 98. Oxford University Press did publish two other Soyinka titles in the late 1960s (*Kongi's Harvest* in 1967 and *Three Short Plays* in 1969), but Collings had been the one to acquire both works.

67. Toyne to Lewis, 26 September 1966; P. J. Chester, 5 April 1967, AOUP, LG229/221(1).

68. Lewis to Toyne, 31 October 1966, AOUP, LG229/221(1).

69. Markham to Currey, 1 May 1970, URSC, HEB 54/10.

70. Alamin Mazrui includes Heinemann's translations as part of what he labels the third wave of Swahili literary translations that began in the early postcolonial period. See Alamin M. Mazrui, *Cultural Politics of Translation: East Africa in a Global Context* (New York: Routledge, 2016), 4–5, 148–49.

71. At this same time, OUP Eastern Africa inquired about the rights with HEB as well (Lewis to Currey, 30 May 1967; Abdilahi Nassir to Hill, 15 November 1967, URSC, HEB 54/10.)

72. Markham to Hill, 26 August 1971, URSC, HEB 54/10.

73. Markham to Currey, 7 December 1972, URSC, HEB 54/10.

74. Currey to David Bolt, 14 August 1970, URSC, HEB 06/06; Currey to Markham, 9 March 1972, URSC, HEB 06/08.

75. For Ngũgĩ's *Weep Not, Child,* see Amy Hoff to David Machin, 22 April 1970, URSC, HEB 08/01. For Achebe's *Man of the People,* see URSC, HEB 06/06.

76. Currey to Markham, 23 November 1970, USRC, HEB 06/06.

77. Currey to Markham, 12 February 1970, USRC, HEB 10/03.

78. Markham to Currey, 11 December 1969, URSC, HEB 06/08.

79. Currey to Markham, 9 March 1972, URSC, HEB 06/08.

80. Markham to Currey, 16 March 1972, URSC, HEB 06/08.

81. Kole Omotoso, "The Missing Apex: A Search for the Audience" (paper presented at the international conference on publishing and book development, Ife, Nigeria, December 16–20, 1973), in *Publishing in Africa in the Seventies: Proceedings of an International Conference on Publishing and Book Development*, ed. Edwina Oluwasanmi, Eva McLean, and Hans Zell (Ile-Ife, Nigeria: University of Ife Press, 1975), 257–58.

82. Soyinka's novel *The Interpreters*, which Andre Deutsch published in hardback in 1965, was reprinted in the African Writers Series in 1970.

83. J. P. Clark's agreement with Oxford University Press was for royalties of 15 percent on UK and overseas sales (Davis, *Creating Postcolonial Literature*), which was significantly greater than the 7.5 percent royalties that Heinemann offered Ngũgĩ for the African Writers Series paperback and the 10 percent royalties it offered for the hardcover edition.

84. Ayi Kwei Armah, "Larsony or Fiction as Criticism of Fiction," *Asemka: A Journal of Literary Studies* 4 (1976): 1–14, quoted in Currey, *Africa Writes Back*, 75.

85. "Mbari—A New Venture in Nigerian Culture," *Nigeria Magazine* 30, no. 74 (September 1962); Robert M. Wren, *Those Magical Years: The Making of Nigerian Literature at Ibadan: 1948–1966* (Washington, DC: Three Continents Press, 1990).

86. The Congress for Cultural Freedom (CCF) funded a wide variety of cultural organizations and publications around the world. Other than the annual grant, the CCF was not too involved in the early operations of the Mbari Club. When Mbari became a bigger name after the 1962 Makerere conference, which was completely paid for by the CCF, the latter asked its name be mentioned in future publicity and publication articles. In 1966 an editorial in the *New York Times* revealed the funding link between the CCF, the Fairfield Foundation (another source of Mbari funds), and the American CIA. Although the initiative for Mbari's establishment had been conceived in West Africa, its output and its role in forging transnational connections were also part of the global Cold War over culture. For more on the relationship between the CIA and its front organizations, see Frances Stonor Saunders, *Who Paid the Piper? The CIA and the Cultural Cold War* (London: Granta, 1999); Hugh Wilford, *The Mighty Wurlitzer: How the CIA Played America* (Cambridge, MA: Harvard University Press, 2009); Patrick Iber, *Neither Peace nor Freedom: The Cultural Cold War in Latin America* (Cambridge, MA: Harvard University Press, 2015), 83–115.

87. Ezekiel Mphahlele, "The Makerere Writers' Conference," *Africa Report* (July 1962): 7–8, Transcription Centre Records, container 1.3.

88. Mphahlele, "Makerere Writers' Conference"; Bernard Fonlon, *Afrika* 8 (August 1962).

89. Mphahlele, "Makerere Writers' Conference."

90. Ibid.

91. Dennis Duerden, "Mbari Writers' Conference in Uganda," Transcription Centre Records, container 1.3.

92. Mphahlele, "Makerere Writers' Conference."

93. Conference of African Writers of English Expression, Makerere University College, Kampala, 11–17 June 1962.

94. *Mbari Newsletters*, Transcription Centre Records, container 3.5.

95. Longmans' proposals for cooperation with the Bureau of Ghana Languages, March 1962, NAG, RG 3/5/1063; Simon D. Allison, "State Participation in Publishing: The Zambian Experience," and A. K. Brown, "State Publishing in Ghana: Has It Benefited Ghana?" in Olyuwasanmi et al., *Publishing in Africa in the Seventies*, 59–69, 113–27.

96. The East African Institute of Social and Cultural Affairs set up the EAPH through a partnership with Andre Deutsch, although the agreement was soon modified (East African Publishing House, press release, 16 February 1965, Transcription Centre Records, container 3.6).

97. Soyinka to Collings, 25 January 1965, AOUP, LG229/221(1).

98. Neale to Soyinka, 16 June 1965, AOUP, LG229/221(1).

99. B. E. to Collings, 17 May 1965, AOUP, LG229/221(1).

100. Ibid.; Collings to Neale, 1 February 1965, AOUP, LG229/221(1).

101. Currey, *Africa Writes Back*, 33.

102. Omotoso, "The Missing Apex: A Search for the Audience," in Olyuwasanmi et al., *Publishing in Africa in the Seventies*, 254.

103. Ibid., 252.

104. Chinua Achebe, "Publishing in Africa: A Writer's View," in Olyuwasanmiet al., *Publishing in Africa in the Seventies*, 45–46.

105. Currey, *Africa Writes Back*, 34.

106. Henry Chakava, "Dealing with the British," *LOGOS* 10, no. 1 (1999): 52, doi: 10.2959 /logo.1999.10.1.52.

CHAPTER 6. FROM CULTURE TO AID TO PAID

1. Colin Perchard, interview by David Waterhouse, 5–6 November 2006, C1083/37, audio file, British Council Oral History Collection.

2. James Mulholland, Narrative review of the year 1981/82: Malawi, 4 May 1982, UKNA, BW 157/18.

3. Perchard, interview.

4. For some examples of this with regard to Ghana's independence, see deputy controller to Hollyer, 20 March 1957, UKNA, BW 93/7; for Malawi's independence, see C. A. F. Dundas to Harrison, 14 September 1962, UKNA, BW 157/3.

5. "Foreign Language Studies: Their Place in the National Life," *English Language Teaching* 1, no. 1 (October 1946): 3–6.

6. "Balance and Proportion," *English Language Teaching* 1, no. 2 (November 1946): 31–33.

7. Richard C. Smith, ed., *Teaching English as a Foreign Language, 1936–1961: Foundations of ELT* (London: Routledge, 2005), civ.

8. R. J. Quinault, "English by Radio," *English Language Teaching* 1, no. 5 (1 March 1947): 119–25; "B.B.C. English Lessons for Foreign Students," *English Language Teaching* 3, no. 2 (1 October 1948): 47–52.

9. Paul Sinker, "The Main Tasks," in British Council, *Annual Report 1958–59* (London: British Council, 1959).

10. Ministry of Education, *Report of the Official Committee on the Teaching of English Overseas*, 23 March 1956, UKNA, CAB 21/4292.

11. Second Commonwealth Education Conference, EC (61) 56, 5 December 1961, UKNA, BW 68/19.

12. Conference on University Teaching and Research in the Use of English as a Second/ Foreign Language, 15–17 December 1960, EC (61) 5, UKNA, BW 68/19.

13. Second Commonwealth Education Conference, EC (61) 56, 5 December 1961, UKNA, BW 68/19.

14. Third Commonwealth Education Conference, EC (64) 35, 6 October 1964, UKNA, BW 68/22.

15. Aid to Commonwealth English (ACE) recruitment of English language officers, EC (62) 49, 6 November 1962, UKNA, BW 68/20.

16. L. R. Phillips to Richard Frost, 15 May 1963, UKNA, BW 95/10.

17. Frost to Arthur King, 5 August 1963, UKNA, BW 95/10.

18. Ibid.

19. King to Phillips, 3 September 1963, UKNA, BW 95/10.

20. See, for example, Executive Committee, 2 May 1961, UKNA, BW 68/19; K. R. Johnstone, Deputy Director General's tour of Southern and Central Africa, EC (62) 8, 23 January 1962, UKNA, BW 68/20; Executive Committee, draft minutes, 2 November 1965, UKNA, BW 68/23.

21. See, for example, minutes and papers of Executive Committee from 1961, UKNA, BW 68/19; W. H. Earle, The council's work in Pakistan, EC (62) 43, 2 October 1962, UKNA, BW 68/20; Paul Sinker, Director-General's report on his visit to Washington, EC (66) 29, 5 July 1966, UKNA, BW 68/24.

22. English language teaching: Anglo-American Conference at Cambridge, 3 October 1961, EC (61) 40, UKNA, BW 68/19.

23. Randolph Quirk and Albert Marckwardt, *A Common Language: British and American English* (London: British Broadcasting Corporation and the United States Government, 1964).

24. R. A. Butler, circular no. 0115, 25 November 1963, UKNA, FO 924/1495.

25. Executive Committee, draft minutes, 5 October 1965, UKNA, BW 68/23.

26. Anglo-American Conference on English language teaching, 2 July 1963, EC (63) 30, UKNA, BW 68/21.

27. David Crystal, interview by Brian Hedger, 19 November 2007, C1083/47, tape, British Council Oral History Collection.

28. Report by the director-general on his tour of Nigeria 11 February—6 March 1962, EC (62) 13, UKNA, BW 68/20.

29. Ibid.

30. Ibid.

31. For more explanation of this, see David Birmingham, *Kwame Nkrumah: The Father of African Nationalism* (Athens: Ohio University Press, 1998), 49–50.

32. Council work in Ghana, EC (63) 44, 1 October 1963, UKNA, BW 68/21.

33. Estimates 1963/64, EC (63) 4, 19 February 1963, UKNA, BW 68/21.

34. Executive Committee, draft minutes, 1 November 1966, UKNA, BW 68/24.

35. For a more detailed examinations that show how British technical assistance in the postcolonial context was embedded in its understanding of its colonial legacy, see Charlotte Lydia Riley, "'The Winds of Change Are Blowing Economically': The Labour Party and British Overseas Development, 1940s–1960s," in *Britain, France and the Decolonization of Africa: Future Imperfect?*, ed. Andrew W. M. Smith and Chris Jeppesen (London: UCL Press, 2017), 54–61; Sarah Stockwell, *The British End of the British Empire* (Cambridge: Cambridge University Press, 2018), 59–60 and 73–77. While the remainder of the chapter refers to the ODM or ODA according to which was in operation at the time, it must be noted that the discussion relies on British Council oral history interviews in which retired council officers use ODM and ODA interchangeably.

36. J. D. B. Fowells, "What the Council Is About," May 1974, PRC (74) 26 Annex A, UKNA, BW 1/653.

37. Report of the working party set up to review coordination between the Ministry of Overseas Development and the British Council, 1969, UKNA, FCO 13/417. From 1965 to 1975, the Hedley-Miller formula stipulated that the ODM would fund approximately one-third and FCO two-thirds of the council's overseas divisions. Then, starting in 1975, the council started a banding formula where it applied different ratios to different countries in which it worked, meaning that in a developing nation such as Kenya the ODA funded 90 percent of the council's operation. Throughout the period, the agency work the council did for the ODA (and others) was outside these formulas.

38. Brian Vale, interview by David Marler, 14 March 2005, C1083/28, tape, British Council Oral History Collection.

39. *Report on Non-Departmental Public Bodies* (Pliatzky Report), Cmnd. 7797, London: HMSO, 1980; also see Martin Kolinsky, "The Demise of the Inter-University Council for Higher Education Overseas: A Chapter in the History of the Idea of the University," *Minerva* 21, no. 1 (March 1983): 37–80.

40. Marler in Vale, interview.

41. Julian Andrews, interview by Tim Butchard, 23 April 2007, C1083/41, tape, British Council Oral History Collection.

42. To see the ways the Colonial Office and the British Council's recruitment and training overlapped and/or diverged during the 1950s and 1960s, see Chris Jeppesen, "A Worthwhile Career for a Man Who Is Not Entirely Self-Seeking": Service, Duty, and the Colonial Service during Decolonization," in *Britain, France and the Decolonization of Africa: Future Imperfect?*, ed. Andrew W. M. Smith and Chris Jeppesen (London: UCL Press, 2017), 133–55. There is also an intriguing overlap in council's emphasis on enthusiasm, friendliness, and absence of expertise with the early VSOs (Jordanna Bailkin, *The Afterlife of Empire* [Berkeley: University of California Press, 2012], 55–94), especially given that the council became the in-country agents for the VSO program.

43. *The British Council: A World-Wide Service* (London: British Council Recruitment Division, 1965), UKNA, BW 68/23. Although the council advertised that it was going to recruit women for these positions, the generalists hired during the early to mid-1960s were largely men, and there were no women in senior positions in the council. Audrey Lambert,

a woman who entered the council in the mid-1960s, remembered the thrill she felt partway into her career when she heard that a woman had been assigned a representative post (Audrey Lambert, interview by Stan Moss, 21 October 2003, C1083/15, tape, British Council Oral History Collection.)

44. John Day, interview by Arthur Sanderson, 7 October 2003, C1083/32, tape, British Council Oral History Collection.

45. John Tod, interview by Tim Butchard, n.d., C1083/62, audio file, British Council Oral History Collection.

46. Peter Elborn, interview by Helen Meixner, 1 November 2007, C1083/46, tape, British Council Oral History Collection.

47. Andrews, interview. The only exceptions, in Andrews's eyes, were the few such as Brian Vale, who were able to demonstrate after they arrived that they were not as insensitive and regimented as might be believed, but rather were, as one council official later put it, "really terribly cuddly . . . very cultural relations-y" (Marler in Vale, interview.) For more on colonial administrators' second careers, see A. H. M. Kirk-Greene, *Britain's Imperial Administrators, 1858–1966* (New York: St. Martin's Press, 1999): 260–73; Joseph Morgan Hodge, "British Colonial Expertise, Post-Colonial Careering and the Early History of International Development," in *Modernizing Missions: Approaches to 'Developing' the Non-Western World after 1945*, ed. Andreas Eckert, Stephan Malinowski, and Corinna R. Unger, (Munich: Beck, 2010), 24–44.

48. Perchard, interview.

49. David Waterhouse, interview by Helen Meixner, 30 November 2007 and 1 October 2008, C1083/48, audio file, British Council Oral History Collection.

50. Frances Donaldson, *The British Council: The First Fifty Years* (London: Jonathan Cape, 1984), 277–78.

51. Charles Troughton, "The Contest for Influence Overseas: Why Britain Must Compete," *Journal of the Royal Society for the Arts* 132, no. 5339 (October 1984): 736.

52. The Heath government established the CPRS in 1971 as part of an effort to modernize and reorganize the central government. It is not to be conflated with the influence or maneuvering of the "think tank archipelago" that Ben Jackson writes about during the same era, most distinctly because the CPRS was largely ineffective at mobilizing important groups of elites. See Simon James, "The Central Policy Review Staff, 1970–1983," *Political Studies* 34, no. 3 (1986): 423–40; Ben Jackson, "The Think-Tank Archipelago: Thatcherism and Neo-Liberalism," in *Making Thatcher's Britain*, ed. Ben Jackson and Robert Saunders (Cambridge: Cambridge University Press, 2012), 43–61.

53. Central Policy Review Staff, *Review of Overseas Representation* (London: HMSO, 1977), ix.

54. Ibid.

55. Trevor Rutter, interview by Helen Meixner, 25 June 2006, C1083/34, tape, British Council Oral History Collection.

56. Ibid.

57. I found Brown's portrayal of neoliberalism to be valuable for this portion of the discussion. Wendy Brown, *Undoing the Demos: Neoliberalism's Stealth Revolution* (Cambridge, MA: Zone Books, 2015).

58. Rutter, interview.

59. John Burgh, interview by Barry Brown, 9 January 2003, C1083/27, tape, British Council Oral History Collection. These accounts of Thatcher's personality, preferences, and leadership style can all be balanced out by the recent appearance of works that examine Margaret Thatcher's administration. For a sample, see Jackson and Saunders, *Making Thatcher's Britain*; Jon Agar, *Science Policy under Thatcher* (London: UCL Press, 2019); and the three volumes by Charles Moore, *Margaret Thatcher: The Authorized Biography* (London: Allan Lane, 2015–2019).

60. Burgh, interview.

61. Rutter, interview.

62. Ibid.

63. Ibid.

64. Fowells, "What the Council Is About."

65. P. A. I. Tahourdin to director-general, 24 June 1974, UKNA, BW 1/653.

66. Waterhouse, interview.

67. Rutter, interview.

68. Ibid.

69. Waterhouse, interview.

70. Burgh, interview.

71. Vale, interview.

72. Ibid.

73. Lambert, interview.

74. Elborn, interview.

75. Rutter, interview.

76. Fowells, "What the Council Is About."

77. Elborn, interview.

78. Ibid.

EPILOGUE

1. Graham Huggan, *The Postcolonial Exotic: Marketing the Margins* (New York: Routledge, 2001); Luke Strongman, *The Booker Prize and the Legacy of Empire* (New York: Rodopi, 2002).

2. Mark Brown, "Man Booker to Allow US Entries from Next Year," *Guardian*, 18 September 2013, https://www.theguardian.com/books/2013/sep/18/man-booker-prize-allow-us-american-entries.

3. Philip Hensher, "'Well, That's the End of the Booker Prize, Then,'" *Guardian*, 18 September 2013, https://www.theguardian.com/books/booksblog/2013/sep/18/booker-prize-us-writers-end.

4. Qtd. in "'A Surprise and a Risk': Reaction to Booker Prize Upheaval," *BBC News*, 18 September 2013, https://www.bbc.com/news/entertainment-arts-24126882.

5. Chinua Achebe, "English and the African Writer," *Transition* 18 (1965): 27–30, reprinted in Ali A. Mazrui, *The Political Sociology of the English Language: An African Perspective* (Mouton: The Hague, 1975), 216–22; Arundhati Roy, "What Is the Morally

Appropriate Language in Which to Think and Write?" W. G. Sebald Lecture, 5 June 2018, British Library.

6. Frances Donaldson, *The British Council: The First Fifty Years* (London: Jonathan Cape, 1984), 35; John Burgh qtd. in William Greaves, "Selling English by the Pound," *Times*, 24 October 1989: 14.

7. John Burgh, "Creating Anglophiles," *English Today* 1, no. 3 (July 1985), 18–19.

8. *BBC Group Annual Report and Accounts 2018/19*, 50.

9. Human Capital 2010, *BBC Global News: International Research Report for the BBC*, January 2010, 52, cited in Marie Gillespie and Alban Webb, "Corporate Cosmopolitanism," in *Diasporas and Diplomacy: Cosmopolitan Contact Zones at the BBC World Service (1932–2012)*, ed. Gillespie and Webb (New York: Routledge, 2013), 3.

10. British Council, *Trust Pays: How International Cultural Relationships Build Trust in the UK and Underpin the Success of the UK Economy* (London: British Council, 2012).

BIBLIOGRAPHY

ARCHIVAL COLLECTIONS

Archive of British Publishing and Printing, University of Reading
Special Collections, Reading, United Kingdom

Heinemann Educational Books Papers (HEB)
Longman Group Papers

British Broadcasting Corporation Written Archives Centre,
Caversham Park, Reading, United Kingdom

British Library Sound Archive, London, United Kingdom

African Writers' Club Collection
British Council Oral History Collection
NLSC: Leaders of National Life Oral History Collection

Harry Ransom Center, University of Texas at Austin, Austin, Texas, USA

Transcription Centre Records

Institute of Commonwealth Studies Library, Senate House, London, United Kingdom

Graham Mytton Papers (ICS 115)

Kenya National Archives, Nairobi, Kenya

Church Missionary Society of Kenya Collection (MSS 61)
District Commissioner Records: Isiolo (ISO), Kakamega (KMG), and Tambach (TAMB)
District Officer Records: Taveta (TAV)
Kenya Literature Bureau Records (RW)

Ministry of Education Records (XJ)
Ministry of Information and Broadcasting Files (AHC)

The National Archives, Kew, United Kingdom
British Council Files (BW)
Cabinet Office Files (CAB)
Colonial Office Files (CO)
Dominions Office Files (DO)
Foreign and Commonwealth Office Files (FCO)
Foreign Office Files (FO)
Ministry of Education Files (ED)
Ministry of Information Files (INF)
Ministry of Overseas Development and Overseas Development Administration Files (OD)
Treasury Files (T)

National Archives and Records Administration, College Park, Maryland, USA
Records of the United States Information Agency (RG 306)

Oxford University Press Archives, Oxford, United Kingdom
Three Crowns Series Files

Oxford University Press Eastern Africa, Nairobi, Kenya

*Public Records and Archives Administration Department
(National Archives of Ghana), Accra, Ghana*
Colonial Secretary's Office Records (CSO)
Ministry of Education Records (RG)

*School of Oriental and African Studies (SOAS) Special Collections Library,
Archives and Special Collections, London, United Kingdom*
Papers of Charles Granston Richards (PP MS 12)

NEWSPAPERS AND MAGAZINES

Africa Abroad
Afrika
Daily Times [Lagos]
East African Standard
Guardian [Manchester]
London Calling
Nigeria Magazine
Stage and Television Today
Times [London]
Times Literary Supplement

INTERVIEWS

Henry Chakava (publisher). 5 July 2013. Nairobi, Kenya.
Tom Hebert (United States Peace Corps). 9–12 June 2017. Telephone.

PUBLISHED SOURCES

Achebe, Chinua. "English and the African Writer." *Transition*, no. 18 (1965): 27–30. Reprinted in Ali A. Mazrui. *The Political Sociology of the English Language: An African Perspective*. Mouton: The Hague, 1975.

Adi, Hakim. *West Africans in Britain, 1900–1960: Nationalism, Pan-Africanism, and Communism*. London: Lawrence and Wishart, 1998.

Agar, Jon. *Science Policy under Thatcher*. London: UCL Press, 2019.

Ahlman, Jeffrey. *Living with Nkrumahism: Nation, State, and Pan-Africanism in Ghana*. Athens: Ohio University Press, 2017.

Ahmad, Aijaz. "Jameson's Rhetoric of Otherness and the 'National Allegory'." *Social Text* 17 (Autumn 1987): 3–25.

Allman, Jean. "Phantoms of the Archive: Kwame Nkrumah, a Nazi Pilot Named Hanna, and the Contingencies of Postcolonial History-Writing." *American Historical Review* 118, no. 1 (February 2013): 104–29.

Anderson, David. *Histories of the Hanged: The Dirty War in Kenya and the End of Empire*. New York: W.W. Norton, 2005.

Apter, Emily. *Against World Literature: On the Politics of Untranslatability*. London: Verso, 2013.

Armah, Ayi Kwei. "Larsony or Fiction as Criticism of Fiction." *Asemka: A Journal of Literary Studies* 4 (1976): 1–14.

Armour, Charles. "The BBC and the Development of Broadcasting in British Colonial Africa, 1946–1956." *African Affairs* 83, no. 332 (July 1984): 359–402.

Austin, Dennis. *Politics in Ghana: 1946–1960*. London: Oxford University Press, 1970.

Bailey, John. *A Theatre for All Seasons: Nottingham Playhouse, The First Thirty Years 1948–1978*. Gloucestershire, UK: Alan Sutton Publishing, 1994.

Bailkin, Jordanna. *The Afterlife of Empire*. Berkeley: University of California Press, 2012.

Barber, Karin, ed. *Africa's Hidden Histories: Everyday Literacy and the Making of the Self*. Bloomington: Indiana University Press, 2006.

Baughan, Emily. *Saving the Children: Humanitarianism, Internationalism and the British Empire, 1914–1970*. Forthcoming. 2021.

Bejjit, Nourdin. "Heinemann's African Writers Series and the Rise of James Ngugi." In *The Book in Africa: Critical Debates*, edited by Caroline Davis and David Johnson, 223–44. London: Palgrave Macmillan, 2015.

Birmingham, David. *Kwame Nkrumah: The Father of African Nationalism*. Athens: Ohio University Press, 1998.

Bourdieu, Pierre. "The Field of Cultural Production; or, The Economic World Reversed." *Poetics* 12, nos. 4–5 (November 1983): 311–56.

Branch, Daniel. *Kenya: Between Hope and Despair, 1963–2011*. New Haven, CT: Yale University Press, 2011.

Branch, Daniel, and Nicholas Cheeseman. "The Politics of Control in Kenya: Understanding the Bureaucratic-Executive State, 1952–1978." *Review of African Political Economy* 33, no. 107 (2006): 11–31.

Brasnett, Clive. *Mr. Nirmal's Guru and Other True Tales*. London: Peris Press, 2009.

Brennan, James R. "The Cold War Battle over Global News in East Africa: Decolonization, the Free Flow of Information, and the Media Business, 1960–1980." *Journal of Global History* 10 (2015): 333–56.

———. "A History of Sauti ya Mvita [Voice of Mombasa]: Radio, Public Culture, and Islam in Coastal Kenya, 1947–1966." In *New Media and Religious Transformations in Africa*, edited by Rosalind I. J. Hackett and Benjamin F. Soares, 19–38. Bloomington: Indiana University Press, 2015.

———. "Radio Cairo and the Decolonization of East Africa, 1953–64." In *Making a World after Empire: The Bandung Moment and Its Political Afterlives*, edited by Christopher J. Lee, 173–95. Athens: Ohio University Press, 2010.

Bridge, Carl, and Kent Fedorowich, eds. *The British World: Diaspora, Culture and Identity*. London: Frank Cass, 2003.

Briggs, Asa. *The History of Broadcasting in the United Kingdom*. 5 vols. Oxford: Oxford University Press, 1961–1995.

British Broadcasting Corporation. *BBC Handbooks*. London: BBC, 1931–1972.

———. *The Empire Broadcasting Service*. London: BBC, 1935.

———. *Overseas Presentation Handbook*. London: BBC, 1944–1955.

British Council. *Annual Reports*. London: British Council, 1942–1980.

———. *Trust Pays: How International Cultural Relationships Build Trust in the UK and Underpin the Success of the UK Economy*. London: British Council, 2012.

Brown, Wendy. *Undoing the Demos: Neoliberalism's Stealth Revolution*. Cambridge, MA: Zone Books, 2015.

Buckner, Phillip, and R. Douglas Francis, eds. *Rediscovering the British World*. Calgary, AB: University of Calgary Press, 2005.

Buettner, Elizabeth. *Europe after Empire: Decolonization, Society, and Culture*. Cambridge: Cambridge University Press, 2016.

Burgh, John. "Creating Anglophiles." *English Today* 1, no. 3 (July 1985): 18–19.

Burke, Timothy. *Lifebuoy Men, Lux Women: Commodification, Consumption, and Cleanliness in Modern Zimbabwe*. Durham, NC: Duke University Press, 1996.

Burns, James. *Cinema and Society in the British Empire, 1895–1940*. Basingstoke, UK: Palgrave Macmillan, 2013.

Burton, Antoinette, ed. *Archive Stories: Facts, Fictions, and the Writing of History*. Durham, NC: Duke University Press, 2006.

Burton, Antoinette, and Isabel Hofmeyr, eds. *Ten Books That Shaped the British Empire: Creating an Imperial Commons*. Durham, NC: Duke University Press, 2014.

Butler, Larry, and Sarah Stockwell, eds. *The Wind of Change: Harold Macmillan and British Decolonization*. Basingstoke, UK: Palgrave Macmillan, 2013.

Cain, P. J., and A. G. Hopkins. *British Imperialism: 1688–2000*. New York: Longman, 2002.

Carruthers, Susan L. *Winning Hearts and Minds: British Governments, the Media, and Colonial Counterinsurgency, 1944–1960*. Leicester, UK: Leicester University Press, 1995.

Caute, David. *The Dancer Defects: The Struggle for Cultural Supremacy during the Cold War*. Oxford: Oxford University Press, 2003.

Central Policy Review Staff. *Review of Overseas Representation*. London: HMSO, 1977.

Chakava, Henry. "Dealing with the British." *LOGOS* 10, no. 1 (1999): 52–54.

———. "Kenyan Publishing: Independence and Dependence." In *Publishing and Development in the Third World*, edited by Philip G. Altbach, 119–50. London: Hans Zell, 1992.

Clarke, Becky. "The African Writers Series: Celebrating Forty Years of Publishing Distinction." *Research in African Literatures* 34, no. 2 (2003): 163–74.

Clarke, Sabine. "A Technocratic Imperial State? The Colonial Office and Scientific Research, 1940–1960." *Twentieth Century British History* 18, no. 2 (2007): 453–80.

Constantine, Stephen. *The Making of British Colonial Development Policy, 1914–1940*. London: Frank Cass, 1984.

Cook, David. "Theatre Goes to the People!" *Transition*, no. 25 (1966): 23–33.

Cooper, Frederick. *Africa in the World: Capitalism, Empire, Nation-State*. Cambridge, MA: Harvard University Press, 2014.

———. *Colonialism in Question: Theory, Knowledge, History*. Berkeley: University of California Press, 2005.

———. *Decolonization and African Society: The Labor Question in French and British Africa*. Cambridge: Cambridge University Press, 1996.

———. *On the African Waterfront: Urban Disorder and the Transformation of Work in Colonial Mombasa*. New Haven, CT: Yale University Press, 1987.

———. "Possibility and Constraint: African Independence in Historical Perspective." *Journal of African History* 49, no 2 (2008): 167–96.

Cooper, Frederick, and Randall M. Packard, eds. *International Development and the Social Sciences: Essays on the History and the Politics of Knowledge*. Berkeley: University of California Press, 1997.

Cordeaux, Shirley. "The BBC African Service's Involvement in African Theatre." *Research in African Literature* 1, no. 2 (1970): 147–55.

Cull, Nicholas J. *The Cold War and the United States Information Agency, 1945–1989*. New York: Cambridge University Press, 2008.

———. "Public Diplomacy: Taxonomies and Histories." In "Public Diplomacy in a Changing World," edited by Geoffrey Cowan and Nicholas J. Cull. Special issue, *Annals of the American Academy of Political and Social Science* 616, no. 1 (March 2008): 31–54.

Cullen, Poppy. *Kenya and Britain after Independence: Beyond Neo-Colonialism*. Cham: Palgrave Macmillan, 2017.

Currey, James. *Africa Writes Back: The African Writers Series and the Launch of African Literature*. Athens: Ohio University Press, 2008.

Darian-Smith, Kate, Patricia Grinshaw, and Stuart Macintyre, eds. *Britishness Abroad: Transnational Movements and Imperial Cultures*. Melbourne: Melbourne University Publishing, 2007.

Darwin, John. *The Empire Project: The Rise and Fall of the British World-System, 1880–1970*. Cambridge: Cambridge University Press, 2009.

———. "A Third British Empire? The Dominion Idea in British Politics." In *The Oxford History of the British Empire, Volume 4: The Twentieth Century*, edited by Judith Brown and Wm. Roger Louis, 64–87. Oxford: Oxford University Press, 1999.

Davis, Caroline. *Creating Postcolonial Literature: African Writers and British Publishers.* New York: Palgrave Macmillan, 2013.

———. "The Politics of Postcolonial Publishing: Oxford University Press's Three Crowns Series 1962–1976." *Book History* 8 (2005): 227–34.

Davis, Caroline, and David Johnson, eds. *The Book in Africa: Critical Debates.* London: Palgrave Macmillan, 2015.

Davis, Stephen R. "The African National Congress, Its Radio, Its Allies, and Exile." *Journal of Southern African Studies* 35, no. 2 (June 2009): 349–73.

Dench, Judi. *And Furthermore.* New York: St. Martin's Press, 2011.

Dick, Archie L. *The Hidden History of South Africa's Book and Reading Cultures.* Toronto: University of Toronto Press, 2013.

Donaldson, Frances. *The British Council: The First Fifty Years.* London: Jonathan Cape, 1984.

Dudziak, Mary L. *Cold War Civil Rights: Race and the Image of American Democracy.* Princeton, NJ: Princeton University Press, 2002.

East African Literature Bureau. *Annual Reports.* Nairobi: East Africa High Commission, 1949–1965.

Elkins, Caroline. *Imperial Reckoning: The Untold Story of Britain's Gulag in Kenya.* New York: Henry Holt, 2005.

Ellerman, Evelyn. "The Literature Bureau: African Influence in Papua New Guinea." *Research in African Literatures* 26, no. 4 (Winter 1995): 206–15.

Faucett, Lawrence. *The Oxford English Course.* London: Oxford University Press, 1933.

Foreign Relations of the United States, 1917–1972, Volume 6: Public Diplomacy, 1961–1963, edited by Kristin L. Ahlberg and Charles V. Hawley. Washington, DC: Government Publishing Office, 2017.

Fraser, John. *The Bard in the Bush.* London: Granada Publishing, 1978.

Frémont, Isabelle, F. G. French, and Laurence Faucett. *The Oxford Readers for Africa.* Books 1–6. London: Oxford University Press, 1938–1943.

French, F. G. *New Oxford English Course (Ghana).* Books 1–6. London: Oxford University Press, 1955-1960.

Gadsden, Fay. "Wartime Propaganda in Kenya: The Kenya Information Office, 1939–1945." *International Journal of African Historical Studies* 19, no. 3 (1986): 401–20.

Gaines, Kevin K. *American Africans in Ghana: Black Expatriates and the Civil Rights Era.* Chapel Hill: University of North Carolina Press, 2006.

Gans, Herbert J. *Deciding What's News: A Study of CBS Evening News, NBC Nightly News, Newsweek, and Time.* New York: Pantheon, 1979.

Gillespie, Marie, and Alban Webb, eds. *Diasporas and Diplomacy: Cosmopolitan Contact Zones at the BBC World Service.* New York: Routledge, 2013.

Gillespie, Marie, Alban Webb, and Gerhard Baumann, eds. "BBC World Service, 1932–2007: Cultural Exchange and Public Diplomacy." Special issue, *Historical Journal of Film, Radio and Television* 28, no. 4 (2008): 441–623.

Griffith, Glyne. *The BBC and the Development of Anglophone Caribbean Literature, 1943–1958*. Basingstoke, UK: Palgrave Macmillan, 2016.

Hadjiathanasiou, Maria. "Colonial Rule, Cultural Relations and the British Council in Cyprus, 1935–55." *Journal of Imperial and Commonwealth History* 46, no. 6 (2018): 1096–124.

Hampton, Mark. "Projecting Britishness to Hong Kong: The British Council and Hong Kong House, Nineteen-Fifties to Nineteen-Seventies." *Historical Research* 85 (2012): 691–709.

Havinden, Michael, and David Meredith. *Colonialism and Development: Britain and Its Tropical Colonies, 1850–1960*. New York: Routledge, 1993.

Head, Sydney W. "British Colonial Broadcasting Policies: The Case of the Gold Coast." *African Studies Review* 22, no. 2 (September 1979): 39–47.

Headrick, Daniel R. *The Invisible Weapon: Telecommunications and International Politics*. New York: Oxford University Press, 1991.

Heil, Alan L. Jr. *VOA: A History*. New York: Columbia University Press, 2003.

Hill, Alan. *In Pursuit of Publishing*. London: J. Murray in association with Heinemann Educational Books, 1988.

Hodge, Joseph Morgan. "British Colonial Expertise, Post-Colonial Careering and the Early History of International Development." In *Modernizing Missions: Approaches to 'Developing' the Non-Western World after 1945*, edited by Andreas Eckert, Stephan Malinowski, and Corinna R. Unger, 22–44. Munich: Beck, 2010.

———. *Triumph of the Expert: Agrarian Doctrines of Development and the Legacies of British Colonialism*. Athens: Ohio University Press, 2007.

Hofmeyr, Isabel. "From Book Development to Book History: Some Observations on the History of the Book in Africa." *SHARP News* 13, no. 3 (2004): 3–4.

———. *The Portable Bunyan: A Transnational History of* The Pilgrim's Progress. Princeton, NJ: Princeton University Press, 2004.

Holland, R. F. *Britain and the Commonwealth Alliance, 1918–1939*. Basingstoke, UK: Macmillan, 1981.

Horne, Janet. "'To Spread the French Language Is to Extend the *Patrie*': The Colonial Mission of the Alliance Française." *French Historical Studies* 40, no. 1 (2017): 95–127.

Howe, Stephen. *Anticolonialism in British Politics: The Left and the End of Empire 1918–1964*. Oxford: Oxford University Press, 1993.

Howsam, Leslie. *Cheap Bibles: Nineteenth-Century Publishing and the British and Foreign Bible Society*. Cambridge: Cambridge University Press, 1991.

Huggan, Graham. *The Postcolonial Exotic: Marketing the Margins*. New York: Routledge, 2001.

Hyam, Ronald. *Britain's Declining Empire: The Road to Decolonisation, 1918–1968*. Cambridge: Cambridge University Press, 2006.

Iber, Patrick. *Neither Peace nor Freedom: The Cultural Cold War in Latin America*. Cambridge, MA: Harvard University Press, 2015.

Jackson, Anthony. "1958–1983: Six Reps in Focus." In *The Repertory Movement: A History of Regional Theatre in Britain*, edited by George Rowell and Anthony Jackson, 130–73. Cambridge: Cambridge University Press, 1984.

Jackson, Ben, and Robert Saunders, eds. *Making Thatcher's Britain*. Cambridge: Cambridge University Press, 2012.

James, Leslie, and Elisabeth Leake, eds. *Decolonization and the Cold War: Negotiating Independence*. London: Bloomsbury, 2015.

James, Simon. "The Central Policy Review Staff, 1970–1983." *Political Studies* 34, no. 3 (1986): 423–40.

Jameson, Fredric. "Third-World Literature in an Era of Multinational Capitalism." *Social Text* 15 (Autumn 1986): 65–88.

Jeppesen, Chris. "'A Worthwhile Career for a Man Who Is Not Entirely Self-Seeking': Service, Duty, and the Colonial Service during Decolonization." In *Britain, France and the Decolonization of Africa: Future Imperfect?*, edited by Andrew W. M. Smith and Chris Jeppesen, 133–55. London: UCL Press, 2017.

Johnson, Lemuel A. *Shakespeare in Africa (and Other Venues): Import and the Appropriation of Culture*. Trenton, NJ: Africa World Press, 1998.

Johnston, Gordon, and Emma Robertson. *BBC World Service: Overseas Broadcasting, 1932–2018*. London: Palgrave Macmillan, 2019.

Kayanja, Lydia. "The Makerere Travelling Theatre in East Africa." *Journal of Modern African Studies* 5, no. 1 (May 1967): 141–42.

Kennedy, Dennis. "British Theatre, 1895–1946: Art, Entertainment, Audiences–An Introduction." In *Cambridge History of British Theatre, Volume 3: Since 1895*, edited by Baz Kershaw, 1–33. Cambridge: Cambridge University Press, 2008.

Kerr, David. "Participatory Popular Theatre: The Highest State of Cultural Under-Development?" *Research in African Literatures* 22, no. 3 (Autumn 1991): 55–75.

Kirk-Greene, A. H. M. *Britain's Imperial Administrators, 1858–1966*. New York: St. Martin's Press, 1999.

Kolinsky, Martin. "The Demise of the Inter-University Council for Higher Education Overseas: A Chapter in the History of the Idea of the University." *Minerva* 21, no. 1 (March 1983): 37–80.

Landau, Paul S. "Empires of the Visual: Photography and Colonial Administration in Africa." In *Images and Empires: Visuality in Colonial and Postcolonial Africa*, edited by Paul S. Landau and Deborah D. Kaspin, 141–71. Berkeley: University of California Press, 2002.

Le Mahieu, D. L. *A Culture for Democracy: Mass Communication and the Cultivated Mind in Britain between the Wars*. Oxford: Oxford University Press, 1988.

Le Roux, Elizabeth. "Book History in the African World: The State of the Discipline." *Book History* 15 (2012): 248–300.

Leavis, F. R. *Mass Civilization and Minority Culture*. Cambridge: Minority Press, 1930.

Lee, Christopher J. "Between a Moment and an Era: The Origins and Afterlives of Bandung." In *Making a World after Empire: The Bandung Moment and Its Political Afterlives*, edited by Christopher J. Lee, 1–42. Athens: Ohio University Press, 2010.

———, ed. *A Soviet Journey: A Critical Annotated Edition*, by Alex La Guma. New York: Lexington Books, 2017.

Lee, J. M. "British Cultural Diplomacy and the Cold War: 1946–61." *Diplomacy and Statecraft* 9, no. 1 (1998): 112–34.

Lewis, Joanna. *Empire State-Building: War and Welfare in Kenya, 1925–52*. Athens: Ohio University Press, 2000.

Lindfors, Bernth. *Critical Perspectives on Amos Tutuola*. Washington, DC: Three Continents Press, 1975.

Lingaga, Dina. "Radio Theatre: The Moral Play in the Historical Context of State Control and Censorship of Broadcasting in Kenya." In *Radio in Africa: Publics, Cultures, Communities*, edited by Liz Gunnar, Dina Lingaga, and Dumisani Moyo, 149–62. Suffolk, UK: James Currey, 2011.

Lizarríbar, Camille. *Something Else Will Stand Beside It: The African Writers Series and the Development of African Literature*. Ann Arbor: University of Michigan Press, 1998.

Louis, Wm. Roger. *Ends of British Imperialism: The Scramble for Empire, Suez, and Decolonization*. Oxford: Oxford University Press, 2006.

———, ed. *The History of Oxford University Press, Volume 3: 1896–1970*. Oxford: Oxford University Press, 2013.

Louis, Wm. Roger, and Ronald Robinson. "The Imperialism of Decolonization." *Journal of Imperial and Commonwealth History* 22, no. 3 (1994): 462–511.

Low, D. A., and John Lonsdale. "Introduction." In *History of East Africa, Volume 3*, edited by John Lonsdale and Alison Smith, 1–64. Oxford: Clarendon Press, 1976.

Low, Gail. *Publishing the Postcolonial: Anglophone West African and Caribbean Writing in the UK 1948–1968*. New York: Routledge, 2011.

Lynn, Martin, ed. *The British Empire in the 1950s: Retreat or Revival?* New York: Palgrave Macmillan, 2006.

Macmillan, Harold. *Pointing the Way, 1959–1961*. London: Macmillan, 1972.

Mansell, Gerard. *Let Truth Be Told: 50 Years of BBC External Broadcasting*. London: Weidenfeld and Nicolson, 1982.

Matera, Marc. *Black London: The Imperial Metropolis and Decolonization in the Twentieth Century*. Oakland: University of California Press, 2015.

Mazrui, Alamin M. *Cultural Politics of Translation: East Africa in a Global Context*. New York: Routledge, 2016.

Moore, Charles. *Margaret Thatcher: The Authorized Biography*. 3 vols. London: Allan Lane, 2015–2019.

Mpe, Phaswane. "The Role of the Heinemann African Writers Series in the Development and Promotion of African Literature." *African Studies* 58 (1999): 112–34.

Murphy, Philip. *Party Politics and Decolonization: The Conservative Party and British Colonial Policy in Tropical Africa, 1951–1964*. Oxford: Oxford University Press, 1995.

Mytton, Graham. "Audience Research at the BBC World Service 1932–2010." *Participations: Journal of Audience and Reception Studies* 8, no. 1 (May 2011): 75–103.

———. "40 Years of Broadcasting from London in African Languages." In *Africa Bibliography 1996*, edited by Chris H. Allen, vi–xxiii. Edinburgh: Edinburgh University Press, 1997.

Nelson, Michael. *War of the Black Heavens: The Battle of Western Broadcasting in the Cold War*. Syracuse, NY: Syracuse University Press, 1997.

Newell, Stephanie. "Paradoxes of Press Freedom in Colonial West Africa." *Media History* 22, no. 1 (2016): 101–22.

Newton, Darrell. "Calling the West Indies: The BBC World Service and *Caribbean Voices*." *Historical Journal of Film, Radio and Television* 28, no. 4 (October 2008): 489–97.

Ngũgĩ wa Thiong'o. *Decolonising the Mind: The Politics of Language in African Literature*. Portsmouth, NH: Heinemann, 1986.

———. *Writers in Politics*. London: Heinemann, 1981.

Nicholls, C. S. *Elspeth Huxley: A Biography*. New York: Thomas Dunne, 2003.

Nottingham, John. "Establishing an African Publishing Industry: A Study in Decolonization." *African Affairs* 68, no. 271 (April 1969): 139–44.

Nye, Joseph S. *Soft Power: The Means to Success in World Politics*. New York: Public Affairs, 2004.

Nyerere, Julius K. "Utangulizi." Introduction to *Julius Caezar*, by William Shakespeare, 3–6. Translated by Julius K. Nyerere. Nairobi: Oxford University Press, 1963.

Olyuwasanmi, Edwina, Eva McLean, and Hans Zell, eds. *Publishing in Africa in the Seventies: Proceedings of an International Conference on Publishing and Book Development*. Ile-Ife, Nigeria: University of Ife Press, 1975.

Osborne, Myles. "'The Rooting Out of Mau Mau from the Minds of the Kikuyu Is a Formidable Task': Propaganda and the Mau Mau War." *Journal of African History* 56, no. 1 (March 2015): 77–97.

Pankhurst, Richard. "Shakespeare in Ethiopia." *Research in African Literatures* 17, no. 2 (Summer 1986): 169–96.

Petersen, Kirsten Holst, and Anna Rutherford, eds. *Chinua Achebe: A Celebration*. Oxford: Heinemann International Literature and Textbooks, 1991.

Peterson, Derek R. *Creative Writing: Translation, Bookkeeping, and the Work of Imagination in Colonial Kenya*. Portsmouth, NH: Heinemann, 2004.

Peterson, Derek R., Emma Hunter, and Stephanie Newell, eds. *African Print Cultures: Newspapers and their Publics in the Twentieth Century*. Ann Arbor: University of Michigan Press, 2016.

Potter, Simon J. *Broadcasting Empire: The BBC and the British World*. Oxford: Oxford University Press, 2012.

———. *News and the British World: The Emergence of an Imperial Press System, 1876–1922*. Oxford: Clarendon Press, 2003.

Prevots, Naima. *Dance for Export: Cultural Diplomacy and the Cold War*. Middletown, CT: Wesleyan University Press, 1998.

Quirk, Randolph, and Albert Marckwardt. *A Common Language: British and American English*. London: BBC and the United States Government, 1964.

Rathbone, Richard. "The Government of the Gold Coast after the Second World War." *African Affairs* 67, no. 268 (July 1968): 209–18.

Reith, John. *Broadcast over Britain*. London: Hodder and Stoughton, 1924.

———. *Into the Wind*. London: Hodder and Stoughton, 1949.

Report on Non-Departmental Public Bodies (Pliatzky Report). Cmnd 7797. London: HMSO, 1980.

Riley, Charlotte Lydia. "Monstrous Predatory Vampires and Beneficent Fairy Godmothers: Postwar British Colonial Development in Africa." PhD diss., University College, London, 2013.

———. "'The Winds of Change Are Blowing Economically': The Labour Party and British Overseas Development, 1940s–1960s." In *Britain, France and the Decolonization of Africa: Future Imperfect?*, edited by Andrew W. M. Smith and Chris Jeppesen, 43–61. London: UCL Press, 2017.

Rivera, Tim. *Distinguishing Cultural Relations from Cultural Diplomacy: The British Council's Relationship with Her Majesty's Government*. USC Center on Public Diplomacy Perspectives Series. Los Angeles: Figueroa Press, 2015.

Robertson, Emma. "'I Get a Real Kick out of Big Ben': BBC versions of Britishness on the Empire and General Overseas Service, 1932–1948." *Historical Journal of Film, Radio and Television* 28, no. 4 (October 2008): 459–73.

Roy, Arundhati. "What Is the Morally Appropriate Language in Which to Think and Write?" W. G. Sebald Lecture. 5 June 2018. British Library.

Rush, Anne Spry. *Bonds of Empire: West Indians and Britishness from Victoria to Decolonization*. Oxford: Oxford University Press, 2011.

Said, Edward W. *Culture and Imperialism*. New York: Vintage Books, 1994.

Sander, Reinhard, Bernth Lindfors, and Lynette Cintrón, eds. *Ngũgĩ wa Thiong'o Speaks: Interviews with the Kenyan Writer*. Trenton, NJ: Africa World Press, 2006.

Saunders, Frances Stonor. *Who Paid the Piper? The CIA and the Cultural Cold War*. London: Granta, 1999.

Schaffer, Gavin. "The Limits of 'Liberal Imagination': Britain, Broadcasting and Apartheid South Africa, 1948–1994." *Past & Present* 240, no. 1 (2018): 235–66.

Schwarz, Bill. *The White Man's World*. Oxford: Oxford University Press, 2011.

Shakespeare, William. *Julius Caezar*. Translated by Julius K. Nyerere. Nairobi: Oxford University Press, 1963.

———. *Mabepari wa Venisi*. Translated by Julius K. Nyerere. Dar es Salaam: Oxford University Press, 1969.

Shaw, Tony, ed. "Britain and the Cultural Cold War." Special issue, *Contemporary British History* 19, no. 2 (2005).

Sinha, Mrinalini. "Whatever Happened to the Third British Empire? Empire, Nation Redux." In *Writing Imperial Histories*, edited by Andrew S. Thompson, 168–87. Manchester: Manchester University Press, 2014.

Smith, Andrew W. M. "'Information after Imperialism': British Overseas Representation and Francophone Africa (1957–1967)." In *Imagining Britain's Economic Future, c. 1800–1975: Trade, Consumerism, and Global Markets*, edited by David Thackeray, Andrew Thompson, and Richard Toye, 205–229. Cham: Palgrave Macmillan, 2018.

Smith, Richard C., ed. *Teaching English as a Foreign Language, 1936–1961: Foundations of ELT*. London: Routledge, 2005.

Smyth, Rosaleen. "The Development of British Colonial Film Policy, 1927–1939, with Reference to East and Central Africa." *Journal of African History* 20, no. 3 (July 1979): 437–50.

———. "A Note on the 'Saucepan Special': The People's Radio of Central Africa." *Historical Journal of Film, Radio and Television* 4, no. 2 (1984): 195–201.

Soyinka, Wole. "Towards a True Theatre." *Transition*, no. 8 (March 1963): 21–22.

Spivak, Gayatri Chakravorty. "Can the Subaltern Speak?" In *Marxism and the Interpretation of Culture*, edited by Cary Nelson and Lawrence Grossberg, 271–313. Urbana: University of Illinois Press, 1989.

Stockwell, Sarah. *The British End of the British Empire*. Cambridge: Cambridge University Press, 2018.

Strongman, Luke. *The Booker Prize and the Legacy of Empire*. New York: Rodopi, 2002.

Summary of the Report of the Independent Commission of Enquiry into the Overseas Information Services (Drogheda Report). Cmd. 9138. London: HMSO, 1954.

Sutcliffe, Peter H. *The Oxford University Press: An Informal History*. Oxford: Clarendon Press, 1978.

Tallents, Stephen G. *The Projection of England*. London: Faber and Faber, 1932.

Taylor, Philip M. *The Projection of Britain: British Overseas Publicity and Propaganda, 1919–1939*. Cambridge: Cambridge University Press, 1981.

Thomas, Lynn M. *Politics of the Womb: Women, Reproduction, and the State in Kenya*. Berkeley: University of California Press, 2003.

Tignor, Robert. *Capitalism and Nationalism at the End of Empire: State and Business in Decolonizing Egypt, Nigeria, and Kenya, 1945–1963*. Princeton, NJ: Princeton University Press, 1997.

Tomlin, Gregory M. *Murrow's Cold War: Public Diplomacy for the Kennedy Administration*. Lincoln, NE: Potomac Books, 2016.

Troughton, Charles. "The Contest for Influence Overseas: Why Britain Must Compete." *Journal of the Royal Society for the Arts* 132, no. 5339 (October 1984): 732–40.

Tusa, John. *A World in your Ear: Reflections on Changes*. London: Broadside Books, 1992.

Tworek, Heidi J. S. *News from Germany: The Competition to Control World Communications, 1900–1945*. Cambridge, MA: Harvard University Press, 2019.

Vaughan, James R. *The Failure of American and British Propaganda in the Arab Middle East, 1945–57: Unconquerable Minds*. Basingstoke, UK: Palgrave Macmillan, 2005.

Von Eschen, Penny M. *Race against Time: Black Americans and Anticolonialism, 1937–1957*. Ithaca, NY: Cornell University Press, 1997.

———. *Satchmo Blows Up the World: Jazz Ambassadors Play the Cold War*. Cambridge, MA: Harvard University Press, 2006.

Walker, Andrew. *A Skyful of Freedom: 60 Years of the BBC World Service*. London: Broadside Books, 1992.

Waters, Rob. *Thinking Black: Britain, 1964–1985*. Oakland: University of California Press, 2019.

Webb, Alban. *London Calling: Britain, the BBC World Service, and the Cold War*. London: Bloomsbury, 2014.

Westad, Odd Arne. *The Global Cold War: Third World Interventions and the Making of Our Times*. Cambridge: Cambridge University Press, 2005.

Wilford, Hugh. *The Mighty Wurlitzer: How the CIA Played America*. Cambridge, MA: Harvard University Press, 2009.

Willinsky, John. *Empire of Words: The Reign of the OED*. Princeton, NJ: Princeton University Press, 1994.

Willis, Justin, Gabrielle Lynch, and Nic Cheeseman. "Voting, Nationhood, and Citizenship in Late-Colonial Africa." *Historical Journal* 61, no. 4 (2018): 1113–35.

Wilson, G. H. "The Northern Rhodesia-Nyasaland Joint Publications Bureau." *Africa: Journal of the International African Institute* 20 (1950): 60–69.

Wilson, John. "Gold Coast Information." *African Affairs* 43, no. 172 (July 1944): 111–15.

Winseck, Dwayne R., and Robert M. Pike. *Communication and Empire: Media, Markets, and Globalization, 1860–1930*. Durham, NC: Duke University Press, 2007.

Wren, Robert M. *Those Magical Years: The Making of Nigerian Literature at Ibadan*. Washington, DC: Three Continents Press, 1990.

Wrong, Margaret. *Africa and the Making of Books: Being a Survey of Africa's Need of Literature*. London: International Committee on Christian Literature for Africa, 1934.

Zimmern, Alfred. *The Third British Empire: Being a Course of Lectures Delivered at Columbia University, New York*. London: Oxford University Press, 1927.

Note: figures are indicated by page numbers followed by *fig.*

BERKELEY SERIES IN BRITISH STUDIES

Edited by James Vernon

Founded in 1893,
UNIVERSITY OF CALIFORNIA PRESS
publishes bold, progressive books and journals
on topics in the arts, humanities, social sciences,
and natural sciences—with a focus on social
justice issues—that inspire thought and action
among readers worldwide.

The UC PRESS FOUNDATION
raises funds to uphold the press's vital role
as an independent, nonprofit publisher, and
receives philanthropic support from a wide
range of individuals and institutions—and from
committed readers like you. To learn more, visit
ucpress.edu/supportus.